W9-CAL-132

Cooking
Under Cover

Cooking Under Cover

One-Pot Wonders—
A Treasury of Soups, Stews,
Braises and Casseroles

Linda & Fred Griffith

Photography by Alan Richardson

CHAPTERS PUBLISHING LTD., SHELBURNE, VT 05482

Copyright © 1996 by Linda and Fred Griffith
Photography copyright © 1996 by Alan Richardson

All rights reserved. No part of this book may be reproduced or transmitted
in any form or by any electronic or mechanical means, including information storage
and retrieval systems, without permission in writing from the Publisher, except for
the inclusion of brief quotations in a review.

Published by Chapters Publishing Ltd., 2085 Shelburne Road, Shelburne, VT 05482

Library of Congress Cataloging-in-Publication Data
Griffith, Linda
    Cooking under cover : one-pot wonders, a treasury of soups, stews,
braises, and casseroles / Linda and Fred Griffith : photography by Alan
Richardson
    p.   cm.
    Includes bibliographical references and index.
    ISBN 1-57630-015-3 (hardcover)
    1. Entrées (Cookery) 2. Soups. 3. Stews. 4. Casserole Cookery. I
Griffith, Fred. II. Title.
TX740.G725 1996
641.8—dc20   96-28427

Printed and bound in the U.S.A. by World Color, Taunton, Massachusetts

Designed by Susan McClellan

Front cover: Potted Stuffed Chicken & Vegetables (recipe on page 118);
photograph by Alan Richardson
Food Stylist: Anne Disrude
Prop Stylist: Betty Alfenito

10 9 8 7 6 5 4 3

As we have come to appreciate the creativity of cooks past,
may our own grandchildren come to understand and celebrate that legacy.

Madison Newman Myers

Mackenzie Weller Hanauer Myers

Forrest Jennings Drucker

Sydney Tate Drucker

May they find pleasure in the books we write and the recipes we record
and take care to preserve them for those who will follow.

Contents

INTRODUCTION 9

COOKING PREFERENCES 15

Chapter 1

STARTERS 17

Chapter 2

SOUPS 39

Chapter 3

SHELLFISH & FISH 61

Chapter 4

POULTRY & GAME 111

Chapter 5

BEEF 151

Chapter 6

VEAL 181

Chapter 7

LAMB 201

Chapter 8

PORK 223

Chapter 9

GRAINS, BEANS & BREADS 245

Chapter 10

VEGETABLES 271

Chapter 11

DESSERTS 301

Appendix

BASICS 323

SOURCES 334

BIBLIOGRAPHY 337

INDEX 341

Acknowledgments

U SUALLY, AUTHORS THANK THEIR AGENTS AND EDITORS LAST. This time, however, let the last be first. We shall be eternally grateful to Judith Weber, our agent, for introducing us to Chapters, to editor-in-chief Barry Estabrook, Linda's favorite mystery writer, and to our favorite editor, Rux Martin.

Culinary historians and antiquarians Jan and Dan Longone have opened their Wine and Food Library to us, and Jan has given freely of her time and knowledge. We thank them for their generosity of spirit and for opening our eyes to the exceptionally rich heritage of 200 years of American food writers.

Because we believe that good food and good wine go hand in hand, we continue to give wine suggestions when they seem appropriate. Partner in Napa Valley's Patz & Hall Wine Company, our good friend Donald Patz has stimulated our palates with wide-ranging recommendations.

Sanford Herskovitz, aka Mr. Brisket, has generously shared his considerable expertise, helping us to understand exactly where in the animal each cut of meat originates and patiently correcting our misconceptions and *mishigas*. He managed to find everything we needed for recipe testing (or talked us out of needing it). We also thank Sanford and his wife Frances for being our best tasters and for being there whenever we needed them.

Thanks go to tasters Brenda and Evan Turner, Deborah and David Klausner, Sandy and Peter Earl, Anne Sethness and Jack Smith, Russell Trusso and the late John Carey, Alan Chong, Larry Berman, Meg and Wes Gerlosky, Mario Vitale and Diann and John Yambor. Linda's mother, Gert LeVine, gets the prize for finally moving to Cleveland so she could help eat what we cook and wash the dishes for us.

Other folks have helped us in a variety of ways: Selana and Fred Shaheen; Dr. Peter Gail of Goosefoot Press; the Grapevine's Bob Fishman; Steve Connolly and Nick Journey from Boston's Steve Connolly Fish; our fish guru, Jon Rowley; Ford Motor Company's Bill Carroll; Ed Chanantry, now General Manager of Cleveland's Ritz-Carlton Hotel; Continental Airline's Sandra Zabinski-Lontkowski; West Point Market's Russ Vernon; and Cleveland's ultimate bookseller, Richard Guildenmeister; Dr. Alan R. Hirsch, neurological director of the Smell and Taste Treatment and Research Foundation in Chicago; Bob Bowersox and Paula Piercy of QVC; and Molly Bartlett of Silver Creek Farm, who reminds us that everything starts in the dirt.

We thank Mardee Haidin Regan, our copy editor, photographer Alan Richardson, designer Susan McClellan and Chapters' wonderful supporting cast: the ever-dedicated Melissa Cochran and the patient and cheerful Cristen Brooks.

Finally, our love and our thanks to our family for much patience and encouragement.

Introduction

A S WE WORKED ON THIS BOOK, STANDING OVER A SIMMERING SOUP OR STEW, jotting down notes, we often found ourselves thinking more about our parents and our favorite childhood dishes than the spattered pages of the recipe in progress.

Linda's grandmother Mary Weller always seemed to have an Old World Jewish dish simmering on the stovetop. Most often, it would be a plump kosher chicken, cut into pieces, in a heavy covered soup pot. She used lots of onions, which she fried in chicken fat, and added heaping spoonfuls of paprika. The aromas were extraordinary. After several hours, the skin would be golden and the flesh succulently moist. When the chicken was gone, everyone would mop up the stewing juices with chunks of her homemade challah. Linda says she still can smell and taste what Grandma Weller was cooking by the mere thought of it.

At other times, Grandma Weller's pot would contain *tzimmes*, a stew of beef, potatoes and carrots. She used boneless flanken, the succulent meat cut from the short ribs, and dried lima beans in place of the more common dried apricots. In the middle was a feathery light dumpling of grated potatoes mixed with eggs, flour, onion and a little chicken fat. She'd pour in a suitable amount of liquid, set the heavy lid in place and heft the pot into the oven, where it would bake for hours.

Grandma Weller's background couldn't have been more different from that of Fred's father, who was born into a West Virginia coal-mining family. But they both shared a fondness for simple slow-cooked food. As the owner of a restaurant for working people in Charleston, where the price had to be right, Fred Griffith, Sr., was a master of the economical cut. On the menu of the MacFarland Lunch, as the restaurant was known, was corned beef with cabbage. Chicken stew with dumplings. Pot roast of beef served with a powerful freshly grated horseradish. Spareribs so tender and tasty that customers sent back only polished bones. And always, there was "baked steak," slices of round or chuck that were pounded and braised in the oven.

Slow moist-cooking techniques are almost universal, imparting rich flavors and tenderness to even the toughest cuts of meat. The key is the cover that retains the heat, captures the steam, contains the aromas and enhances the flavors. This is convenient, economical cooking that requires little labor. Covered dishes yield plenty of easily reheated leftovers, which are often tastier the second day when the seasonings have had time to develop. Many cooks, in fact, prefer to make such meals in advance and chill them overnight before serving, not only to take advantage of the magnified flavors but to make it easier to remove any fat.

The most famous of these sorts of dishes—the ones that prompt memories—are one-pot soups and stews, like gumbos and chilis. Many are hearty, long-simmered preparations especially suitable for winter. But these are only the most prominent members of the covered-cooking clan. Others are delicate and light, low in fat and can be prepared in minutes. The tradition embraces appetizers, like pâtés, which are cooked, covered, in a water bath, small cocktail meatballs, stuffed grape leaves and the Chinese dumplings we know as pot stickers. Side dishes, including baked beans and that New England classic accompaniment steamed brown bread, are part of the extended family as well.

Though we don't normally associate desserts with this cooking method, some of the best ones are made this way. Poached pears, fruit mulled in wine, and plum pudding, made by mixing preserved fruit with nuts, flour and a little suet and steaming it in a mold, are a few of our own favorites.

Once considered strictly family fare, these old-fashioned dishes are perfect for company— convenient, easy and economical. Nothing matches the appeal of baby chickens braised on a bed of root vegetables, a dish that can be served on its own or with a simple salad. It is fun to spend an hour in the kitchen browning chicken and vegetables and letting the pot bubble along unattended, the flavors developing and deepening and sending pleasing aromas out from the kitchen, while you relax like one of the guests.

In addition, the once humble dishes like those served up at the MacFarland Lunch are now among the most popular items on the menus of restaurants so sophisticated that Fred's father would be amazed. In our hometown, Cleveland, Osso Bucco Milanese—thick veal shanks braised in a garlic, onion and white wine sauce—is among the most requested winter entrées at Johnny's Downtown, one of the city's most fashionable restaurants. In New York, the celebrated Montrachet and Union Square Cafe offer a host of covered dishes, ranging from lamb and veal shanks to seafood stews. In Paris at the acclaimed Taillevent, a plump chicken braised in a pastry-sealed casserole, opened tableside, is one of the specialties of the house.

T HE FAMILY OF COVERED DISHES embraces a multiplicity of cooking methods: not only stewing and braising but also steaming, poaching, baking in parchment paper and foil, even indoor smoking in a covered wok. Some depend on hybrid techniques, such as roasting under cover or frying under cover.

Braising is the slow cooking of meats, fish, poultry or vegetables in a covered pot with relatively little liquid. The term comes from the French word *braiser*, meaning "charcoal," referring to the original practice of setting the pot into the hot embers of the fire, with more coals placed on top of the lid to provide heat from two directions. Today, a braise is any dish cooked slowly in moist heat in a covered container. Steam rising from the hot broth swirls about the food, bringing it close to 212 degrees F, the temperature at which water boils, but never higher. This temperature is sufficient to break down tough fibers and render them tender and palatable.

Stewing works in much the same way but involves more liquid, usually enough to cover whatever is being cooked. Generally, the food to be stewed is cut into smaller chunks and browned in a skillet before it goes into the stew pot.

Steaming is an ideal technique for thorough cooking without browning. Foods cooked by steaming often develop a silky, light texture and have a delicate flavor. A variety of cookware has been designed to steam foods, usually involving a rack to hold the food just above the liquid that will produce the steam.

In *poaching*, a variant of *boiling*, water or a stock is kept just at or under the boiling point so that the liquid barely swirls—important when you are trying to keep an egg together or a fish from falling apart.

Smoking carries not only heat to food but flavor too, whether from burning wood, charcoal or tea leaves. Frequently, the temperature of the smoke is moderated by water or some other liquid in the smoker.

In *parchment-* or *foil-baking*, the food is sealed in a package with seasonings and a little liquid and is cooked in a hot oven so that it quickly steams, causing the paper to puff up. Presentation is impressive: The parchment paper, or foil, is slit and opened at the table.

Putting a lid on a dish that is traditionally cooked uncovered often improves both texture and flavor. Chicken fried in a covered skillet will become crisp but will be more evenly cooked and tender than when fried uncovered. Baking corn bread in a cast-iron Dutch oven, as our ancestors did, results in a moister, more full-flavored bread. And meat loaf, similarly cooked, becomes juicier in the steamy atmosphere of the pot. Risotto, an Italian rice dish that is cooked and continually stirred so that it becomes creamy, can be made by bringing it to a boil on the stovetop, then covering and baking it in a slow oven, transforming it from a labor-intensive offering to an exceptionally easy one. The oven does the work while you spend time with your guests.

VIRTUALLY EVERY IMMIGRANT GROUP BROUGHT ITS OWN VERSIONS of covered dishes to this country, using cuts of meat that improved in the pot. In Europe, covered cookery was for centuries the primary method of food preparation. Dishes were cooked for long hours so working families could come home to a hot, hearty meal. This was the food of the common folk, prepared with whatever simple ingredients were available, stewed or braised until everything was tender and delicious. It was not uncommon, especially in the winter, to have a pot on the stove or near the fire all the time, with dinner ladled out onto plates and replacement cuts and parts put in. Nothing spoiled because it was too hot, and nothing burned in the gentle simmer. This kind of cooking had to conform to local limitations, to what was available and when. The food was almost certainly produced in the neighborhood, and perhaps there was only one pot in the household and only one heat source.

In central and eastern Europe, where much of Jewish cooking has its roots, celebrated dishes that could be cooked unattended in a still warm stove evolved out of the prohibition of cooking on the Sabbath. Still other covered dishes come from the French countryside, where daubes and ragouts are important; and from countries around the Mediterranean, from Portugal, Italy and Greece to the North African coast and the Middle East, where lamb and grain dishes abound; and from within the African continent, where meals of beans, rice and vegetables are staples. In China, where the wok is king, delicate steamed and braised fish and poultry dishes have had an important place for centuries.

Spurred by creative instincts and simple necessity, American settlers recrafted these Old World approaches, coming up with such disparate specialties as New England boiled dinners, Cajun jambalayas and étouffées. They put their own mark on chowders, made by layering the catch of the day with potatoes in a deep, covered pot; and on sauerbraten, beef cured with a little vinegar and salt in advance of cooking; and on Hungarian goulash, to name just a few. Eventually, the venerable institution we call the Covered Dish Supper developed as an important social event. When people gathered together to celebrate or worship or build a barn, they brought a hearty meal in a dish that could be reheated.

COMMON TO MANY OF THE MAIN-COURSE DISHES is a reliance on inexpensive but tasty cuts of meat, like eye of round, brisket, shanks, short ribs or shoulder. Cleveland butcher Sanford Herskovitz calls such cuts "the meat of locomotion." Generally speaking, says Herskovitz, the farther the meat is from the middle, the tougher it is likely to be. The chuck part in the front and the round at the rear are almost always working; the brisket and the flank, the tip and the shank also are usually in motion. "Middle meat," tender cuts like standing rib roasts, steaks and sirloin, makes up only one-fifth of the cow. Save that for your grill, not the stew pot.

The hips, shoulders and legs, on the other hand, are tougher but more flavorful. They are full of connective tissue that gives strength and resiliency to working muscle. To break down this tissue requires slow, moist cooking. Meat that is braised will reach an internal temperature of 212 degrees F, which converts the collagen, a major component of the tissue, into soluble gelatin. Roasting or broiling may confront the outside of the meat with higher temperatures, but wet heat penetrates better.

Most recipes call for browning the main ingredients before braising or stewing them. Cookbooks have told us for centuries that browning seals in juices. In his 1984 book, *On Food and Cooking*, Food writer Harold McGee quietly asserted that this notion was false, and other researchers have confirmed his findings. No juices are trapped inside by the searing process. The real reason for browning is to heighten flavor.

Louis-Camille Maillard, a French biochemist and physician, was the first to study what happens when food browns. He knew that sugars and amino acids occur naturally in most foods. In 1912, he heated glucose, a simple sugar, with lysine, a common amino acid. The experiment produced brown pigments and a pleasant aroma. Maillard's was the first experiment in flavor chemistry and one of the most important culinary breakthroughs of the century. Variations on this apparently simple chemical reaction, in which sugars and amino acids form hundreds of new flavor-producing compounds, are at the heart of the taste of most cooked food.

THE TECHNIQUES AND CUTS OF MEAT USED IN COVERED DISHES are humble ones, and so is the cookware. You undoubtedly have most, if not all, of the right pots in your kitchen now. The simplest are often the best.

The *Dutch oven* is perhaps the most important because it is deep enough so you can brown a quantity of ingredients and because it can go directly into the oven. Its origins are unclear, but it probably goes back to medieval times in the low countries when craftsmen first developed techniques for pouring molten iron into sand molds, letting the iron cool to form a thick pot. Traditionally, the Dutch oven was a wide, heavy, tightly covered container with straight sides, usually wider at the top than at the bottom. Often, it was crafted with legs to keep it above the coals on the hearth and with a bail so it could be hung over the fireplace. To allow for better distribution of the heat, the lid was made with a flange around it so hot coals could be put on top. Foods were placed directly in the Dutch oven, or they might be put in smaller containers first and then set in. Today, in kitchenware stores and catalogs, "Dutch oven" indicates any covered cooking vessel that can be placed directly on the stovetop or in the oven. Our favorites are made of cast aluminum or cast iron, both of which distribute the heat evenly, so the contents are less likely to scorch. The Dutch oven has been an essential tool in American kitchens from the beginning. (John Winthrop, the governor of Massachusetts, sent a letter reminding his wife in England not to forget hers when she started her journey to join him.)

One of the best-known brands is Le Creuset from France, cast metal clad in a baked enamel or porcelain coating. Magnalite (heavy cast aluminum) and Wagner cast iron are also outstanding brands. We find the 5½-quart and 8-quart sizes most useful.

The *electric slow cooker* is the modern-day equivalent of the cast-iron Dutch oven. It comes in a number of sizes, from one to six quarts, costs as little as $19 and uses about as much electricity as an ordinary light bulb. If you haven't tried yours lately, dust it off.

A *casserole* can be of any material, as long as it conducts the heat efficiently from the oven through its sides, bottom and lid. Commonly available in ovenproof glass, ceramic or earthenware, with small handles on each side to make them easier to carry, casseroles also come in cast iron, copper, enameled iron, aluminum and stainless steel. We like the ceramic, enameled iron and cast-iron models for their even distribution of heat.

Pottery cooking vessels are the direct descendants of humankind's earliest cookware. Artisans learned early that if the sides of the pot bulged out, the pot would cook the food more efficiently, because a larger portion of the surface is exposed to the heat than with a straight-sided vessel. Today's bean pot is a part of this tradition.

A *wok* with a cover is often handy. We use ours a lot, coupling it with bamboo steamers for some dishes. For delicate dishes of chicken, seafood or vegetables cooked in broth, the *Yunnan steam pot*, widely used in parts of China and available in Chinese specialty shops in this country, works something like a double boiler. It is a small, hard-fired, unglazed clay vessel with an inner chimney, shaped like a rounded angel food cake pan. The food, including some broth, is put in the pot around the center chimney. The pot is covered and placed in a wok. Steam from the boiling water in the wok travels up the chimney and spreads out over whatever is being braised, intensifying the flavors and aromas.

IN WRITING THIS BOOK, we have come to realize that we owe far more to the folk cook than to the sophisticated chef. Friends have generously shared their own traditions with us. Often, their specialties required what our friend Larry Stone calls "*Fingerspitzengefuehl,*" which can be loosely translated as intuition but really means a combination of intuition and experience—a touch of this, a bit of that. Neither of us can recall seeing cookbooks in the kitchens of Grandma Weller and Fred Griffith, Sr. They cooked with what was there, never from a recipe. Our goal has been to pay homage to that older style of cooking, while providing guidelines along the way. In so doing, we hope to recover lost connections and bring new enjoyment to the simple act of eating.

Cooking Preferences

CONNECTIONS INSPIRE US. We celebrate our connections to cooks of the past—not just in our family, but to those writers whose works belong to history. We also believe it is important to recognize the connections between the food we eat and the farmers who produce it. We try to eat seasonally and regionally, using the freshest organically grown produce whenever possible. If you need help finding organic growers in your region, check with the agricultural extension service or with chefs at fine restaurants, who are apt to know local growers.

We prefer organic stone-ground flours, meal, grains and beans. We use fresh herbs, since they impart full flavor without the harshness that often characterizes dried.

We always cook with kosher salt because we like its light, clean flavor and its coarse texture. Sea salt, which also has a light, fresh taste, is equally good. Neither of these salts contains any additives. Ordinary table, or common, salt is fine-grained, with additives, which we feel lend a definite medicinal flavor.

For chile powder, we prefer pure ground chiles, found in specialty food markets. Commercial chili powder, which can be substituted, is usually a blend incorporating other seasonings.

In keeping with our concerns for healthful food, we use hormone-free poultry, which is dipped in cold rather than hot water before plucking. Not only does it taste fresher than ordinary chicken, but it is nearly impossible to overcook, because it retains moisture during cooking. We are equally particular about the quality of our meats. When it comes to bacon, we generally use well-smoked bacon that is very lightly cured and not injected with water and chemicals.

For cookware, we rely on our fine assortment of cast-iron skillets, many of which were acquired for pennies at flea markets and antique shops. Two cast-iron Dutch ovens, one 5½ quarts and the other 8½ quarts, are almost as old. We often turn to our ancient Magnalite sauté pan, whose tight cover fits beautifully on our well-seasoned skillet. Two large, oval roasters serve us well: one cast aluminum made by Magnalite, the other enamel over steel. We have an old, well-seasoned wok with a battered, but tight, cover. Our casseroles are flameware, which is similar in cooking properties to stoneware and is made by Massachusetts potter Bill Sax. Don Drumm's handsome cast-aluminum pots are also useful, going from stove directly to buffet table. (See Sources, page 336.)

Finally, we never cook with a wine we do not enjoy drinking. Our cooking wine of choice continues to be R.H. Phillips California Night Harvest Sauvignon Blanc (white) and Mistura (a Rhône-style red). The specific wines suggested to accompany our main- or first-course recipes are among many fine choices that one could make. Some of these wines may not be available where you live. Your local retailer can suggest alternatives that are similar.

Starters

Tea-Smoked Scallops 18

Venetian-Style Shrimp with Olive Paste Croutons 20

Rustic Terrine (Country Pork Loaf) 22

Stuffed Grape Leaves Shaheen (*Yub ' Ruck*) 24

Grandma Bess's Meatballs 26

Foil-Baked Sweet Onions with Mushrooms, Shallots & Herbs 28

Salt Cod in Garlic Sauce with Potatoes & Raisins 30

Pot Stickers with Cabbage, Scallions & Carrots 32

Artichokes Barigoule 34

Casserole of Artichokes Provençal 36

Tea-Smoked Scallops

Serves 6-8

THE CHINESE TRADITION OF SMOKING FOODS over tea instead of wood has become popular in this country, especially as more home cooks have learned how simple it can be. Done right on the stovetop, it makes no mess. The smoking ingredients—a mixture of dried black tea leaves and spices—are put in a foil-lined wok. The food is placed on a rack above the mixture and covered until the distinctively flavored smoke cooks the scallops.

A simple soy, ginger and cilantro marinade gives a delicate lift to big sea scallops. The light, slightly sweet smoke cooks them to silky perfection. After chilling, we serve them with a creamy mustard sauce. You might also want to slice the smoked scallops and serve them on endive spears, garnished with a dollop of the sauce.

Scallops and Marinade
- 3 tablespoons dry white wine
- 3 tablespoons soy sauce
- 1 tablespoon Asian sesame oil
- 4 scallions, trimmed to include 1 inch of green and minced
- 1 tablespoon minced fresh ginger
- 1 tablespoon minced fresh cilantro
- 1 teaspoon sugar
- 1½ pounds sea scallops

Smoking Mixture
- ½ cup packed dark brown sugar
- 2 tablespoons smashed star anise (or substitute aniseeds)
- ½ cup black tea leaves

Sauce
- 2 tablespoons Colman's dry English mustard
- 2 tablespoons Dijon mustard
- 1½ cups low-fat sour cream
- 1 cup whole-milk yogurt (available in natural-food stores)
- 2 tablespoons Worcestershire sauce
   Freshly ground white pepper

- 1 tablespoon Asian sesame oil

To marinate scallops: Combine wine, soy sauce, sesame oil, scallions, ginger, cilantro and sugar in a large Pyrex pie plate. Whisk well to combine. Add scallops and turn to coat well with marinade. Cover dish with plastic, and refrigerate, turning several times, for 1½ to 3 hours.

To make smoking mixture: Line a wok with heavy foil; also line inside of wok's cover. Combine brown sugar, anise and tea leaves in wok. Place a rack or steaming basket about 3 inches above steaming mixture.

Rearrange scallops in a single layer. Place pie plate on rack; cover wok. If it does not have a lid, cover tightly with heavy-duty foil.

Cook over high heat until you can smell smoke, 2 to 3 minutes. Reduce heat to medium and cook for 10 minutes. Turn off heat and let scallops rest, still covered, for 5 minutes.

Meanwhile, make sauce: In a medium bowl, combine mustards and blend well. Whisk in sour cream, then yogurt, Worcestershire and white pepper. Chill until needed. Sauce will keep, covered and refrigerated, for up to 1 week.

Carefully transfer scallops to a clean plate. Toss with sesame oil. Chill for several hours. Serve cold, with sauce.

Wine: Trimbach Gewürztraminer (France: Alsace) or another full-bodied Alsatian Gewürztraminer

Venetian-Style Shrimp with Olive Paste Croutons

Serves 6

T HESE SHRIMP ARE BRAISED IN A LIGHT SWEET-AND-SOUR SAUCE. The preparation is a traditional Venetian one, but we've adapted it, using shrimp in place of the usual fillet of sole. As an alternative, dust small fillets of sole or perch and cook them as you do the shrimp, reducing the cooking time in the first step by 2 minutes if the fillets are very thin. A simple tapenade, or olive paste, on a toasted crouton makes a pleasing accompaniment. You can also serve this as a summer supper.

Olive Paste

1	cup pitted Kalamata olives
6	oil-packed sun-dried tomatoes
3	plump garlic cloves
	About ¼ cup extra-virgin olive oil

Shrimp

¼	cup unbleached flour
1¼	pounds large shrimp (21-24 per pound), shelled and deveined
4	tablespoons (½ stick) unsalted butter
1	tablespoon olive oil
½	small dried red chile, crumbled
1	plump garlic clove, minced
1	medium-sized yellow onion, thinly sliced
1	plump shallot, minced
3	tablespoons pine nuts
1	bay leaf
½	cup dry white wine
¼	cup red wine vinegar
¼	cup fish or chicken stock (page 327 or page 325)
⅓	cup golden raisins
⅛	teaspoon ground cinnamon
2	grindings of nutmeg
	Kosher salt and freshly ground black pepper to taste

12   ½-inch-thick slices French baguette

To make olive paste: Combine olives, sun-dried tomatoes and garlic in a food processor fitted with the metal blade. Pulse until pureed. With motor running, slowly add enough oil to make a smooth paste. Add more oil if you prefer a thinner paste. Set aside.

To make shrimp: Combine flour and shrimp in a paper bag and toss until shrimp are lightly coated with flour. In a large nonreactive skillet with a tight-fitting lid, heat butter and oil over medium heat until butter melts. Add shrimp, dried chile, garlic, onion, shallot and pine nuts; stir to coat lightly. Cover and cook shrimp mixture, shaking skillet, until shrimp are somewhat firm to the touch, about 3 minutes. Add bay leaf, wine, vinegar, stock, raisins, cinnamon and nutmeg. Increase heat and cook until liquids begin to boil. Reduce heat, cover and simmer for 5 minutes.

Remove skillet from heat. Uncover and allow shrimp and sauce to cool for about 20 minutes. Discard bay leaf; season with salt and pepper.

While shrimp are cooling, preheat broiler.

Arrange bread slices on a cookie sheet, and toast until medium-dark on both sides. Generously spread each crouton with olive paste.

Serve shrimp lukewarm on heated plates accompanied by 2 croutons for each person.

Wine: Ca' Del Solo Il Pescatore (California) or a citrusy, dry white Italian wine or an Aligoté from Burgundy

Rustic Terrine

(*Country Pork Loaf*)

Serves 12-14

A FRENCH COUNTRY TERRINE is a type of meat loaf that is covered and baked in a water bath, then chilled under weights to make it firm and smooth. The water bath maintains the heat at a temperature so low that the meat cooks but does not brown. Slices of this delicately spiced terrine, a chunk of crusty bread and a glass of chilled wine are all you need for a picnic lunch. A single serving garnished with small pickles and a crust of bread is a terrific prelude to a simple supper. When cooked and served, the sliced pistachios and chicken livers make a handsome pattern surrounded by the ground meats. Thoroughly wrapped, this terrine will keep nicely in the refrigerator for more than a week; the flavors deepen as it stands.

1¾	pounds lean pork butt, ground
¾	pound lean veal, ground
½	pound bacon, ground, plus 6 slices
1	cup dry white wine
¼	pound chicken livers, trimmed
1	tablespoon applejack or brandy
⅓	cup minced shallots
2	plump garlic cloves, minced
2	tablespoons unbleached flour
1	large egg, lightly beaten
1	tablespoon kosher salt
1	tablespoon freshly ground black pepper
1	teaspoon *quatre épices* (or ¼ teaspoon *each* ground cloves, nutmeg, cinnamon and ginger)
½	teaspoon dried thyme
⅓	cup shelled pistachio nuts
2	bay leaves
	Cornichons, pickled onions and French bread, for serving

Combine ground meats in a bowl. Toss with wine, wrap with plastic and refrigerate.

In another bowl, combine livers with applejack or brandy, seal with plastic and refrigerate. Marinate for at least 4 hours, or up to 12.

Preheat oven to 350 degrees F. Line a 6-cup terrine or loaf pan with bacon slices so that slices cover bottom and come up sides. Reserve 1 slice for top.

Drain liquid from meats and discard. In a large mixing bowl, combine ground meats with shallots, garlic, flour, egg, salt, pepper, spices, thyme and pistachios. Blend thoroughly. Pat half of mixture into terrine or loaf pan. Make a layer of livers, gently pressing them into mixture. Cover with remaining meat mixture, pressing firmly to fill any air pockets. Smooth top and draw any bacon "tails" over top. Place reserved bacon slice on top of terrine. Arrange bay leaves in center.

Cover tightly with heavy-duty foil; if your terrine has a lid, place it over foil. Place terrine or loaf pan in a deep roasting pan filled with enough boiling water to reach halfway up sides. Bake for 2 hours.

Remove terrine or loaf pan from oven and water bath. Let cool to room temperature with cover on. Remove lid. Place a heavy weight (we use a brick) on top of foil. Chill for at least 8 hours before serving.

Serve terrine in thin slices, with cornichons, pickled onions and French bread.

Wine: Marcel Deiss Gewürztraminer (France: Alsace) or Adelsheim Vineyards Riesling (Oregon: Willamette Valley) or any complex Alsatian Gewürztraminer

Stuffed Grape Leaves Shaheen

(Yub ' Ruck)

Makes 48-50 Grape Leaves

BORN IN CANTON, OHIO, more than 70 years ago, sisters Wedad and Helen Shaheen are excellent home cooks who continue the rich traditions taught them by their Syrian mother and grandmother. They are famous for their stuffed grape leaves—filled with a simple mixture of ground lamb and rice, seasoned with a hint of allspice and cooked in a buttery lemon-juiced water bath. If you cook the grape leaves over rhubarb, as the Shaheens sometimes do, it lends a subtle tang. In the spring and early summer, grape leaves can be found on vines growing in the woods. Choose the silky ones, the heavier ones don't taste as good. Canned leaves can be purchased at Middle Eastern markets all year long; be sure to rinse the vinegar from them. Wedad and Helen remind us that stuffed grape leaves make great finger food.

6	rhubarb stalks (if available), cut to fit across bottom of saucepan
60	grape leaves, more if available, drained or blanched
1	cup raw white rice, rinsed
2	pounds coarsely ground lamb or beef
½	cup minced fresh flat-leaf parsley
½	cup melted unsalted butter or oil
¼	teaspoon ground allspice
	Kosher salt and freshly ground black pepper
	Juice of 2 lemons

Select a large, heavy-bottomed nonreactive saucepan with a tight-fitting lid. Place near your work area. Line bottom with a layer of grape leaves. If you are using rhubarb, pack stalks in a layer across bottom.

In a large bowl, blend together rice, lamb or beef, parsley, butter or oil, allspice and salt and pepper.

Arrange a batch of grape leaves, rough sides up, on a work surface. Use pieces of torn leaves as filler for any large holes in the better leaves. Place about 1 tablespoon filling across stem side of leaf, distributing evenly, in an oval shape, 1 to 1½ inches long. Fold a very small part of sides over filling; roll up to make a neat package. Continue until all stuffing is used.

Arrange grape leaves close together in layers in saucepan; be certain not to squeeze too tightly. Alternate directions of each layer. When all rolls are placed in saucepan, sprinkle some salt over the top. Cover with a layer of grape leaves.

Invert a ceramic or stoneware plate on top to press down on rolls. Add water to reach plate. Tightly cover and cook over medium heat until water boils, about 10 minutes.

Reduce heat to low and cook for 20 minutes. Sprinkle on lemon juice and cook until stuffed grape leaves feel firm to the touch, about 10 minutes more. Discard rhubarb and grape leaves on bottom.

Serve stuffed grape leaves hot or at room temperature. Refrigerate leftovers with the cooking broth.

Wine: Azalea Springs Merlot (California: Napa Valley) or Edna Valley Vineyards Chardonnay (California: Edna Valley) or any fruity Merlot

Grandma Bess's Meatballs

Serves 8-10

THIS OLD-FASHIONED COVERED DISH featuring tender meatballs cooked in a tangy cabbage sauce is excellent for potluck parties or school suppers. Clevelander Bess Klausner prepared these meatballs for more than 70 years before she turned the recipe over to her son and daughter-in-law David and Deborah Klausner. While the meatballs were originally served as a main dish, we've enjoyed them in recent years as an appetizer when dining at the Klausner home. Bess always made these with Sauce Arturo tomato sauce, distributed by the Red Wing Company, Fredonia, New York 14063. If you can find Arturo's in your area, use it, but omit the brown sugar and vinegar. If you choose to offer the meatballs as an appetizer, serve them from a heated chafing dish.

Meatballs

¾	pound ground beef
¾	pound ground veal
¾	cup coarse fresh bread crumbs
½	cup minced onion
1	plump garlic clove, minced
1½	teaspoons kosher salt
1½	teaspoons freshly ground black pepper
½	teaspoon dried marjoram
2	large eggs
	Up to ¼ cup vegetable oil
8	cups coarsely chopped cabbage (1 head)

Sauce

1	1-pound can whole cranberry sauce
2	8-ounce cans tomato sauce, preferably Sauce Arturo
1	tablespoon packed light brown sugar
1	teaspoon red wine vinegar

Preheat oven to 350 degrees F. Lightly oil a shallow 3- or 4-quart baking dish.

To make meatballs: Combine ground meats, bread crumbs, onion, garlic, salt, pepper, marjoram, eggs and ¼ cup water in a large mixing bowl. Mix vigorously until ingredients are thoroughly blended.

Form meatballs the size of plump walnuts. Lightly coat a large cast-iron skillet with oil. Brown meatballs over medium heat, 5 to 6 minutes, adding more oil if needed.

While meatballs are browning, distribute cabbage evenly over bottom of oiled baking dish. Scatter browned meatballs over cabbage.

To make sauce and bake: Blend together cranberry and tomato sauces, brown sugar and vinegar. Pour over meatballs; do not add extra liquid. Tightly cover with foil and bake until cabbage is softened into sauce, about 1½ hours.

Serve hot on small plates with forks.

Wine: Georges Duboeuf Beaujolais-Villages (France) or Peachy Canyon Zinfandel (California: Paso Robles) or another medium-bodied fruity red wine

Foil-Baked Sweet Onions with Mushrooms, Shallots & Herbs

Serves 4

THESE TENDER SWEET ONIONS are oven-steamed in a flavorful mushroom sauce, their protective outer skin pulled back and crisped into jaunty topknots. We serve them with their tops upright on plates. This recipe is inspired by the specialty of the house at the restaurant Vidalia in Washington, D.C. While the chef was never able to talk with us, we finally made our own version. You will love this succulent onion in its fragrant and delicious mushroom sauce.

4	medium-sized sweet onions, such as Vidalias, unpeeled
½	pound fresh shiitake or portobello mushrooms, stemmed
1	medium carrot, cut into pieces
1	plump shallot
1	plump garlic clove
1	tablespoon fresh tarragon leaves or 2 teaspoons dried
4	tablespoons (½ stick) unsalted butter
2	teaspoons soy sauce
2	teaspoons freshly ground black pepper, plus more
8	tablespoons dry Marsala
	Freshly grated nutmeg
2	tablespoons minced fresh chives

Preheat oven to 425 degrees F.

Carefully slice off tops of onions. Without cutting into flesh, score onion skin from top down to root in order to make about 6 "petals." Gently pull onion-skin petals back toward root into a loose ponytail. Set aside.

Combine mushrooms, carrot, shallot, garlic and tarragon in a food processor fitted with the metal blade. Pulse until finely chopped.

In a small skillet, melt butter over medium heat. Stir in mushroom mixture, soy sauce and 2 teaspoons pepper. Cover, reduce heat and braise until mushrooms have absorbed liquid, about 4 minutes.

Arrange 4 foil squares, each 12 x 10 inches, on a work surface. Divide mushroom mixture among squares, spooning some into center of each. Pour 2 tablespoons Marsala over each. Add a few grindings of nutmeg. Place 1 onion, top side down over the mushroom mixture. Carefully pull corners of foil over onion so that bulb is tightly covered, but ponytail of onion skin is exposed. Crunch foil together to close.

Place onions on a cookie sheet, flattened top sides down, ponytails upright. Bake until onion feels tender when gently pressed, about 45 minutes.

To serve, carefully open package. Using a spatula, scoop up mushroom mixture and onion and place it in the center of a heated serving plate. Carefully pour collected juices around onion. Add a few grindings of pepper. Repeat for remaining packages. Sprinkle onions with chives and serve.

Wine: Rosemont Estate Shiraz-Cabernet (southeastern Australia) or Truchard Vineyard Chardonnay Carneros (California: Napa Valley) or another full-bodied Shiraz-Cabernet from Australia

Salt Cod in Garlic Sauce with Potatoes & Raisins

Serves 8

acala, COOKED SALT COD, is an integral part of Christmas Eve dinner in traditional Italian celebrations. Members of Cleveland's Minnillo family gather at their beautiful Baricelli Inn to enjoy their customary feast of fish and shellfish. They begin their meal with this simple dish of salt cod braised with olive oil, garlic and potatoes and tossed with golden raisins. This is Chef Paul Minnillo's lighter version of a recipe that has been handed down over the decades. Because one needs to reconstitute and desalt the fish, Paul prefers to soak his for 5 days, but we find that 1 day is sufficient.

4	pounds salt cod
1	head garlic
1	tablespoon plus ¼ cup olive oil
1¾	pounds red or Yukon gold potatoes, peeled
1	bunch fresh flat-leaf parsley, finely chopped, plus sprigs, for garnish
	Freshly ground white pepper
½	cup golden raisins

The day before serving, place salt cod in a colander under a faucet in your sink. Trickle cold water over cod for 1 to 2 hours, occasionally moving pieces around from bottom to top. Transfer to a large bowl and cover with cold water. Refrigerate for 24 hours, changing water at least 4 times. Drain, rinse and pat dry. Cover with plastic wrap and chill for 2 to 6 hours.

While cod is chilling, caramelize garlic: Preheat oven to 325 degrees F. Slice off top of garlic. Gently remove heavier outer papery skin from sides of head. Place head in a small oven-proof dish. Spoon 1 tablespoon oil over garlic; drizzle with 1 teaspoon water. Tightly cover with foil. Bake garlic for 1¼ hours.

Uncover, baste with any remaining pan juices, and bake, uncovered, until golden, about 15 minutes more. Remove from oven and set aside; leave oven on.

Meanwhile, cut potatoes into 1-inch cubes; boil until tender, about 15 minutes. Drain, let cool and chill while you prepare fish.

Increase oven temperature to 375 degrees.

Cut fish into 1-inch cubes. Combine cubed potatoes and fish in a shallow 3-to-4-quart ovenproof casserole. Carefully separate cloves from garlic head. To remove garlic from skin, gently squeeze bottom of each clove. Mince garlic and parsley together; sprinkle evenly over fish. Pour remaining ¼ cup oil over parsley mixture. Season with white pepper.

Cover casserole with foil. Bake until fish and potatoes are hot and oil is bubbling, about 25 minutes.

Remove casserole from oven, uncover and toss fish mixture with raisins. Serve, garnished with fresh parsley sprigs.

Wine: Long Vineyards Pinot Grigio (California: Napa Valley) or Alpine Vineyards Riesling (Oregon: Willamette Valley) or a Pinot Grigio from Italy

Pot Stickers with Cabbage, Scallions & Carrots

Makes 36-40; serves 8-10

THESE DELIGHTFUL CHINESE DUMPLINGS have a gingered filling of cabbage, scallions and carrots, instead of the usual ground pork. The zesty dipping sauce is refreshed by lots of minced cilantro. The most important part of cooking pot stickers is the final braising in a thin mixture of cornstarch and water; they steam and glaze simultaneously. While we always make our pot stickers in an electric frying pan, a heavy-bottomed skillet with a tight-fitting lid will work equally well. (See photograph, page 82.)

Pot Stickers

2   cups finely chopped napa cabbage
3   medium carrots, cut into chunks
2   plump garlic cloves
4   scallions, trimmed to include 1 inch of green,
        cut into pieces
2   ¼-inch-thick slices peeled fresh ginger
1   tablespoon minced fresh cilantro
1   tablespoon dark soy sauce, preferably black
1   tablespoon rice wine
1   teaspoon dark sesame oil
    Up to ¼ cup cornstarch
1   10-ounce package gyoza wrappers
        (a round wrapper made without eggs)

Dipping Sauce

2   tablespoons soy sauce, preferably mushroom soy sauce
2   tablespoons Chinese black vinegar
3   tablespoons rice wine
2   tablespoons red wine vinegar
2   teaspoons Chinese chili paste
1   teaspoon Asian sesame oil
2   tablespoons minced fresh cilantro
1   tablespoon minced scallions, green parts included
1   teaspoon minced fresh ginger

Up to ¼ cup peanut oil

To make pot stickers: In a food processor fitted with the metal blade, combine cabbage, carrots, garlic, scallions, ginger and cilantro. Pulse until finely chopped. Add soy sauce, rice wine and sesame oil; pulse until mixture is fairly smooth.

Lightly dust a large flat tray or plate with cornstarch. Arrange wrappers, floured sides up, on a work surface. Put ⅓ cup cold water in a small bowl. Place a rounded teaspoonful of filling in center of each wrapper. Dip your finger into water and moisten outer edge of each filled wrapper. Fold each piece in half, using your thumb and index finger to pinch a few folds across each dumpling top where edges come together. Place dumpling, plump side down, on prepared tray and repeat until 36 to 40 dumplings are made. Cover well with wax paper until time to fry.

In a small dish, combine 1 teaspoon cornstarch and a scant ½ cup cold water. Blend thoroughly; set aside.

To make dipping sauce: In a small serving bowl, combine all ingredients and whisk well to blend. Set aside.

To cook pot stickers: Preheat an electric frying pan to 400 degrees F, or set a large cast-iron skillet over medium-high heat. Brush skillet with enough oil to coat bottom generously, and heat until oil shimmers. Arrange all dumplings close together, but not touching, in pan. Fry, uncovered, until bottoms just begin to brown, 3 to 5 minutes.

Quickly pour reserved water-cornstarch mixture over tops of dumplings. Cover pan, reduce heat to 375 degrees or to medium-low and cook until dumpling bottoms are well browned and tops have a nice shine to them, 2 to 4 minutes.

Carefully remove pot stickers from pan and arrange on a heated serving platter. Serve with dipping sauce.

Wine: Veuve Cliquot Brut Champagne (France: Champagne) or another dry sparkling white wine

Artichokes Barigoule

Serves 4-6

Barigoule IS A PROVENÇAL NAME FOR THE MUSHROOM originally used in this dish. But the term has come to mean a particular method of braising on a bed of vegetables. There are numerous variations on this time-honored dish of braised artichokes. The constants appear to be onions and bacon. Here, we braise the artichokes on a bed of onions and carrots, cooking them long and slow so they form a tender "sauce" for the artichokes. The bacon, meanwhile, lends a delightful smoky quality. It's a delicious preparation, great as a first course for dinner or a main dish for lunch. (See photograph, page 95.)

	Juice of 1 lemon, plus 1 whole lemon,
	cut into quarters or sixths, for garnish
4-6	large artichokes
3	tablespoons olive oil
2	cups thinly sliced yellow onions
2	medium carrots, grated
2	thick slices bacon, cut into small matchsticks
2	cups chicken stock (page 325)
½	cup dry white wine
1	bouquet garni (page 331)
	Kosher salt and freshly ground black pepper
⅛	teaspoon freshly grated nutmeg

Fill a large mixing bowl with cold water. Add lemon juice and set aside. With a sharp knife, remove artichoke stem. Cut off and discard top third of artichoke; remove and discard tough lower leaves. Using sharp kitchen scissors, cut off upper pointed tips of all remaining leaves. Immediately plunge artichoke into lemon water. Repeat until all artichokes are prepared and soaking in lemon water.

In a heavy, nonreactive saucepan or deep skillet just large enough to hold artichokes, combine oil, onions and carrots. Arrange artichokes on vegetables and sprinkle evenly with bacon. Add ⅔ cup stock, wine and bouquet garni. Sprinkle artichokes with salt, pepper and nutmeg. Cover pan with a tight-fitting lid and place over high heat until liquid begins to bubble.

Reduce heat to low and braise, basting from time to time and adding more of remaining 1⅓ cups stock as needed to keep artichokes moist. Cook until artichokes are very tender, about 1 hour. To test for doneness, gently tug a lower artichoke leaf; when you meet with only the barest suggestion of resistance, artichokes are done.

Discard bouquet garni. Serve artichokes on heated plates surrounded by some of vegetable mixture and pan juices for dipping. Garnish with lemon wedges.

Wine: Ferrari-Carano Fumé Blanc (California: Sonoma County) or another citrusy Sauvignon Blanc

Casserole of Artichokes Provençal

Serves 4

T HESE TENDER ARTICHOKES are stuffed with a light herb-enriched fresh bread crumb filling. They are then slowly braised on a bed of onions and tomato puree that cooks into a kind of marmalade by the time the artichokes are tender. This makes a superb first course. Or, should you wish to serve them for a luncheon main course, add some smoked ham to the filling.

	Juice of 1 lemon
4	large artichokes
1¼	cups coarse fresh bread crumbs
⅓	cup minced fresh flat-leaf parsley
⅓	cup pitted Niçoise olives, minced
10	oil-packed anchovy fillets, drained and minced
4	plump garlic cloves, minced
1	teaspoon herbes de Provence or mixture of dried rosemary, savory, thyme, basil and crumbled bay leaf
	Kosher salt and freshly ground black pepper
4	tablespoons olive oil
2	large yellow onions, finely diced
½	cup dry white wine, plus more if needed
2	cups tomato puree (page 324) or canned crushed tomatoes

Fill a large mixing bowl with cold water. Add lemon juice and set aside. With a sharp knife, remove artichoke stem. Cut off and discard top third of artichoke; remove and discard tough lower leaves. Using sharp kitchen scissors, cut off upper pointed tips of all remaining leaves. With a small spoon, remove choke from center of artichoke. Carefully scrape out all of fuzz from center. Immediately plunge artichoke into lemon water. Repeat with remaining artichokes.

In a small mixing bowl, combine bread crumbs, parsley, olives, anchovies, garlic, herbes de Provence, salt and pepper and 1 tablespoon oil. Mix thoroughly and divide into 4 portions.

Put some stuffing into center of each artichoke. Using your fingers to pull petals open, carefully insert some stuffing around base of artichoke leaves; make certain that some stuffing is distributed throughout artichoke. Repeat until all 4 are prepared.

Pour 2 tablespoons oil into a heavy, nonreactive saucepan or deep skillet just large enough to hold artichokes. Sprinkle evenly with onions. Add wine and tomato puree or crushed tomatoes. Arrange prepared artichokes over onions. Drizzle with remaining 1 tablespoon oil. Season with salt and pepper.

Cover pan with a tight-fitting lid and place over high heat until liquid begins to bubble. Reduce heat to low and braise, basting from time to time and adding more wine if needed to keep artichokes moist, until artichokes are very tender, 1 to 1¼ hours. To test for doneness, gently tug a lower artichoke leaf; when you meet with only the barest suggestion of resistance, artichokes are done. About the time artichokes are done, tomato and onion mixture should be thick and creamy.

Serve artichokes on heated plates. Spoon some tomato and onion mixture over each.

Wine: Reserve St.-Martin Marsanne (France: Roussillon) or a Marsanne from Australia

Soups

Summer Asparagus Soup with Tarragon 40

Fresh Pea Soup with Mint 41

Potage Crécy (Puree of Carrot Soup) 42

Salmon & Spinach Chowder with Yellow Potatoes & Scallions 43

New England Clam Chowder 44

Creamy Fish Chowder with Chard & Corn 46

Potato & Leek Soup with Sage 47

Fresh Pumpkin & Apple Bisque with Crispy Leeks 48

Pokagama Soup 50

Big Soup of Split Peas 52

Kentucky Black Bean Soup with Sherry 54

Spicy Hungarian Sauerkraut Soup 56

Creamy Rutabaga Soup with Caramelized Shallots 57

Cauliflower Bisque 58

Winter Vegetable Stew 59

Summer Asparagus Soup with Tarragon

Serves 4-6

SPINACH AND TARRAGON add a light, fresh "green" note to this simple soup of asparagus and onion. For an even more delicate flavor, use vegetable stock instead of chicken stock as the base. Should you prefer the soup cold, blend a cup of yogurt into the chilled soup just before serving.

2   tablespoons unsalted butter
1   pound asparagus, trimmed and coarsely chopped
1   pound spinach, cleaned and trimmed
1   large sweet onion, coarsely chopped
2   tablespoons fresh tarragon leaves
3   cups chicken stock (page 325), plus more if needed
     Kosher salt and freshly ground white pepper
     Freshly grated nutmeg

Melt butter in a large nonreactive skillet with a tight-fitting lid. Add asparagus and stir to coat well. Add spinach, onion, tarragon, 3 cups stock and salt and white pepper. Cover and cook over medium heat until liquid begins to bubble.

Reduce heat and simmer until vegetables are soft, about 30 minutes.

Place a large strainer over a 3-quart saucepan. Using a slotted spoon, transfer solids to strainer. Pour liquid through. Transfer solids to a food processor. Add 1 cup liquid and pulse until pureed. Return mixture to saucepan and blend thoroughly. Soup should be quite thick; add more stock only if needed to create a pleasing texture. Adjust seasonings and add generous grindings of nutmeg. Reheat just before serving.

Wine: Harpersfield Vineyards Gewürztraminer (Ohio: Lake Erie) or a full-bodied Alsatian Gewürztraminer

Fresh Pea Soup with Mint

Serves 4

THIS FRESH SOUP IS PERFECT IN THE SUMMER when the peas are available locally and have a special sweetness. To emphasize their flavor, we add a touch of mint before serving.

2   pounds whole fresh pea pods, shelled, pods reserved
1   medium-sized white onion, cut in half
1   head Boston lettuce, leaves separated and cleaned,
         plus 1 cup shredded
2   tablespoons unsalted butter
     Kosher salt and freshly ground white pepper
1   tablespoon minced fresh mint, preferably a fruit mint
         such as pineapple, apple or orange

In a large saucepan, combine pea pods, onion and whole lettuce leaves with 6 cups water. Cover and bring to a boil over high heat. Reduce heat to low and simmer for 30 minutes.

Pour mixture through a large strainer; reserve stock and discard solids.

Melt butter in saucepan over medium heat. Add peas, cover and cook, shaking pan frequently, for 3 minutes. Add strained stock, cover and simmer briskly for 3 minutes. Stir in shredded lettuce and salt and white pepper to taste. Cover and simmer for 1 minute.

Ladle into heated soup plates and sprinkle with mint.

Wine: Kunde Estate Winery Sauvignon Blanc (California: Sonoma County) or another nonherbaceous Sauvignon Blanc

Potage Crécy

(*Puree of Carrot Soup*)

Serves 6-8

FRENCH IN ORIGIN, THIS DELICIOUS CARROT SOUP is simple, light and fragrant. If you wish to finish the soup in the traditional manner, force the solids through a fine mesh strainer instead of pureeing in a food processor. There will be somewhat more texture in the food processor soup. What is "Crécy?" According to *Larousse Gastronomique*, the soup might be named for a small French town noted for the quality of its carrots, or it could be named for a different little town that was near where the Battle of Crécy was fought in 1346.

3	tablespoons unsalted butter
½	cup minced shallots
2	pounds carrots, thinly sliced
7	cups chicken or vegetable stock (pages 325 or 330)
½	cup cooked white rice (from ¼ cup raw)
	Juice and grated zest of 1 lemon
	Kosher salt and freshly ground white pepper
¼	cup minced fresh chives, for garnish

In a large, heavy-bottomed pot, melt butter over low heat. Add shallots, cover and braise until softened, about 3 minutes. Stir in carrots, cover and continue to braise over very low heat until carrots begin to soften, about 15 minutes.

Add stock and rice, cover, increase heat to medium-high and cook until liquid begins to bubble, about 5 minutes. Reduce heat to low and simmer for 30 minutes. Remove soup from heat and let cool.

Puree soup in a food processor fitted with the metal blade. Return puree to pot, stir in lemon juice and zest and salt and white pepper.

Reheat soup before serving and serve in warmed soup plates garnished with chives.

Wine: Paul Cotat Sancerre Chavignol Les Culs de Beaujeu (France: Loire) or another flinty dry wine from the Loire

Salmon & Spinach Chowder with Yellow Potatoes & Scallions

Serves 4

THIS SIMPLE SOUP OF SALMON AND SPINACH retains its fresh flavor because the ingredients are cooked as briefly as possible. The combination of yellow potatoes, pink salmon and green spinach looks smashing. This soup makes a good prelude to a meal or a supper for two.

3	tablespoons unsalted butter
3	plump shallots, finely diced
1	teaspoon fresh thyme leaves or ½ teaspoon dried
2	large Yukon gold or red potatoes, peeled and cut into ½-inch dice
4	cups chicken stock (page 325)
⅓	cup dry white wine
½	pound fresh spinach, cleaned, trimmed and coarsely chopped
4	4-ounce salmon fillets, skinned, left whole Kosher salt and freshly ground white pepper
3	scallions, trimmed to include 1 inch of green, finely sliced

In a large nonreactive pot, melt butter over low heat. Add shallots and thyme, cover with a tight-fitting lid and braise over low heat until shallots are very tender, about 10 minutes. Add potatoes, stock and wine, cover and bring to a boil over medium heat. Reduce heat to low and simmer until potatoes are tender, 15 to 20 minutes.

Add spinach and salmon. Simmer, covered, until spinach wilts and salmon is done, about 5 minutes. To check salmon, uncover and gently insert tines of a fork into thickest part of fish; flesh should be opaque but slightly translucent in center.

Season soup with salt and white pepper. Divide salmon among heated soup plates; ladle over hot soup. Sprinkle with scallions and serve.

Wine: Knudsen Erath Winery Pinot Noir (Oregon: Willamette Valley) or Dry Creek Vineyard Sauvignon Blanc (California: Sonoma County) or another American Pinot Noir or Sauvignon Blanc

New England Clam Chowder

Serves 6-8

BEING FROM MASSACHUSETTS, Linda has always been devoted to a creamy, yet chunky, clam chowder. Her recipe also has a pleasing smoky quality that comes from a judicious use of bacon. Serve with thick slices of warm Under-Cover Corn Bread (page 267). If you use soft-shell clams, be certain to remove the tough dark membrane over the long siphon after the clams are steamed.

4	dozen littleneck (about 4½ pounds) or soft-shell clams (about 4 pounds), cleaned
2	tablespoons unsalted butter, melted
2	thick slices bacon, finely diced
⅓	cup minced fennel or celery
1	cup minced yellow onion
2	large russet potatoes, cut into ½-inch cubes
½	teaspoon dried thyme
	Kosher salt and freshly ground white pepper
⅔	cup fresh or frozen yellow corn kernels
2	cups whole milk, heated
1½	cups heavy cream, heated
	Several grindings of fresh nutmeg
⅓	cup minced fresh flat-leaf parsley and chives

To clean soft-shell clams, scrub them under cold running water; drain.

Combine clams and 2 cups cold water in a large saucepan. Cover, place pan over high heat and bring to a boil. Reduce heat to low and simmer until clams open, 8 to 10 minutes for littlenecks and about 4 minutes for soft-shells. Remove from heat. Reserve broth in saucepan.

Working quickly, discard any unopened clams and remove meat from shells of open ones. Place clams in a small bowl, toss with butter and cover until needed.

Combine bacon, fennel or celery and onion in a small skillet. Cover and cook over low heat until onion becomes translucent but not browned, about 10 minutes.

Add potatoes, onion mixture, thyme and salt and white pepper to clam broth. Cover, increase heat to medium and cook until stock begins to boil. Reduce heat to low and simmer until potatoes are almost tender, about 20 minutes.

Add corn; slowly stir in hot milk and cream. Cover and cook, without boiling, until very hot, about 5 minutes. Add reserved clams, heat through and adjust seasonings, adding salt and white pepper if needed.

Ladle chowder into heated soup plates, sprinkle with nutmeg and herbs and serve.

Wine: Au Bon Climat Chardonnay Bien Nacido Vineyard Reserve (California: Santa Barbara County) or another full-bodied California Chardonnay, preferably from the Santa Barbara region

Creamy Fish Chowder with Chard & Corn

Serves 4-6

THIS SIMPLE BUT SUBSTANTIAL FISH SOUP gets a special lift from tangy chard. Sea bass and red snapper are also good in it, and you can replace the butter with the fat rendered from 3 slices of bacon cut into matchsticks. (See photograph, page 91.)

3	large Yukon gold potatoes, peeled, cut into ½-inch cubes
3	tablespoons unsalted butter
1	cup thinly sliced yellow onions
6	large Swiss chard leaves, thick stems removed, shredded
1	teaspoon dried thyme
3	cups fish stock (page 327) or bottled clam juice
2	cups half-and-half or milk
1	pound monkfish, skinned and cut into 2-inch cubes
1	pound thick fresh cod fillet, cut at least 1 inch thick, skinned and cut into 2-inch rectangles
⅔	cup fresh or frozen yellow corn kernels
	Kosher salt and freshly ground white pepper
¼	cup minced fresh flat-leaf parsley

Combine potatoes and 4 cups water in a medium saucepan; bring to a boil over high heat. Cook for 5 minutes; drain and set aside.

In a large saucepan, melt butter over medium heat. Add onions and chard, cover and cook until onions are somewhat softened, about 5 minutes. Add potatoes, thyme, stock or clam juice and half-and-half or milk. Cover and cook over high heat until liquid begins to bubble, about 5 minutes. Reduce heat to low and cook until onions are exceptionally tender, about 20 minutes.

Add fish, corn and salt and white pepper; cover and bring to a boil over high heat. Reduce the heat to low and simmer until fish is opaque, 8 to 10 minutes.

Ladle into heated soup plates, dividing fish evenly. Sprinkle with parsley.

Wine: Frog's Leap Winery Sauvignon Blanc (California: Napa Valley) or another austere Napa Valley Sauvignon Blanc or a white wine from Bordeaux (France)

Potato & Leek Soup
with Sage

Serves 8-10

WHAT COULD BE BETTER FOR AUTUMN than a thick, hearty potato and leek soup? We take a box of pristine leeks and combine them with fresh-from-the-farm large white potatoes. Because we grow lots of sage in the garden, we like to add it fresh to fall dishes, but dried sage is just fine too. This fragrant soup is perfect for a bone-chilling winter's night. While any leek will do, for a great treat, we order the exceptional long-shafted, organically grown ones from Kingsfield Gardens (see Sources, page 334).

6	tablespoons (¾ stick) unsalted butter
6	large leeks, including tender green, well washed and thinly sliced
½	cup finely sliced shallots
1	rounded teaspoon minced fresh sage or ½ teaspoon dried
3	pounds large white potatoes, peeled and diced
11	cups chicken stock (page 325), plus more if needed
1	cup heavy cream or milk
	Kosher salt and freshly ground white pepper
	Minced scallions or fresh chives, for garnish

In a large, heavy pot over low heat, melt butter; add leeks, shallots and sage. Cover, reduce heat to low and cook until leeks are fairly tender, stirring from time to time, about 30 minutes.

Add potatoes and stock, cover and bring to a boil over medium heat. Reduce heat to low and simmer until potatoes are very tender, about 30 minutes.

Remove soup from heat. Using a slotted spoon or skimmer, transfer solids to a food processor fitted with the metal blade. Add about 1 cup cooking liquid and puree until smooth. (You may have to do this in several batches.)

Stir pureed mixture back into liquid in pot. Cook over low heat, stirring in cream or milk and salt and white pepper to taste. Simmer for a few minutes before serving, just to heat through.

Ladle into heated soup plates and sprinkle with minced scallions or chives.

Wine: Pine Ridge Winery Chenin Blanc (California: Napa Valley) or a medium-dry white wine from Vouvray (France)

Fresh Pumpkin & Apple Bisque with Crispy Leeks

Serves 8-10

DESPITE ITS INTENSE COLOR, pumpkin has a more subtle flavor than most of its squash cousins. Roasted apples and hints of cinnamon and ginger add a tinge of sweetness, making this bisque just right for the fall holidays. It is topped with crunchy fried leeks. (See photograph, page 84.)

5	pounds fresh pumpkin, unpeeled, but seeded and quartered
2	very large, tart apples (Rome, Jonathan, Gala), peeled and cored
5	cups chicken stock (page 325), plus more if needed
1	large leek, white part only
3	tablespoons unsalted butter
½	cup minced shallots
½	teaspoon ground ginger
¼	teaspoon ground cinnamon
2	cups whole milk
	Kosher salt and freshly ground white pepper
1½	cups canola oil, for frying
	Freshly grated nutmeg, for garnish

Preheat oven to 425 degrees F. Place pumpkin and apples in a foil-lined roasting pan. Add 1 cup stock; tightly cover with foil and bake until pumpkin is tender, about 1 hour.

Cut leek into 2-inch lengths. Finely julienne each length. Soak leek julienne in cold water for at least 30 minutes and up to 2 hours.

Meanwhile, melt butter in a large pot. Add shallots, cover and cook over very low heat until softened, about 4 minutes. Add remaining 4 cups stock and set aside.

When pumpkin is cool enough to handle, scrape flesh from skin and add to pot. Add whole apples and any remaining pan juices. Stir in ginger and cinnamon; cover pot.

Place pot over medium heat and cook until mixture begins to bubble, about 5 minutes. Reduce heat to low and simmer for 20 minutes.

Remove pot from heat. Carefully spoon mixture into a food processor fitted with the metal blade; puree until smooth. Stir puree back into pot. Stir in milk and more stock, if soup is too thick. Season with salt and white pepper. Cook slowly over low heat until just at the point of simmering.

Before serving, drain and carefully dry leeks. Place oil in a saucepan or wok and heat to 225 degrees, or until oil is hot enough to brown a cube of bread tossed into it. Deep-fry leeks in 2 batches until browned, 2 to 4 minutes. Drain well on paper towels; season with salt and white pepper.

Ladle hot soup into heated soup plates. Season with a few grindings of nutmeg and garnish with a handful of crispy leeks.

Wine: Fetzer Vineyards Gewürztraminer (California) or another American Gewürztraminer

Pokagama Soup

Serves 6

PRONOUNCED "PO-KAG-A-MA," this is a simple and traditional tomato, beef and barley soup. It was a childhood favorite of Wayne Marshall, husband of cookbook author Lydie Marshall. Thanks to Lydie's encouragement and help, Wayne's sister Marilyn Dabner has successfully developed recipes for some of their family dishes. According to Marilyn's notes, this soup was first replicated by their mother after the whole family enjoyed it in a hotel in Albert Lea, Minnesota, when returning from a family fishing trip to the northern part of the state. "Next to chicken soup," writes Marilyn, "this soup is best for severe colds and flu. And, when served with a large salad, good bread and apple pie à la mode, it is true comfort food." Neither she nor Wayne has any idea why the hotel named it Pokagama, because there is no such place in or around Minnesota now. But maybe 50 years ago, there was.

2	tablespoons olive oil
3	pounds beef soupbones with meat or 2 pounds boneless flanken or boneless short ribs
1	small cabbage wedge
1	large yellow onion, studded with 3 cloves, plus 1 medium onion, cut in half and thinly sliced
1	carrot, coarsely chopped, plus 1 large carrot, grated
	Tops of several celery stalks
3	whole allspice
3	black peppercorns
1	bay leaf
4	cups tomato juice
½	cup pearl barley
	Kosher salt and freshly ground black pepper
¼	cup minced fresh flat-leaf parsley

Heat oil in a large, heavy, nonreactive pot. Brown meat on all sides, 10 to 12 minutes.

Add 4 cups water, cabbage, whole onion, chopped carrot, celery tops, allspice, peppercorns and bay leaf; bring to a boil. Reduce heat to low and skim froth until it stops appearing. Add ½ cup more water.

Tightly cover pot and simmer over low heat until meat is very tender, about 2½ hours, being certain to replenish any liquid that evaporates. When meat is very tender, remove pot from heat and let meat cool in broth.

Remove all meat from bones. Discard bones and all fat and shred meat; set meat aside. Strain broth and discard solids. Return meat and broth to saucepan. Add sliced onion, grated carrot, tomato juice, barley and salt and pepper.

Bring soup to a boil over high heat. Reduce heat to low and simmer with the lid slightly ajar until barley is tender, about 30 minutes.

Ladle into heated soup plates and sprinkle with parsley.

Wine: E. Guigal Côtes du Rhône (France: Rhône) or a medium-bodied Rhône-style red wine

Big Soup of Split Peas

Serves 12-18

BIG IN FLAVOR, big in texture and big in quantity! And, in our house, it celebrates the end of another big, aged, smoked Virginia ham from S. Wallace Edwards & Sons, our favorite purveyors of smoked-pork products (see page 335). You can use any hambone, but it's best to use one that has been smoked. Yellow and green split peas and carrots contribute color, while the caramelized onions bring an irresistible sweetness, complementing the smoky flavor. The soup is generously seasoned with curry powder and freshly ground black pepper. (If you wish to omit the hambone, add more onions and oil and caramelize them until they are very dark.) Serve with thick slices of hearty bread.

4	tablespoons (½ stick) unsalted butter
1	tablespoon vegetable oil
1	jumbo Spanish onion, finely diced
2	medium carrots, finely chopped
2	celery stalks, finely diced
1	tablespoon minced garlic
2	tablespoons curry powder
1	teaspoon freshly ground black pepper
1	pound *each* yellow and green split peas
2	teaspoons kosher salt, plus more if needed
1	teaspoon dried thyme
16	cups (4 quarts) chicken stock (page 325) or water, plus more if needed
1	large smoked hambone or smoked ham hock (about 2 pounds), trimmed of any fat

In a large, heavy pot, combine butter and oil over medium heat until butter melts. Add onion and cook, stirring often, until onion is golden, 15 to 20 minutes.

Add carrots, celery and garlic; cook, stirring, until softened, about 5 minutes. Add curry powder and pepper; cook, stirring, for 2 minutes to release flavors. Add split peas, salt, thyme, stock or water and hambone or ham hock.

Cover pot, increase heat and bring to a boil. Reduce heat to very low and simmer, stirring occasionally, until split peas fall apart and soup is very thick, about 2 hours. If soup is too thick, add more stock or water.

Remove bone or hock from soup. Dice any meat and return it to pot.

Serve in heated soup plates.

Wine: Bonny Doon Vineyard Le Cigare Volant (California), Domaine Tempier Bandol Rosé (France: Bandol) or a rich California Rhône-style red or rosé

Kentucky Black Bean Soup with Sherry

Serves 8-10

LEMON AND VEAL are the unusual components of this delicious, spice-filled black bean soup. Sautéed onions and sherry add more layers of flavor. Marion Flexner's *Out of Kentucky Kitchens* (Franklin Watts, 1949) describes this soup as a pre-Civil War recipe and "another Kentucky masterpiece." We think you'll agree.

1	pound black beans, picked over
1	pound boneless veal, trimmed of all fat
2-3	pounds veal knucklebone with meat
4	whole cloves
1	lemon, cut into 8 wedges, plus 3 lemons, thinly sliced, for garnish
2	tablespoons Worcestershire sauce
1	tablespoon kosher salt, plus more if needed
½	teaspoon freshly ground black pepper
½	teaspoon freshly grated nutmeg
¼	teaspoon ground allspice
2	tablespoons unsalted butter
3	medium-sized yellow onions, finely chopped
1	cup dry sherry
2	hard-cooked eggs, thinly sliced, for garnish

Combine beans and enough water to cover them in a large pot. Cover and bring to a boil over high heat. Remove pot from heat and let beans stand, covered, for 1 hour. Drain thoroughly and transfer beans to a heavy soup pot.

Add 12 cups (3 quarts) water, meat and bones to soup pot. Put cloves into half of lemon wedges; place all wedges in soup pot. If beans and meat are not covered, add more water. Add Worcestershire sauce, 1 tablespoon salt, pepper, nutmeg and allspice. Cover and bring to a boil over high heat. Reduce heat and simmer, covered, until beans are very mushy, about 3 hours. Remove from heat.

When soup has cooled, carefully transfer meat and bones to a large platter; set aside. Remove and discard lemon wedges. Drain soup in a colander; reserve liquid. Transfer beans to a food processor fitted with the metal blade. Add 2 cups cooled bean liquid and puree until smooth. Return puree to pot and add enough liquid, about 4 cups, to make a pleasingly thick soup.

Melt butter in a large skillet over medium-high heat. Add onions and cook, stirring often, until very golden, 15 to 20 minutes.

Add onions to soup. Shred meat and return to soup. Cover and cook over low heat until hot, about 5 minutes.

Stir in sherry. Increase heat to medium-high and cook until mixture begins to bubble. Adjust seasonings.

Ladle soup into heated soup plates. Garnish with several slices of lemon and egg.

Wine: Scherrer Vineyards Zinfandel (California: Alexander Valley) or another spicy California Zinfandel

Spicy Hungarian Sauerkraut Soup

Serves 6

S AUERKRAUT SOUP," YOU ASK? It's wonderful. When cooked with tomato, smoked sausage and caraway, the sauerkraut becomes a slightly tangy, mellow base for a sturdy soup that's perfect for cold weather. As for the smoked sausage, a good kielbasa will be just fine. Serve with thick slices of bread.

1	tablespoon vegetable oil
1	pound smoked sausage, cut into ½-inch slices
1	large yellow onion, finely chopped
1	tablespoon hot Hungarian paprika
1	teaspoon caraway seeds
¼	cup dry white wine
2½	cups sauerkraut, rinsed
1	large russet potato, cut into ½-inch cubes
2	tablespoons tomato paste
7	cups beef or veal stock (page 328)
	Kosher salt and freshly ground black pepper

Heat oil in a large, heavy-bottomed, nonreactive pot over medium heat. Add sausage and onion and cook, stirring often, until onion begins to soften, about 5 minutes. Add paprika, caraway seeds and wine and cook, stirring constantly, for 2 minutes so that flavors are released. Stir in sauerkraut, potato and tomato paste. Add stock, stirring to blend.

Cover pot and cook until liquid begins to bubble, about 5 minutes. Reduce heat and simmer, stirring from time to time, for 1 hour. Season with salt and pepper, cover and simmer for another 30 minutes.

Serve in heated soup plates.

Wine: Schuetz-Oles Petit Sirah Rattlesnake Acres (California: Napa Valley) or a fruity, tannic Australian Shiraz

Creamy Rutabaga Soup with Caramelized Shallots

Serves 6-8

P LEASING CREAMY TEXTURE, robust flavor and a hint of apple make this autumn soup a standout, especially when you add the topping of caramelized shallots. The soup was inspired by a favorite side dish created by our friend Chef Ali Barker when he opened Piperade, his former Cleveland restaurant. Save the butter left over from caramelizing the shallots for mashed potatoes.

1	tablespoon kosher salt, plus more to taste
3	pounds rutabagas, peeled and quartered
2	large tart apples, peeled, cored and quartered
4	tablespoons (½ stick) unsalted butter
6	plump shallots, thinly sliced
6	cups chicken stock (page 325)
½	teaspoon freshly ground white pepper
1	cup low-fat sour cream
2	cups plain low-fat yogurt

Fill a 3-quart saucepan with cold water; add 1 tablespoon salt, rutabagas and apples. Tightly cover and bring to a boil over high heat. Reduce heat to low and cook until rutabagas are tender, 20 to 25 minutes.

Meanwhile, melt butter in a small saucepan over low heat. Add shallots, increase heat to medium-high and cook, stirring often, until shallots are golden brown, about 15 minutes. Using a slotted spoon, transfer shallots to paper towels to drain; set aside.

Drain rutabagas well, cut into small pieces and place in a food processor fitted with the metal blade. Add 1 cup stock and white pepper; puree until smooth. Return mixture to saucepan and slowly whisk in remaining 5 cups stock.

Cover saucepan, place over medium heat and cook until mixture begins to bubble, about 5 minutes. Reduce heat to low, stir in sour cream and yogurt. Stir over low heat until mixture is thoroughly heated and just beginning to simmer. Adjust seasonings.

Ladle soup into heated soup plates, garnish with caramelized shallots and serve.

Wine: Honig Cellars Sauvignon Blanc (California: Napa Valley) or another complex Sauvignon Blanc

Cauliflower Bisque

Serves 6

THE CAULIFLOWER takes on a special sweetness from the braised leeks and shallots. While cauliflower is available year-round, we like to think of this as a soup for autumn, when the cauliflower and leeks are fresh from the garden and at peak flavor.

2	tablespoons vegetable oil
2	large leeks, whites and tender greens, trimmed, well washed and chopped
1	plump shallot, chopped
	Pinch dried thyme
1	medium cauliflower, cleaned, cored and broken into florets
1	large russet potato, peeled and coarsely chopped
5	cups chicken stock (page 325)
1½	cups milk
	Kosher salt and freshly ground black pepper
1	tablespoon minced fresh chives

Heat oil in a large, heavy-bottomed pot over low heat. Add leeks, shallot and thyme, tightly cover and braise over low heat until leeks are very tender, about 10 minutes.

Add cauliflower, potato and 4 cups stock, increase heat to medium-high and cook, uncovered, until stock just begins to boil, about 5 minutes. Tightly cover pot, reduce heat to low and cook until cauliflower is very tender, 20 to 25 minutes.

Let soup cool slightly, about 15 minutes. Carefully spoon solids into a food processor fitted with the metal blade. Add 1 cup warm stock and process until solids are very smooth.

Return puree to pot and whisk in remaining 1 cup stock and milk. Cook over medium heat until soup is hot but not boiling. Season with salt and pepper. Ladle into heated soup plates and sprinkle with chives.

Wine: Foxen Vineyard Chardonnay (California: Santa Barbara County) or another full-bodied California Chardonnay, preferably from the Santa Barbara region

Winter Vegetable Stew

Serves 6-8

THE COMBINATION OF TURNIPS AND WINTER SQUASH with chard and beans in this tomato-based dish is as attractive as it is tasty. The basil added at the end gives it a light, fresh quality. We like to serve it with baguette slices that have been rubbed with garlic butter, sprinkled generously with cheese and toasted.

3	tablespoons olive oil
1½	cups finely diced yellow onions
2	plump garlic cloves, minced
1	tablespoon minced fresh basil, plus 6 leaves, shredded, for garnish
1	tablespoon tomato paste
1	cup chicken or vegetable stock (page 325 or 330)
4	cups tomato puree (page 324) or canned crushed tomatoes
½	pound Swiss chard, cleaned, trimmed and coarsely chopped
1	large (½ pound) turnip, cut into ½-inch cubes
½	pound butternut squash, peeled and cut into ½-inch cubes
1	cup frozen or fresh lima beans
	Kosher salt and freshly ground black pepper
½	cup freshly grated Parmesan cheese

Heat oil in a large, heavy-bottomed, nonreactive soup pot over low heat. Add onions, tightly cover, and braise over low heat until onions soften, about 4 minutes. Stir in garlic and minced basil, cover and braise until garlic softens, 2 to 3 minutes more. Add tomato paste and blend.

Stir in stock and tomato puree or crushed tomatoes. Cover, increase heat to medium and cook until liquid begins to bubble, 5 to 6 minutes. Add chard, turnip and squash, cover, reduce heat to low and simmer until turnip and squash are tender, 30 to 40 minutes.

Stir in lima beans, cover and cook for 15 minutes more. Season with salt and pepper.

Ladle soup into heated soup plates. Sprinkle generously with Parmesan and garnish with shredded basil.

Wine: Cloudy Bay Sauvignon Blanc (New Zealand: Marlborough) or another austere and flinty Sauvignon Blanc

Shellfish & Fish

Oyster & Sausage Gumbo with Okra & Corn 62

Shrimp & Smoked Ham Jambalaya 64

Shrimp with Snow Peas & Corn 66

Mussel Stew with Tomatoes & Tarragon 68

Squid Marinara 69

Spicy Steamed Lobsters & Clams with Corn 70

Mediterranean Fish Stew 72

Portuguese Fish Stew (*Caldeirada*) 74

Braised Trout with Onions & Peppers 76

Herbed Salmon Poached in Red Wine 77

Ginger-Steamed Bluefish with Pepper & Cilantro 78

Fragrant Lemon Sole en Papillote 79

Steamed Asian-Style Stuffed Flounder 80

Salmon Teriyaki with Spinach & Scallions 97

Parchment-Braised Snapper with Fennel 98

Orange & Ginger Steamed Salmon 100

Oven-Braised Salmon with *Labnee* (Yogurt Cheese)
& Herb-Cucumber Sauce 102

Tuna Provençal 104

Braised Halibut with Sake 106

Tomato-Braised Swordfish with Onions & Anchovies 107

Shad Roe with Crispy Bacon & Lemon Sauce 108

Oyster & Sausage Gumbo with Okra & Corn

Serves 4-6

OUR FIRST GUMBO LESSON was from Connie Scheer, owner of Sportsman's Paradise, a fishing lodge and restaurant in Chauvin, Louisiana. She uses okra for thickening instead of a roux. Her suggestions have helped us to create many satisfying gumbos over the years, including this one, which has a lot of zip and color to it. We love the combination of briny oysters and spicy andouille sausage. This is a stick-to-your-ribs dish. Add some good bread and a nice salad, and you'll have a terrific meal.

4	tablespoons vegetable oil
1	pound andouille sausage, cut into ½-inch rounds
3	medium-sized yellow onions, finely diced
1	pound fresh okra, trimmed and cut into ¼-inch rounds
2	medium-sized red bell peppers, seeded, deribbed and cut into medium dice
1	fresh hot chile, seeded and finely diced
1	tablespoon minced garlic
2	teaspoons kosher salt, plus more if needed
2	teaspoons freshly ground black pepper
1	teaspoon freshly ground white pepper
1	teaspoon cayenne pepper
1	teaspoon dried thyme
2	bay leaves
2	cups tomato puree (page 324) or canned crushed tomatoes
3	cups fish stock (page 327) or bottled clam juice
½	teaspoon Tabasco sauce, plus more to taste
1¼	cups fresh or frozen corn kernels
1½	pounds shucked oysters and liquor
½	cup chopped fresh flat-leaf parsley
2½	cups hot cooked jasmine rice (see Sources, page 335) or other long-grain aromatic rice (from 1 cup raw)
4	scallions, trimmed to include 1 inch of green, thinly sliced

In a medium cast-iron skillet, heat 1 tablespoon oil over medium heat. Add sausage and cook, stirring often, until browned on both sides, about 10 minutes. Using a slotted spoon, remove sausage from skillet and drain on paper towels. Set aside.

Heat remaining 3 tablespoons oil in a heavy-bottomed, nonreactive soup pot over medium heat. Stir in onions, reduce heat to low, cover and cook until onions begin to soften, 3 to 4 minutes. Add okra, peppers and chile; cover and cook over low heat, stirring often, until mixture is mushy, about 1 hour.

Add sausage, garlic, 2 teaspoons salt, black and white peppers, cayenne, thyme and bay leaves. Cook, uncovered, stirring frequently, over low heat for 10 minutes. Increase heat to high and add tomato puree or crushed tomatoes and stock or clam juice. When mixture begins to bubble, reduce heat to low, cover and simmer for 1 hour. Taste and add ½ teaspoon Tabasco; adjust seasonings. Stir in corn. (You can make gumbo ahead to this point.)

Shortly before serving, bring contents to a boil over medium-high heat. Add oysters and liquor, cover, reduce heat to low and cook just until edges of oysters curl, 4 to 5 minutes. Stir in parsley.

Fill large, heated soup plates with generous portions of rice. Ladle gumbo over rice, sprinkle with scallions and serve.

Wine: Sterling Vineyards Sauvignon Blanc (California: Napa Valley) or another Napa Valley Sauvignon Blanc

Shrimp & Smoked Ham Jambalaya

Serves 10-12

T HIS LUSTY COMBINATION of rice, smoked ham, spices and shrimp is a real crowd pleaser. If you have access to tasso, a highly seasoned Cajun smoked ham, use it—just brown it first—or you can add browned andouille sausage instead. We like to use jasmine brown rice (see Sources, page 335) because its fragrance and nutty flavors work so well with the seasonings.

3	tablespoons vegetable oil
1	dried red chile, crumbled
2	medium-sized yellow onions, finely diced
2	cups diced smoked ham
1	teaspoon kosher salt
1	teaspoon freshly ground white pepper
½	teaspoon dried thyme
½	teaspoon dried oregano
¼	teaspoon cayenne pepper
2	cups raw long-grain brown rice
2	plump garlic cloves, minced
1½	cups finely chopped scallions, including green parts
2	large tomatoes, peeled, seeded and coarsely chopped
1	large green bell pepper, seeded, deribbed and finely diced
½	teaspoon Tabasco sauce
2	cups fish stock (page 327) or bottled clam juice
1	cup dry white wine
	Up to 2 cups chicken stock (page 325)
¾	pound large shrimp, peeled and deveined
⅓	cup minced fresh flat-leaf parsley

In a large, deep, nonreactive sauté pan or Dutch oven fitted with a heavy lid, heat oil and chile over medium heat. Add onions, ham, salt, white pepper, thyme, oregano, cayenne and rice. Cook, stirring constantly, until onions soften, about 4 minutes. Stir in garlic, 1 cup scallions, tomatoes and green pepper; cook for 2 minutes. Add Tabasco, fish stock or clam juice, wine and 1 cup chicken stock. Increase heat and bring to a boil. Cover, reduce heat to low and cook, stirring several times, for 40 minutes. Add more chicken stock if rice is too dry.

Stir in shrimp. Cover and cook for 15 minutes. (If rice is dry at this point, add ½ cup more stock.)

Let stand, covered, for 15 minutes so that rice absorbs flavors and liquid; jambalaya should not be soupy.

Stir in remaining ½ cup scallions and parsley. Serve on heated plates.

Wine: Argyle Winery Chardonnay (Oregon) or another barrel-fermented Chardonnay

Shrimp with Snow Peas & Corn

Serves 6 as a first course, 4 as a main dish

THIS CHINESE PREPARATION for shrimp calls for braising instead of stir-frying. It's a light and healthy dish that can be cooked in a flash. As a main course, we like to serve the shrimp with brown rice. If you are serving it as an appetizer, arrange over watercress tossed with a tiny bit of walnut oil.

Marinade and Shrimp

1	egg white
¼	cup cornstarch
¼	cup rice wine
2	scallions, smashed with flat side of a cleaver
1	thin slice fresh ginger, smashed with flat side of a cleaver
1½	pounds large shrimp, peeled and deveined
3	tablespoons vegetable oil
¼	cup minced shallots
1	small dried red chile
1	plump garlic clove, minced
36	snow peas (4-5 ounces), trimmed
½	cup fresh or frozen yellow corn kernels
1	medium tomato, peeled, seeded and cut into medium dice
1	cup chicken stock (page 325), heated
2	tablespoons soy sauce
	Freshly ground white pepper
1	tablespoon minced fresh chives
1	tablespoon minced fresh flat-leaf parsley

To marinate shrimp: Combine egg white and cornstarch in a medium bowl and whisk until blended. Whisk in rice wine; add scallions, ginger and shrimp. Stir until shrimp are thoroughly coated. Marinate at room temperature for 30 to 60 minutes. Remove and discard scallions and ginger.

Heat oil, shallots, chile and garlic in a large nonreactive skillet over medium heat until shallots soften, 3 to 4 minutes. Quickly stir in shrimp mixture; add snow peas, corn, tomato, stock and soy sauce. Cover and cook, shaking skillet briskly from time to time, for 5 minutes. Stir and cook until shrimp are pink and firm, about 2 minutes. Season with white pepper, chives and parsley. Serve on heated plates.

Wine: Eyrie Vineyard Pinot Gris (Oregon: Willamette Valley) or an Italian Pinot Grigio

Mussel Stew with Tomatoes & Tarragon

Serves 4

TOMATOES AND TARRAGON are a winning combination with mussels. If you have fresh basil instead of tarragon, go ahead and use it. This soupy stew should be served with a toothsome bread, followed by a crisp salad. Don't debeard your mussels until you are ready to cook them, or they will die and spoil.

3	tablespoons olive oil
1	dried red chile, crumbled
2	plump garlic cloves, minced
½	cup finely diced yellow onion
1	cup dry white wine
3	cups tomato puree (page 324) or canned crushed tomatoes
2	teaspoons kosher salt
1	teaspoon freshly ground black pepper
1	teaspoon finely minced lemon zest
3-4	pounds mussels, debearded just before cooking
1	tablespoon minced fresh tarragon
¼	cup minced fresh flat-leaf parsley

In a heavy-bottomed, nonreactive soup pot, heat oil and chile over medium heat. Stir in garlic and onion, reduce heat to low, cover and braise until onions are soft, 4 to 6 minutes.

Stir in wine, tomato puree or crushed tomatoes, salt, pepper and zest. Increase heat to high and cook, stirring often, until mixture comes to a vigorous boil. Let boil for 1 minute. Add mussels, cover and reduce heat to medium. Cook until all mussels open, 5 to 6 minutes. Discard any mussels that do not open. Distribute stew among heated soup plates, ladling sauce over mussels. Sprinkle with tarragon and parsley and serve.

Wine: Liparita Vineyard Sauvignon Blanc (California: Napa Valley) or another full-bodied non-Chardonnay white wine

Squid Marinara

Serves 8-10

WE ARE BIG FANS OF SQUID, especially when it is sautéed in a fruity olive oil with lots of garlic and onions. In this recipe, derived from one that has been served at Cleveland's Johnny's Bar on Fulton for more than 20 years, squid, garlic and onions become the base for a luscious marinara sauce. We like to ladle the squid and sauce into a soup plate and serve it on its own, with lots of grilled bread to mop up the sauce. If you wish, however, you can toss it with linguine.

¼	cup olive oil
3	pounds cleaned squid, body sacks cut into ½-inch rings
2	dried red chiles, crumbled
3	tablespoons unsalted butter
1	large yellow onion, finely diced
1	large carrot, grated
5	plump garlic cloves, minced
5¼	cups canned crushed Italian plum tomatoes
1½	teaspoons dried basil
¼	teaspoon dried oregano
	Kosher salt and freshly ground black pepper
¼	cup minced fresh basil
¼	cup minced fresh flat-leaf parsley

Heat oil over high heat in a large nonreactive sauté pan or Dutch oven. Add squid and sauté, stirring often, until rings turn opaque and tentacles are firm, about 5 minutes. Add chiles, butter, onion, carrot and garlic. Stir briskly until carrot softens, about 3 minutes. Stir in tomatoes, dried basil, oregano and salt and pepper. Tightly cover and cook until liquid begins to bubble, 3 to 4 minutes. Reduce heat to low, cover, and simmer until squid is fork-tender, about 25 minutes.

Ladle squid and sauce into heated soup plates. Sprinkle generously with fresh basil and parsley and serve.

Wine: Chalk Hill Winery Chardonnay (California: Chalk Hill) or another full-bodied Chardonnay

Spicy Steamed Lobsters & Clams with Corn

Serves 4

WE CREATED THIS ZIPPY SHELLFISH ONE-POT MEAL in honor of cookbook publicist Lou Ekus, who introduced us to the idea of adding sausage to a steam pot. We've been doing it ever since. The oil from the sausage brings out all the other seasonings in the pot and provides a sauce for the corn.

3	tablespoons olive oil
2	dried red chiles, crumbled
1	tablespoon yellow mustard seeds
1	teaspoon fennel seeds
3	garlic cloves, peeled
1	tablespoon cayenne pepper
2	bay leaves
1	tablespoon kosher salt, plus more as needed
1½	pounds white onions, finely diced
2	pounds good-quality smoked sausage, such as kielbasa
4	1½-pound live lobsters, claw bands removed
3	dozen littleneck clams, cleaned
8	ears sweet corn, shucked
½	pound (2 sticks) melted unsalted butter, for serving
	Honey mustard, for serving
	Freshly ground black pepper
2	lemons, cut into wedges

Heat oil in a 10-to-12-quart soup or lobster pot with a tight-fitting cover. Stir in chiles, mustard seeds, fennel seeds, garlic, cayenne, bay leaves and 1 tablespoon salt. Cook, stirring, over medium heat until garlic is fragrant, 1 to 2 minutes. Stir in onions and cook until softened, 1 to 2 minutes. Add water until it is 2 inches deep. Add sausage and bring to a boil.

Place lobsters, tails tucked under bodies, into boiling water. Cover and steam for 10 minutes. Gently add clams and corn. Cover and steam until clams open and lobsters are done, about 5 minutes more.

To check each lobster for doneness, remove one at a time from pot. Pull curled tail back and let go. If it snaps back, the lobster is cooked. If sluggish, return lobster to pot for a few minutes more.

When lobsters are done, place on a large, heated serving platter. Surround with clams, sausage, cut into chunks, and corn. Divide melted butter among 4 small dishes. Serve a bowl of mustard for the sausage. Sprinkle corn with salt and pepper and pass the lemon wedges.

Wine: Hogue Cellars Chardonnay (Washington: Columbia Valley), Cinnabar Winery Chardonnay (California: Santa Cruz Mountains) or another full-bodied Chardonnay

Mediterranean Fish Stew

Serves 6-8

T HIS TASTY TOMATO-LACED FISH STEW has pleasing overtones from wine, orange peel, fennel and saffron. It's the perfect broth in which to cook fish and shellfish. Serve this lusty meal in large soup bowls with a toasted crouton piled with the creamy, garlicky rouille—a pimiento mayonnaise. Our recipe is based upon a multiplicity of food notes from our first visit to France's Côte d'Azur, where we ate a different bouillabaisse every day. Adapted to American fish, this recipe is quite flexible. Use whatever fish and shellfish combinations you want. Our personal favorite includes mussels. For a special occasion, we also add lobster.

Soup Base

3	tablespoons olive oil
1	large Spanish onion, finely diced
3	plump garlic cloves, minced
12	cups (3 quarts) fish stock (page 327)
2½	pounds fresh tomatoes, quartered
1	cup dry white wine
½	teaspoon saffron threads
1	tablespoon fennel seeds, crushed
1	teaspoon dried marjoram
	Peel of 1 orange
	Kosher salt and freshly ground black pepper

Rouille

2	whole canned pimientos, drained, or peeled roasted red bell peppers
3-4	plump garlic cloves, minced
1	large egg yolk
½	teaspoon cayenne pepper
⅔	cup extra-virgin olive oil
½	cup fine dry bread crumbs
	Kosher salt and freshly ground black pepper

Fish

1   1½-pound lobster (optional)

1½   pounds halibut steak or fillets, left whole

1½   pounds cod fillets, left whole

1½   pounds red snapper, bluefish or sea bass fillets, left whole

2   pounds cleaned mussels, debearded just before cooking

1   loaf French bread, thinly sliced, rubbed with oil and toasted

To make soup base: In a nonreactive pot, heat oil over medium heat. Stir in onion and sauté, stirring often, until softened, 2 to 3 minutes. Add garlic and continue to sauté, stirring often, until garlic begins to soften. Add stock, tomatoes and wine. Cover and cook over high heat until mixture comes to a boil, 8 to 10 minutes. Uncover and ladle some hot liquid into a small bowl; add saffron and stir until dissolved. Return saffron liquid to soup pot. Stir in fennel seeds, marjoram and orange peel. Reduce heat to medium-low and cook, uncovered, until mixture reduces by one-third, 30 to 45 minutes. Season with salt and pepper.

Process soup base mixture through a food mill and return to soup pot. Alternatively, puree in a food processor and strain.

While soup is cooking, make rouille: In a food processor fitted with the metal blade, puree pimientos or roasted peppers, garlic, egg yolk and cayenne. (Alternatively, you can mash them together using a mortar and pestle, and whisk in oil, bread crumbs and stock.) With motor running, add oil, a few drops at a time; mixture will form a mayonnaise. Add bread crumbs and pulse. Add ¼ to ½ cup soup base, a little at a time, just enough to make a lighter but still thick sauce. Season with salt and pepper. Scrape into a bowl, cover with plastic and refrigerate until needed.

To prepare fish: Shortly before serving, bring soup base to a boil. If using lobster, add to pot, cover and boil for 5 minutes. Add any 1-inch-thick or thicker pieces of fish to bubbling liquid. Cover, reduce heat to medium-low and simmer briskly for 5 minutes. Add thinner fish fillets and mussels. Cover and simmer briskly until mussels open, 5 to 6 minutes. Check fish for doneness. Discard any unopened mussels. Carefully remove lobster, drain well and cut into pieces.

Arrange large heated soup plates in a row. Generously spread rouille on a piece of toasted bread for each serving and place in bottom of soup plates. Ladle soup into each. Break fish into large pieces and divide among plates. Add mussels and lobster. Pass more rouille with remaining toasted bread.

Wine: Girard Winery Chardonnay Old Vines (California: Napa Valley) or another full-bodied, complex Chardonnay

Portuguese Fish Stew

(*Caldeirada*)

Serves 10-12

THIS SCRUMPTIOUS TOMATO-BASED FISH STEW, with its colorful cubes of orange squash, can be as lavish or as simple as you wish. It makes a spectacular main dish for a party. Although you should try to include a blend of lean and oily fish, the combinations are up to you. We always add shrimp, which cook in their shells in the soup. (The shells add so much flavor that they are worth the mess.) Occasionally, we also put in clams or mussels, when we can get them. The soup grew out of one included in Jean Anderson's superb book *The Food of Portugal* (William Morrow, 1986). See photograph, page 81.

¼	cup olive oil
1	dried red chile, crumbled
3	large Spanish onions, coarsely chopped
1	large green bell pepper, finely diced
5	plump garlic cloves, minced
¼	cup shredded, loosely packed fresh basil
¼	cup minced fresh flat-leaf parsley
2	teaspoons fresh thyme leaves or 1 teaspoon dried
2	bay leaves
4	cups tomato puree (page 324) or canned crushed tomatoes
2	cups fish stock (page 327) or bottled clam juice
2	cups dry white wine
1½	pounds butternut squash, peeled, cut into 1-inch cubes
1	pound large shrimp in their shells
1½	pounds fresh monkfish fillet
1½	pounds 1½-inch-thick halibut fillet, skin removed
1½	pounds 1½-inch-thick swordfish steak, left whole, skin removed
1½	pounds 1½-inch-thick tuna steak, skin removed
1½	teaspoons kosher salt
1	teaspoon freshly ground black pepper
½	cup minced fresh cilantro

In a large, heavy, nonreactive pot, heat oil and chile. Stir in onions, green pepper and garlic. Cover and cook over low heat, stirring occasionally, until onions are very tender, 15 to 20 minutes.

Stir in basil, parsley, thyme, bay leaves, tomato puree or crushed tomatoes, stock or clam juice, wine and squash. Cover and bring to a boil. Reduce heat to low and simmer for 15 minutes.

Distribute shrimp evenly over tomato mixture; layer fish over shrimp. Season with salt and pepper. Cover and simmer until fish flakes easily, about 20 minutes.

Break fish into large chunks and ladle with soup mixture into serving bowls. Sprinkle generously with cilantro.

Wine: Caymus Vineyards Sauvignon Blanc Barrel Fermented (California: Napa Valley) or another barrel-fermented Sauvignon Blanc

Braised Trout
with Onions & Peppers

Serves 2

THIS SIMPLE PREPARATION FOR TROUT stewed with onions and peppers is adapted from one of the best community cookbooks we've seen, Billie Burn's *Stirrin' the Pots on Daufuskie* (available from Billie Burn Books, P.O. Box 29, Daufuskie Island, SC 29915). A small island between Hilton Head, South Carolina, and Tybee Island, Georgia, Daufuskie is the southernmost tip of South Carolina territory and the first of the Carolina Sea Islands to have been inhabited. It was settled by an Indian trader in 1706, but it was the slaves who were brought to the island from Africa and whose families remain today who made their mark on the island's traditions and history. This slender volume is a collection of their treasured family recipes and vignettes about the people who shared them. Among them are Mrs. Geneva Bryan Wiley and Mrs. Sarah Hudson, both of whom contributed stewed fish recipes that served as the inspiration for this particular dish.

2   thick slices bacon, preferably smoked
2   10-ounce trout, cleaned
1   medium-sized yellow onion, coarsely diced
1   medium-sized green bell pepper, coarsely diced
    Kosher salt and freshly ground black pepper

Fry bacon in a medium cast-iron skillet. When fat is rendered and bacon is browned, remove bacon; set aside.

Add trout to skillet and brown quickly over medium-high heat, 2 to 3 minutes per side. When trout is browned on both sides, cover with onion, green pepper and ⅓ cup water. Season with salt and pepper. Crumble bacon and sprinkle over trout. Tightly cover and cook over low heat until onion and pepper are tender and trout are firm, about 15 minutes.

Serve fish on heated plates garnished with pan sauce and vegetables.

Wine: Markham Vineyards Chardonnay Barrel Fermented (California: Napa Valley) or another fruity barrel-fermented Chardonnay

Herbed Salmon Poached in Red Wine

Serves 4

O UR FRIEND JON ROWLEY, the Seattle-based fish consultant to restaurants around the country, has long advocated pairing an elegant red Pinot Noir with salmon. To us, it has always been a splendid combination. So why not cook the fish in red wine too? We thought ourselves quite innovative until we came across Auguste Escoffier's recipe for *"Darne de Saumon Chambord"* in *Ma Cuisine*, a recipe in which the bay leaf and red wine impart particularly fragrant flavors to the fish. While you can easily use farmed Atlantic salmon, this dish is even more remarkable when made with wild Alaskan salmon.

2	tablespoons unsalted butter
2	medium carrots, finely diced
2	plump shallots, minced
4	6-ounce salmon fillets, each cut about 1 inch thick, pinbones removed
2	tablespoons minced fresh flat-leaf parsley
1	teaspoon fresh thyme leaves or ½ teaspoon dried Kosher salt and freshly ground black pepper
1	750-ml bottle Pinot Noir
1	bay leaf

Melt butter in a medium nonstick skillet over medium heat. Stir in carrots and shallots, cover and braise until shallots soften, 3 to 4 minutes.

Place salmon in a deep, nonreactive skillet just large enough to hold fillets in a single layer. Sprinkle evenly with shallot mixture, parsley, thyme and salt and pepper. Add enough wine to almost cover fish. Add bay leaf. Cover and bring to a boil over high heat. Reduce heat to very low and simmer, covered, until fish feels firm to the touch, 8 to 12 minutes, depending upon thickness of fillets. Gently insert tines of a fork into a thick part of fish to check appearance of flesh; salmon should still be a bit translucent at center.

Serve immediately on heated plates, with pan juices spooned over.

Wine: Benton Lane Winery Pinot Noir (Oregon) or another medium-bodied fruity Pinot Noir

Ginger-Steamed Bluefish with Pepper & Cilantro

Serves 4

THIS GINGER AND SOY MARINADE blends beautifully with the strongly flavored blue-fish. Fresh black pepper and cilantro provide finishing touches.

¾	cup dry white wine
3	tablespoons soy sauce
4	scallions, trimmed to include 1 inch of green, minced
2	tablespoons minced fresh ginger, plus 2 thin slices
2	tablespoons Asian sesame oil
1	teaspoon sugar
2	pounds ¾-to-1-inch-thick bluefish fillets
1	stalk lemongrass, 1 lemon verbena branch or peel of 1 lemon
1	tablespoon freshly ground black pepper
1	tablespoon minced fresh cilantro
	Lemon wedges, for garnish

Whisk together ¼ cup wine, soy sauce, scallions, minced ginger, 1 tablespoon sesame oil and sugar in a large glass or ceramic dish. Add bluefish and turn to coat well. Cover with plastic and refrigerate, turning several times, for 2 to 3 hours.

Just before cooking, add remaining ½ cup wine, ginger slices and lemongrass, lemon verbena or lemon peel to a wok or steamer. Add enough water to create steam without bubbling onto fish. Bring liquid to a boil.

Reduce heat so liquid is at a vigorous simmer, and place a rack or steaming basket about 2 inches above steaming liquid. Quickly arrange fish, skin side down, on rack. Sprinkle fish with pepper, pressing lightly into fish with your fingers; spoon a little marinade over each. Cover and steam until fish feels firm to the touch, about 10 minutes. To check, uncover and gently insert tines of a fork into a thick part of flesh; it should be opaque, with a bit of rare at center.

Carefully transfer fish to heated plates. Brush tops of fish with remaining 1 tablespoon sesame oil, and sprinkle with cilantro. Serve hot or cold, garnished with lemon wedges.

Wine: Waterbrook Winery Chardonnay (Washington: Columbia Valley) or another medium-bodied Chardonnay

Fragrant Lemon Sole
en Papillote

Serves 2

En papillote is a French technique for oven-steaming inside a greaseproof paper or foil packet. Lemon sole, also called "winter sole," lends itself well to this preparation. The fragrance wafts upward when the parchment is slit, and each bite of fish has a green-herb center.

	Olive oil
2	tablespoons unsalted butter, softened
3	tablespoons minced fresh flat-leaf parsley
1	tablespoon minced fresh chives
1	tablespoon minced fresh tarragon
1	teaspoon minced lemon zest
4	4-to-6-ounce lemon sole fillets
	Kosher salt and freshly ground white pepper
1½	tablespoons dry white wine
2	tablespoons fish stock (page 327) or bottled clam juice
2	fresh tarragon sprigs

Preheat oven to 500 degrees F. Cut parchment paper into two 15-x-15-inch squares. Fold parchment squares in half, crease and re-open. Brush lightly all over with oil; set aside.

In a small bowl, thoroughly cream together butter, parsley, chives, tarragon and zest. Place a fillet along the fold of each piece of parchment; sprinkle lightly with salt and white pepper. Spread each with half of herb butter. Place another fillet directly on top of the first; lightly sprinkle each with more salt and white pepper.

Sprinkle each packet with half of wine and stock or clam juice. Place a tarragon sprig on each. Quickly fold one side of parchment over fish and fold and crimp edges tightly to seal. Place packages on a large baking sheet. (Packets can be stored in refrigerator for several hours, if you wish. Bring to room temperature before baking.)

Bake 8 to 10 minutes for 4-to-5-ounce fillets, 10 minutes for 6-ounce ones, until packages are puffed and browned.

Place packets on heated dinner plates. Open at the table.

Wine: Patz & Hall Chardonnay (California: Napa Valley) or a complex white Burgundy (France)

Steamed Asian-Style Stuffed Flounder

Serves 2

G INGERED FRESH PLUMS are the surprise stuffing for flounder fillets here. An orange butter and cilantro topping makes a refreshing sauce. This delicate fish preparation is the creation of our friend, caterer Kookie Brock.

4	tablespoons (½ stick) unsalted butter, softened
½	teaspoon grated orange zest
2	teaspoons fresh orange juice
2	6-ounce flounder fillets
2-3	tablespoons peeled, grated fresh ginger
	Freshly ground white pepper
2	firm, ripe plums (any kind), pitted and thinly sliced
4	scallions, trimmed to include 1 inch of green, minced
	Minced fresh cilantro, for garnish

Set a bamboo steamer or steaming rack in a wok or soup pot. Fill with water to 1 inch below steamer or rack. Bring water to a boil just before using.

Combine butter, zest and juice in a small bowl and blend thoroughly. Turn out onto wax paper and roll into a thin log. Place in freezer until firm, about 20 minutes.

Place flounder, skin side down, on a work surface. Rub ginger into the fillets. Grind a generous amount of white pepper over. Arrange plum slices over fillets; sprinkle evenly with scallions.

Roll fillets, pressing carefully to keep filling within them. Secure with a skewer (a toothpick is too flimsy); place fillets on a heatproof plate. Place plate in steamer over boiling water, tightly cover and cook over simmering water until flounder is somewhat firm but springy to the touch and opaque, 15 to 18 minutes.

Transfer fish to heated plates. Garnish with several slices of orange butter and sprinkle generously with cilantro.

Wine: Cain Cellars Sauvignon Blanc Monterey Musqué (California: Napa Valley) or another crisp and flinty Sauvignon Blanc from California or France

Portuguese Fish Stew (Caldeirada) ◆ page 74

Pot Stickers with Cabbage, Scallions & Carrots ◆ *page 32*

Orange & Ginger Steamed Salmon ◆ page 100

Fresh Pumpkin & Apple Bisque with Crispy Leeks ◆ *page 48*

Springtime Stew of Lamb (*Printanier Navarin*) ◆ *page 208*

Joey's Osso Bucco Milanese ◆ page 194

Yunnan Pot Chicken with Bok Choy & Snow Peas ◆ page 116

Covered Risotto with Wild Mushrooms & Radicchio ◆ page 246

Corned Beef & Cabbage ◆ page 162

Choucroute Garni (Braised Alsatian Sauerkraut & Pork) ◆ *page 240*

Creamy Fish Chowder with Chard & Corn ◆ page 46

Gingered Carrot Cake ♦ page 320

Mélange of Root Vegetables ◆ page 276

Pork Chops Braised with Apples & Cabbage ◆ page 232

Artichokes Barigoule ◆ *page 34*

Poached Rosemary Pears with Late-Harvest Riesling & Raisins ◆ *page 305*

Salmon Teriyaki with Spinach & Scallions

Serves 4

SALMON BRAISED ON A BED OF SPINACH and scallions receives an Asian twist here. Not only does the gingered soy sauce make a good basting medium for the fish, it serves as a tasty sauce for the vegetables as well. The dish is then lightly sprinkled with sesame seeds.

¼	cup rice wine
2	tablespoons soy sauce
2	teaspoons Asian sesame oil
2	teaspoons firmly packed dark brown sugar
1	tablespoon peeled, minced fresh ginger
1	plump garlic clove, minced
1½	pounds 1¼-inch-thick salmon fillets, skinned
¾	pound fresh spinach, trimmed
1	teaspoon olive oil
10	thin scallions, cut into 2-inch-long julienne
1	tablespoon sesame seeds
	Freshly ground black pepper
2	tablespoons minced fresh chives

In a glass dish just large enough to hold salmon, whisk together rice wine, soy sauce, sesame oil, brown sugar, ginger and garlic. Add fillets and marinate for 30 minutes at room temperature. Turn fish and marinate for 15 minutes more.

Preheat oven to 500 degrees F. Oil an ovenproof casserole just large enough to hold fish and spinach. Rinse spinach, but do not dry thoroughly. Place spinach in casserole; scatter half of scallions on top. Remove fish from marinade and place, skin side down, over spinach. Pour marinade over fillets. Sprinkle evenly with remaining scallions, sesame seeds and pepper.

Tightly cover casserole with foil. Bake until fish is firm to the touch and not quite opaque in center, about 15 minutes.

Divide fish and spinach among 4 heated plates. Spoon some pan juices over fish, if you wish. Sprinkle with a bit more pepper and chives.

Wine: Dehlinger Winery Pinot Noir Russian River Valley (California: Sonoma County) or another full-bodied Pinot Noir from America or France

Parchment-Braised Snapper with Fennel

Serves 8 as a first course, 4 as a main course

WE ENJOY RED SNAPPER prepared in parchment with a colorful garnish of shallots, fennel and bell pepper, with splashes of lime juice and stock. Be sure to let your guests slit their packets themselves at the table. They'll love the splendid aroma that arises. Leave the skin on, since it virtually melts away during the cooking process. But because snapper fillets vary in thickness, increase the cooking time for pieces more than ¾ inch thick. If fillets are 1 inch thick, cook for 12 minutes; if they are 1¼ inches thick, cook for 14 minutes. Mark the exterior of the packets so you know which is which.

4	tablespoons (½ stick) unsalted butter
1	large carrot, finely diced
⅓	cup finely diced shallots
⅓	cup finely diced fennel bulb, plus 2 tablespoons minced fennel fronds
¼	cup finely diced red or yellow bell pepper
¼	cup olive oil
2	pounds red snapper fillet, about ¾ inch thick, cut into 8 portions or 4 portions, if serving as a main course
	Zest of 1 lime, finely minced
	Kosher salt and freshly ground white pepper
2	tablespoons fresh lime juice
½	cup fish stock (page 327) or bottled clam juice

Melt butter in a medium nonstick skillet over low heat. Add carrot, shallots, diced fennel bulb and red or yellow pepper. Cover and cook until tender, about 5 minutes. Let cool.

Cut parchment paper into eight 14-x-15-inch sheets or four 16-x-15-inch sheets. Fold each sheet in half lengthwise, crease and reopen. Arrange on work surface with fold parallel to edge of counter. Lightly brush each sheet with oil.

Place 1 piece of fish, skin side down, in lower half of parchment next to fold line. Spoon equal amounts of shallot mixture over each piece of fish. Sprinkle evenly with fennel fronds, zest and salt and white pepper. Drizzle each with 1 teaspoon oil and ½ teaspoon lime juice.

Working with 1 package at a time, drizzle with 2 tablespoons stock or clam juice, quickly fold top over bottom and fold and crimp edges tightly. Repeat until all packages are prepared. Place on large cookie sheets. Chill until 30 minutes before baking; bring to room temperature.

Preheat oven to 500 degrees F.

Bake packages for 9 minutes if snapper fillets are up to ¾ inch thick or for longer if they are thicker; the packages will be puffed and browned. Place packets on heated dinner plates. Slit open at table.

Wine: Matanzas Creek Winery Chardonnay (California: Sonoma County) or another complex California Chardonnay

Orange & Ginger Steamed Salmon

Serves 6

SALMON'S FLAVOR IS ENHANCED by the fragrant and tasty combination of ginger and orange, and we use them often to marinate and steam the fish. This particular preparation is versatile. In warm weather, it is enjoyable served at room temperature, but it is equally delicious hot. (See photograph, page 83.)

4	tablespoons (½ stick) unsalted butter, softened
	Minced zest of 1 orange
1	tablespoon minced fresh chives, plus 12 long chives
½	teaspoon peeled, minced fresh ginger, plus 2 thin slices, lightly smashed with a cleaver
1	cup dry white wine
¼	teaspoon freshly ground white pepper, plus more to taste
½	large orange, thinly sliced
6	4-ounce center-cut salmon fillets, skinned and pinbones removed
1	bunch watercress, washed
	Kosher salt
6	large lettuce leaves (leaf lettuce best), stems removed

Combine butter, zest, minced chives and minced ginger in a small bowl and blend well. Spoon onto a sheet of wax paper and form into a thin log. Wrap tightly and place in freezer.

Combine wine, sliced ginger, ¼ teaspoon white pepper and orange slices in a glass or ceramic dish large enough to hold salmon in a single layer. Arrange fillets in dish. Marinate at room temperature, turning several times, for 30 minutes.

Scatter watercress over bottom of a large bamboo steamer or steaming rack. Arrange salmon fillets over watercress in a single layer. Divide seasoned butter into 6 pieces and place 1 piece on each fillet; sprinkle each lightly with salt and white pepper. Pour marinade into wok. Add just enough water to create steam without bubbling water onto fillets.

Place steamer in wok; tightly cover. Bring liquid to a boil and steam until salmon is firm, about 10 minutes. To check, insert a fork into center of a piece; it should be opaque, with a bit of rare in center.

Remove steamer from wok and let salmon rest for 1 minute.

Divide lettuce leaves among serving plates. Place 1 fillet on each and garnish with long chives. Spoon 1 tablespoon of steaming liquid over each serving.

Wine: Harpersfield Vineyards Gewürztraminer (Ohio: Lake Erie) or a rich Alsatian Gewürztraminer

Oven-Braised Salmon with Labnee (Yogurt Cheese) & Herb-Cucumber Sauce

Serves 8-12

THIS IS A DISH FOR A SPECIAL PARTY when a poached salmon on a handsome platter should be the star attraction. Linda created it 30 years ago, when she possessed neither a fish poacher nor a stovetop large enough to use one. She wrapped the fish in a lettuce-lined foil package, added some poaching liquid, sealed it tightly and popped it into the oven. The lettuce adds moisture and flavor, and we've poached fish this way ever since. It's great served with this Middle Eastern-style cucumber and herb sauce made from yogurt (*laban*) drained to make a yogurt cheese (*labnee*). The sauce is also excellent spread on pita as an appetizer. Remember, you must begin to make the yogurt cheese one day ahead. Starting with whole-milk yogurt will yield a richer, tastier cheese. Avoid brands made with gums, gelatin or stabilizers, which can retard the draining process.

Labnee

4   cups whole-milk yogurt

Salmon

2   large heads of leaf lettuce, separated, rinsed
      and thick stems removed
2   lemons, thinly sliced
1   6-to-7-pound whole salmon, at room temperature
1   tablespoon olive oil
    Kosher salt and freshly ground black pepper
1   cup fish stock (page 327) or bottled clam juice
1   cup dry white wine

Sauce

2   tablespoons extra-virgin olive oil
½   English (seedless) cucumber, unpeeled, grated and drained
1   very plump shallot, minced
2   teaspoons minced fresh mint
1   rounded tablespoon minced fresh tarragon

2 tablespoons minced fresh dill
   Kosher salt and freshly ground white pepper

   Leaf lettuce, cucumber slices, lemon slices and dill,
     for garnish

To make *labnee*: Line a 4½-cup strainer with 4 layers of dampened cheesecloth, leaving a generous overhang. Spoon in yogurt; gather ends of cheesecloth together and tie. If possible, hang cheese over a bowl, refrigerate and let drain for at least 12 hours and up to 16. Spoon drained yogurt into a container; you will have 1½ cups. Cover and chill until needed.

To prepare salmon: Preheat oven to 375 degrees F. Cut a length of heavy-duty foil 8 inches longer than fish. Using three-fourths of lettuce, make a bed the width and length of fish, leaving 4 inches exposed at either end. Arrange half of lemon slices over lettuce. Rub top of fish with some oil, sprinkle with salt and pepper. Place, seasoned side down, on lettuce bed. Oil and season top of fish, cover with remaining lemon slices and lettuce. Turn up sides and ends of foil, pour stock or clam juice and wine around fish, cover with another long sheet of foil and crimp pieces together. Roll up tightly to enclose fish; seal.

Place fish, crimped edges up, on a large cookie sheet in oven. Fish may have to go in on a diagonal (curve tail up, if necessary). Braise for 50 minutes.

Remove from oven, open gently, and insert an instant-read thermometer into thickest part of fish; it should read about 90 degrees. Reseal fish and return it to the oven for 10 minutes. Check again. Fish is done when it reaches 140 degrees. (A 7-pound fish cooks in about 70 minutes.) When fish is done, remove from oven, carefully open foil, and let cool.

Spoon off as much liquid as you can; discard as much lettuce and lemon as possible. To facilitate handling, wrap cooled fish first in plastic and then in foil. Chill overnight.

To make sauce: In a medium bowl, combine *labnee* and olive oil. Add cucumber, shallot, mint, tarragon, dill and salt and white pepper; blend thoroughly, cover and chill.

To serve: Shortly before serving, skin fish and remove layer of dark flesh and any fat. Cover a large platter with lettuce. Arrange fish attractively on platter. Decorate with thin slices of lemons, cucumber slices and dill fronds. Serve with *labnee* sauce.

Wine: Byron Winery Chardonnay Reserve (California: Santa Barbara County) or Ponzi Vineyards Pinot Noir (Oregon: Willamette Valley) or any rich French red or white Burgundy

Tuna Provençal

Serves 6-8

ONE COULD ALMOST CALL THIS a hot salade Niçoise. The cover is a thick layer of lettuce, which, in the process of cooking, becomes singed and inedible. However, its protective moisture helps to ensure a tender, moist, delectable fish that is braised between layers of onions, tomatoes, olives and garlic. We've prepared tuna and swordfish this way for years, but the first inspiration came from a recipe in the Time-Life series *The Good Cook: Fish* (1979).

5	tablespoons olive oil
2	heads Boston lettuce, separated, washed and dried, plus 1 head, separated, washed, dried and shredded
1	very large Spanish onion, thinly sliced
4	medium-sized ripe tomatoes, thinly sliced
1	large lemon, thinly sliced
2½	pounds 1-inch-thick tuna steaks
3	plump garlic cloves, minced
2	tablespoons drained capers
2	teaspoons herbes de Provence or mixture of dried rosemary, savory, thyme, basil and crumbled bay leaf
	Kosher salt and freshly ground black pepper
½	cup pitted Niçoise olives
	Fresh herbs and lemon slices, for garnish

Preheat oven to 325 degrees F. Thoroughly coat a 4-quart casserole with 2 tablespoons oil. Line casserole bottom with half of whole Boston lettuce leaves. Arrange half of onion, half of tomatoes and half of lemon slices over lettuce. Place tuna on lemon. Drizzle with 2 tablespoons oil. Season evenly with garlic, capers, herbes de Provence and salt and pepper. Cover with shredded lettuce, remaining onion, tomatoes and lemon slices. Scatter olives evenly on top; pour remaining 1 tablespoon oil over all. Cover with remaining lettuce leaves.

Bake for 45 minutes, basting a few times with pan juices. Check for doneness by gently pulling away some vegetables and pressing fish to feel for firmness, or insert tines of a fork into center of fish; flesh should be opaque, with a fine line of rare at center.

Remove casserole from oven. Discard top layer of lettuce. Serve fish and topping on heated plates garnished with fresh herbs, lemon slices and pan juices.

Wine: Saintsbury Pinot Noir Carneros Garnet (California: Carneros), Château Souverain Sauvignon Blanc Alexander Valley Barrel Fermented (California: Sonoma County) or any medium-bodied Pinot Noir (red) or any barrel-fermented Sauvignon Blanc (white)

Braised Halibut with Sake

Serves 4

S AKE, LEMON AND GINGER make a fine marinade and braising medium for tasty halibut. The reduced marinade, in turn, becomes a simple sauce when a little butter is whisked into it, with watercress adding a peppery counterpoint.

½	cup sake
1	teaspoon soy sauce
4	scallions, trimmed to include 1 inch of green, cut into 2-inch matchsticks
2	teaspoons minced lemongrass or 1 teaspoon minced lemon zest
2	¼-inch-thick slices fresh ginger, cut into julienne
2	pounds 1-inch-thick halibut fillets or steaks, skin removed
¼	cup fish stock (page 327) or bottled clam juice
3	tablespoons cold unsalted butter, cut into small pieces
	Kosher salt and freshly ground black pepper
1	bunch watercress, for garnish

In a glass dish just large enough to hold fish, combine sake, soy sauce, scallions, lemongrass or zest and ginger. Add fish and marinate at room temperature, turning once, for 1 hour.

Preheat oven to 500 degrees F.

Pour marinade and stock or clam juice into an ovenproof, nonreactive saucepan just large enough to hold fish. Bring to a boil. Add fish, skin side down. Tightly cover and braise in oven until fish is firm to touch, about 13 minutes. Gently insert tines of a fork into center to check appearance of flesh; it should be opaque.

Remove fish to a heated plate. Place saucepan on high heat and bring sauce to a vigorous boil; reduce by one-third. Remove saucepan from heat and whisk in butter.

Season fish with salt and pepper. Divide among 4 heated serving plates and spoon some sauce over top. Garnish with watercress.

Wine: The Hess Collection Chardonnay (California: Napa Valley) or another medium-bodied California Chardonnay

Tomato-Braised Swordfish with Onions & Anchovies

Serves 4-6

T HIS SUCCULENT SWORDFISH reflects the wonderful flavors of Mediterranean France and Italy—olives, garlic, herbs, tomato and olive oil. While swordfish is more commonly grilled, this covered cooking results in an exceptionally tender and moist fish.

2	large yellow onions, thinly sliced
1	bunch fresh flat-leaf parsley, finely chopped (about 1 cup)
2-3	pounds 1¾-to-2-inch-thick swordfish steak
½	cup pitted Kalamata or Niçoise olives, minced
3	plump garlic cloves, minced
	Minced zest of 1 orange
½	teaspoon herbes de Provence or mixture of dried rosemary, savory, thyme, basil and crumbled bay leaf
	Kosher salt and freshly ground black pepper
6-8	flat oil-packed anchovy fillets, rinsed
⅓	cup olive oil
1	cup tomato puree (page 324) or canned crushed tomatoes
	Buttered boiled potatoes and chopped fresh flat-leaf parsley, for garnish

Preheat oven to 450 degrees F.

Lightly oil a baking dish just large enough to hold fish in a single layer. Sprinkle with a bit more than half of onions and parsley. Add fish. Sprinkle with olives, garlic, zest, herbes de Provence, salt and pepper and remaining onions and parsley. Distribute anchovy fillets over surface. Pour oil over fish. Pour tomato puree or crushed tomatoes around fish, spooning a little over.

Wrap casserole with foil and place in oven. Bake until onions are cooked, fish is firm to the touch and liquid is bubbling, about 25 minutes.

Serve with some pan juices over fish, accompanied by potatoes and fresh parsley.

Wine: Rochioli Vineyard Pinot Noir Russian River Valley (California: Sonoma County) or another complex Pinot Noir from America or France

Shad Roe with Crispy Bacon & Lemon Sauce

Serves 2-4

THIS DISH IS AN INTEGRAL PART of our rites of spring. Soaking the roe in milk eliminates any strong fishy taste and imparts a delicate sweetness. What's left is a pleasing flavor similar to fine calves' liver. While it is more common to cook shad roe uncovered, we learned that a brief covered oven-poaching lightens the texture of the roe. Covered frying speeds and evens the cooking with some steam, while at the same time eliminating the awful splatter. Linda has prepared shad roe this way for more than 30 years. A generous addition of fresh lemon, lots of parsley and chives makes a delicious butter sauce. The whole is enhanced by crispy smoked bacon slices. For brunch, we serve these with eggs and grits. For dinner, we accompany them with mashed potatoes and a green vegetable.

2	pairs shad roe
1	cup milk
	Juice of ½ lemon, plus 2 tablespoons
¼	cup unbleached flour
4	thick slices bacon
4	tablespoons (½ stick) unsalted butter
	Kosher salt and freshly ground black pepper
½	cup minced fresh flat-leaf parsley
2	tablespoons minced fresh chives
4	lemon slices and watercress, for garnish

Arrange roe in an ovenproof glass dish large enough to hold them in a single layer. Cover with milk, refrigerate and let stand for 1 to 2 hours, turning at least once. Drain and pat dry.

Preheat oven to 325 degrees F.

Rinse baking dish, return roe to dish and pour ⅓ cup water around them. Squeeze juice of ½ lemon over roe. Tightly cover with foil. Poach in oven just until roe is firm to the touch, 10 to 15 minutes.

Remove pan from oven. Gently remove roe. With a sharp knife, carefully separate pairs into 4 lobes. Using the tip of a thin bamboo skewer or a needle, gently prick roe in a few places so it will not burst in final cooking. Pour flour onto a plate. Dredge roe in flour and set aside.

Cook bacon in a large cast-iron skillet until crisp. Remove and drain on paper towels. Pour off all but 1 tablespoon bacon fat; add butter and melt over medium heat. Increase heat to medium-high, add roe and cover. Cook until brown, 2 to 3 minutes. Turn and repeat on other side. Remove roe to a heated platter, sprinkle with salt and pepper, and keep warm.

Add remaining 2 tablespoons lemon juice and parsley to pan drippings, and stir vigorously over high heat for 1½ minutes.

Place roe and bacon slices on heated plates. Spoon some pan sauce over each and sprinkle with chives. Garnish with lemon slices and watercress.

Wine: Ferrari-Carano Vineyards Chardonnay Alexander Valley (California: Sonoma County) or another medium-bodied Chardonnay

Poultry & Game

Skillet-Fried Chicken with Creamy Cracklin' Gravy 112

Pot-Roasted Baby Chickens with Garlic, Root Vegetables & Herbs 114

Yunnan Pot Chicken with Bok Choy & Snow Peas 116

Potted Stuffed Chicken & Vegetables 118

Smothered Chicken with Andouille Sausage,
Onions & Peppers 120

Oven-Barbecued Chicken 122

Chicken Hunter's Style (*Pollo alla Cacciatora*) 123

Chicken & Shrimp Gumbo 124

Nana's Chicken Fricassee 126

Peppered Chicken with Curried Onion & Mustard Sauce 128

Casserole of Spanish-Style Chicken & Brown Rice
(*Arroz con Pollo*) 130

Old Kentucky Curried Chicken 132

Chicken Stew with Virginia Ham, Mushrooms, Peas
& Cornmeal Dumplings 134

Silky Slow-Cooked Stew of Chicken, Beans, Garlic & Herbs 136

Deviled Turkey Legs with Olive Pan Sauce 138

Chili of Smoked Turkey & Peppers 140

Casserole of Ducks with Carrots, Onions & Turnips 142

Duck & Wild Rice Casserole 144

Duck Legs Braised with Baby Lettuces 146

Pheasant Stuffed with Wild Rice, Leeks & Cabbage 148

Skillet-Fried Chicken with Creamy Cracklin' Gravy

Serves 6-8

OCCASIONALLY, WE TREAT OURSELVES to this "gather-round-the-table" family treasure. The chicken is packed with flavor—crisp and crunchy on the outside, tender and moist inside. The secrets to success are soaking the chicken in the buttermilk before frying it, covering the pan while it is frying and frying in lard. While one can substitute canola oil, we often don't. Cooking it in lard may not be politically correct, but nothing makes fried foods taste better. The chicken will have a richer flavor and a less greasy exterior than if fried in oil. Buttermilk adds a special moisture and tang, while covering the skillet both speeds up the frying and allows the chicken to cook more evenly. Serve with lots of creamy mashed potatoes.

Chicken

2	3-pound fryers or 4 split chicken breasts
4	cups (1 quart) buttermilk
2½	cups unbleached flour
1½	teaspoons kosher salt
1½	teaspoons coarsely ground black pepper
½	teaspoon cayenne pepper
1-1½	pounds lard, enough to fill a large skillet ½ inch deep

Gravy

¼	cup unbleached flour
2	cups chicken stock (page 325)
	Up to 2 cups milk
½	cup heavy cream
2	teaspoons coarsely ground black pepper
	Kosher salt
2	tablespoons minced fresh chives

To prepare chicken: Cut each fryer, if using, into 8 pieces. Remove backbone and wing tips, discard or hold for stockpot. (Or cut each breast half in half again.) Place chicken pieces in a large bowl, cover with buttermilk, and marinate for 1 to 2 hours.

Drain chicken thoroughly, but do not pat dry. Combine flour, 1½ teaspoons salt, 1½ teaspoons pepper and cayenne in a plastic bag and mix well. Toss chicken pieces in flour mixture a few pieces at a time; place chicken on a rack until ready to cook.

Preheat oven to 225 degrees F.

In a 12-inch cast-iron skillet with a cover or in 2 smaller skillets, heat lard over medium-high heat until a bread cube tossed in browns quickly. Carefully add 6 to 8 chicken pieces; do not crowd. Cover with a lid or heavy-duty foil and fry over medium heat for 10 minutes.

Turn and continue frying until skin is golden brown and meat is very tender when pierced with a fork, about 10 minutes more. Be sure to check chicken several times while cooking to make certain it does not burn. (If pieces are large, they may need a few more minutes on each side.) Remove cooked chicken from skillet, drain well on paper towels and keep warm on a cookie sheet in oven until remaining chicken is done and ready to serve.

To make gravy: When all chicken is fried, pour fat through a strainer into a bowl. Reserve solids ("cracklings") left in strainer; return ¼ cup fat to skillet and discard remaining fat.

Over medium-high heat, whisk in flour, and continue whisking until mixture becomes toasty brown, about 5 minutes. Gradually whisk in stock, 1 cup milk and cream. Cook, whisking frequently, for 5 to 10 minutes, to remove floury taste. If gravy is too thick, gradually whisk in up to 1 cup more milk. Whisk in reserved cracklings, pepper, salt and chives. Pour into a heated gravy boat.

Serve chicken on heated plates. Pass gravy separately.

Wine: Oakville Ranch Vineyards Chardonnay (California: Napa Valley) or another medium-bodied Chardonnay

Pot-Roasted Baby Chickens with Garlic, Root Vegetables & Herbs

Serves 4

THIS CHICKEN AND ROOT VEGETABLE ONE-POT is as delicious as it smells. When the vegetables begin to caramelize, their subtle sweetness blends beautifully with the sun-filled flavors of the herbes de Provence. Serve with mashed potatoes.

2	tablespoons olive oil
3	tablespoons unsalted butter
2	fresh rosemary sprigs or 1 teaspoon dried
2	plump garlic cloves, peeled, plus 1 garlic head, cloves separated, unpeeled
2	plump 1½-pound baby chickens or Cornish hens
4	small parsnips, peeled and cut into 1-inch chunks
2	medium turnips, trimmed and quartered
8	large shallots
½	head Savoy cabbage, cut into 4 wedges, core removed
2	teaspoons herbes de Provence or mixture of dried rosemary, savory, thyme, basil and crumbled bay leaf
	Kosher salt and freshly ground black pepper

Preheat oven to 400 degrees F.

Combine oil and butter in a 5-quart cast-iron Dutch oven and melt over medium-high heat. Meanwhile, place 1 rosemary sprig or ½ teaspoon dried and 1 peeled garlic clove in each chicken cavity. Cook, breast side down, in butter mixture, until golden, about 6 minutes. Turn and brown undersides, about 6 minutes; remove browned birds. Add parsnips, turnips and shallots to butter mixture. Toss in hot butter just until slightly golden, 2 to 3 minutes.

Remove pot from heat. Place cabbage over browned vegetables; position birds on top of cabbage. Scatter unpeeled garlic cloves over, allowing them to tumble into vegetables. Season with herbes de Provence and salt and pepper.

Cover and braise in oven until juices of chicken run clear when thigh is punctured with a sharp fork, about 1¼ hours. Cut birds in half. Serve on heated plates with cooked vegetables and garlic. Sauce with pan juices.

Wine: Ravenswood Winery Zinfandel Old Vine (California: Sonoma County) or another full-bodied Zinfandel

Yunnan Pot Chicken
with Bok Choy & Snow Peas

Serves 4

THIS CHICKEN SOUP with lots of chicken and vegetables makes a full meal. It must be made in a Yunnan steam pot, which is a plain clay pot with a central steaming funnel that rises from the bottom; a tight-fitting lid covers the whole thing. It looks like a smooth Bundt pan with a lid. The Yunnan pot is placed over water in a wok or large pot. The steam rises through the central tube, bathing the pan with moist heat, so that the soup is steamed. These pots are not costly; they retail for about $20 and can be found in most Chinese markets or ordered from The Oriental Pantry (see Sources, page 336). See photograph, page 87.

2	large chicken breasts, split
½	cup matchstick pieces smoked ham
½	teaspoon kosher salt
½	teaspoon finely ground white pepper
	Generous pinch of cayenne pepper
2	medium carrots
3	scallions, smashed with flat side of a cleaver, plus 2 scallions, trimmed to include 1 inch of green, minced
1	tablespoon minced fresh ginger
2¼	cups chicken stock (page 325), boiling
¼	cup dry white wine
1	cup sliced (½ inch) bok choy
16	snow pea pods
1	teaspoon Asian sesame oil
1	tablespoon minced fresh cilantro

Select a wok or pot large enough to hold Yunnan pot; pot should fit partway in like the top of a double boiler. Or place pot inside a large, deep stockpot. Put enough water, about 3 inches, into bottom pot so that plentiful steam will be created.

With a heavy knife or cleaver, whack chicken through bone into small (about 2-inch) pieces. Arrange chicken and ham in bottom of Yunnan pot. Sprinkle with salt, white pepper and cayenne.

Cutting on a slight angle, slice carrots into ¼-inch slices and add to pot. Add smashed scallions, ginger, stock and wine.

Cover Yunnan pot and bring steaming water to a boil. Reduce heat to low and steam for 1 hour. (Check from time to time to make certain that water has not evaporated.)

Add bok choy and snow peas, cover and steam until chicken is fork-tender, about 15 minutes more.

Remove pot from stove; skim off any surface fat. Discard scallions. Stir in sesame oil.

Ladle into heated soup plates and sprinkle with minced scallions and cilantro.

Wine: Dr. Loosen St. Johannishof Riesling Kabinett Mosel-Saar-Ruwer Wehlener Sonnenuhr (Germany: Mosel-Saar-Ruwer) or Preston Vineyards Marsanne Dry Creek Valley (California: Sonoma County)

Potted Stuffed Chicken & Vegetables

Serves 4

THIS TENDER ROASTING CHICKEN with its mushroom stuffing is simmered in a fragrant herb-and-vegetable-filled broth. It is a pleasing version of old-fashioned poached or boiled chicken—a cooking technique that always yields an exceptionally moist bird. Traditionally, the French tenderized old hens in this fashion, cooking them for twice the time our bird requires. Serve the leftover soup another day with noodles. (See photograph on cover.)

Stuffing

3	tablespoons olive oil
1	chicken liver, diced
¼	pound mushrooms, preferably portobello or shiitake, finely chopped
1	plump shallot, minced
1	plump garlic clove, minced
1	cup fine dry bread crumbs
1	tablespoon Dijon mustard
1	large egg
1	teaspoon herbes de Provence or mixture of dried rosemary, savory, thyme, basil and crumbled bay leaf
	Kosher salt and freshly ground black pepper

Chicken

1	4-to-4½-pound roasting chicken, excess fat removed
	Kosher salt and freshly ground black pepper
1	tablespoon hot Hungarian paprika
2	tablespoons olive oil
2	medium carrots, finely chopped, plus 4 medium carrots, cut into thirds
1	large yellow onion, finely chopped
10	cups (2½ quarts) chicken stock (page 325), plus more if needed
2	bouquet garnis (page 331)

2   whole cloves

1   bay leaf

8   small boiling onions, blanched and peeled

2   cups chopped escarole or arugula
    Freshly grated nutmeg

¼   cup chopped fresh flat-leaf parsley

To make stuffing: Heat oil in a large nonstick skillet over medium heat. Add chicken liver and sauté, stirring constantly, until cooked, 2 to 3 minutes. Remove with a slotted spoon and reserve. Add mushrooms, shallot and garlic. Cover and cook, stirring occasionally, until moisture evaporates, 3 to 4 minutes.

Transfer mixture to a mixing bowl. Add bread crumbs, mustard, egg, herbes de Provence and salt and pepper; mix thoroughly. Stir in enough water—about 2 tablespoons—to moisten stuffing.

To prepare chicken: Season chicken cavity with salt and pepper. Fill with stuffing mixture; skewer cavity closed and secure with string. Rub outside of chicken with salt, pepper and paprika. For a neater bird, skewer wings to body and loosely tie legs together with a length of kitchen twine.

Heat oil in skillet over high heat. Carefully brown chicken on all sides, 5 to 7 minutes. Meanwhile, place chopped carrots and chopped onion in a heavy, deep pot just wide enough to hold chicken. Place browned chicken over onions. Add 10 cups stock, bouquet garnis, cloves and bay leaf to pot. If there is not enough stock to reach at least halfway up chicken, add more.

Cover pot and bring to a boil over high heat. Reduce heat to low, cover and simmer for 45 minutes.

Add boiling onions, carrot pieces and escarole or arugula. Cover and cook until chicken is fork-tender, 30 to 45 minutes more.

Carefully transfer chicken to a carving board and keep warm. Skim any fat from soup. Adjust seasonings, adding salt and pepper if needed.

Remove string and skewers from chicken; cut it into quarters. Place some chicken and stuffing in each of 4 heated soup plates. Divide vegetables among them and ladle soup over. Add a few grindings of pepper and nutmeg. Sprinkle with parsley.

Wine: Domaine René et Christian Miolane Beaujolais-Villages Cuvée de la Cotabras (France: Burgundy), R.H. Phillips Viognier EXP (California) or a medium-bodied, fruity red or another California Viognier (white)

Smothered Chicken with Andouille Sausage, Onions & Peppers

Serves 8

A SMOTHERED FOWL is one that is first floured, quickly fried so the skin acquires a delicious flavor from browning, then slowly cooked under cover right in its thick gravy, until it becomes almost falling-apart tender. While Paul Prudhomme's Cajun cooking brought smothered cooking to national prominence, one can find a splendid recipe for smothered chicken in Lettice Bryan's 1839 masterpiece, *The Kentucky Housewife*. Slices of spicy andouille sausage and generous additions of onions, celery and fresh peppers make the gravy dark and addictive. Serve this with mashed potatoes.

1	pound andouille sausage or smoked garlic sausage, cut into ½-inch-thick slices
1⅓	cups unbleached flour
2	3-pound frying chickens, each cut into 8 pieces
	Up to 1 cup vegetable oil
2	plump garlic cloves, minced
2¼	teaspoons kosher salt
1¼	teaspoons freshly ground black pepper
1¼	teaspoons freshly ground white pepper
1	teaspoon cayenne pepper
1	teaspoon dried thyme
1	teaspoon dried oregano
¼	teaspoon ground sage
1	bay leaf
1½	cups coarsely diced yellow onions
8	scallions, trimmed to include 1 inch of green, finely chopped
2	celery stalks, finely diced
1	medium-sized red bell pepper, seeded, deribbed and cut into medium dice
1	jalapeño chile, seeded and finely diced
4	cups chicken stock (page 325)

1   teaspoon Tabasco sauce, or more to taste
2   tablespoons minced fresh flat-leaf parsley, for garnish

Place sausage in a medium saucepan, cover with water and bring to a boil; reduce heat and simmer for 5 minutes. Drain and set side.

Place flour in a plastic bag. Add chicken pieces, a few at a time, and shake to coat evenly. Place chicken on a rack; reserve ½ cup flour.

Pour ½ cup oil into a 12-inch cast-iron skillet or 2 smaller skillets. Cover with a tight-fitting lid or heavy-duty foil. Heat over high heat until hot but not smoking. Add chicken pieces; do not crowd. Reduce heat to medium and cook until golden brown, about 5 minutes; turn and brown other side. Transfer browned chicken to a large platter. Repeat until all pieces are browned, adding more oil as needed.

Discard oil; wipe out skillet. Thinly coat bottom with 3 to 4 tablespoons fresh oil and heat over medium heat until hot. Add garlic, salt, black and white peppers, cayenne, thyme, oregano, sage and bay leaf. Sauté over medium heat for 2 minutes. Add onions, scallions, celery, red pepper and chile. Cook, stirring frequently, just to soften vegetables slightly, 2 to 3 minutes. Remove skillet from heat and return chicken to skillet, spooning pepper mixture over it. Scatter sausage pieces over top and set aside.

Pour stock into a medium saucepan and bring to a lively simmer. Meanwhile, in a small cast-iron skillet, combine ¼ cup oil and reserved flour; whisk well to blend. Place over medium heat and cook, whisking constantly and scraping skillet from time to time with a wooden spoon, until mixture is pecan-colored, 5 to 10 minutes. Quickly whisk half of roux into simmering stock. Add remaining roux and whisk over medium-high heat until gravy thickens. Stir in 1 teaspoon Tabasco.

Pour gravy over chicken and sausage slices. Tightly cover skillet and cook over medium heat until liquid bubbles. Reduce heat and simmer until chicken is very tender when pierced with a fork, about 45 minutes. Taste, adding more Tabasco if desired. Skim off any surface fat.

Serve on heated plates; nap generously with sausage slices and gravy. Sprinkle with parsley.

Wine: Marietta Cellars Old Vine Red (California: Sonoma) or an Australian Cabernet-Shiraz blend

Oven-Barbecued Chicken

Serves 2-4

THIS OLD SOUTHERN PREPARATION, adapted from Marion Flexner's 1941 *Dixie Dishes*, is simple. The chicken is butterflied, lightly coated with a simple and light barbecue sauce and browned under the broiler. Transferred to a skillet, it is braised in more of the sauce. The result is a piquant, buttery bird that is moist and tender.

1   3-to-3½-pound fryer, split down the back, backbone removed
    Kosher salt and freshly ground black pepper
4   tablespoons (½ stick) unsalted butter
1   tablespoon Worcestershire sauce
¼   teaspoon Tabasco sauce, plus more to taste
1   tablespoon red wine vinegar, plus more to taste
    Minced fresh flat-leaf parsley and chives, for garnish

Preheat broiler.

Place chicken, skin side up, on work surface. Bang hard on each side of breast to flatten. Rub each side of bird with salt and pepper. Place on a large broiling pan or cookie sheet covered with foil.

In a small, nonreactive saucepan, combine butter, Worcestershire, ¼ teaspoon Tabasco and 1 tablespoon vinegar. Cook over high heat until butter melts. Remove from heat. Using a pastry brush, coat chicken on both sides with butter sauce.

Place chicken under hot broiler and brown on both sides, brushing often with butter sauce, 10 to 15 minutes.

Preheat oven to 375 degrees F.

Transfer chicken, skin side up, to a large ovenproof skillet. Paint generously with remaining butter sauce. Add ¾ cup hot water to skillet. Tightly cover and braise in oven, basting occasionally and adding more water if needed, until chicken is fork-tender, about 1¼ hours.

Transfer chicken to a carving platter. Add ¼ cup water to skillet and whisk vigorously over high heat to loosen browned particles adhering to pan. Sauce will be thin. Adjust seasonings, adding more Tabasco or vinegar as needed.

Cut chicken into quarters. Serve on heated plates garnished with pan sauce. Sprinkle generously with parsley and chives.

Wine: Burgess Cellars Zinfandel (California: Napa Valley) or another medium-bodied, fruity Zinfandel

Chicken Hunter's Style

(*Pollo alla Cacciatora*)

Serves 4

WE'VE MADE THIS WONDERFUL RAGOUT of chicken, tomatoes, onions and mushrooms for years. It's comfortable family food and truly sublime when served with polenta.

1	3½-to-4-pound frying chicken quartered, wings separated, or 2 chicken breasts, split
⅓	cup unbleached flour
2	tablespoons olive oil
1½	cups diced yellow onions
¼	teaspoon fennel seeds, crushed
1	small dried red chile, crumbled
2	plump garlic cloves, minced
1⅓	cups dry red wine
½	pound cremini mushrooms, thinly sliced
2½	cups tomato puree (page 324) or canned crushed tomatoes
	Kosher salt and freshly ground black pepper
¼	cup minced fresh basil, plus more to taste

Place chicken on a large sheet of wax paper. Sprinkle with flour; rub flour into chicken.

Heat oil in a large, deep, nonreactive skillet over medium heat. Add chicken, skin side down, and cook until golden, 7 to 10 minutes. Turn and brown on other side, about 7 minutes. Transfer chicken to a large, warm platter and set aside.

Add onions, fennel seeds and chile to skillet and stir over medium heat until onions soften, 2 to 4 minutes. Add garlic and stir until garlic begins to soften, 1 to 2 minutes. Add wine, increase heat to high, and stir vigorously to loosen any browned particles adhering to pan. Return chicken pieces to pan, skin side down, and cook for about 2 minutes. Add mushrooms and tomato puree or crushed tomatoes; stir until liquid begins to bubble.

Season with salt and pepper. Cover skillet, reduce heat to low and cook, stirring occasionally, until chicken is fork-tender, about 50 minutes.

Serve chicken and sauce on heated plates with a generous sprinkling of fresh basil.

Wine: Elyse Zinfandel Coeur du Val (California: Napa Valley) or a rich red wine from Tuscany or Piedmont (Italy)

Chicken & Shrimp Gumbo

Serves 8

Like most gumbos, this one is colorful, richly flavored and zesty. It is thickened with both okra and a dark brown roux. You can prepare the gumbo early in the day up to the addition of the chicken and shrimp.

Shrimp
1 large yellow onion, peeled
4 bay leaves
1 tablespoon black peppercorns
1 tablespoon cayenne pepper
1 tablespoon dry mustard
2 whole cloves
2 garlic cloves, peeled
1½ pounds large shrimp

Gumbo
½ cup plus 3 tablespoons canola oil
2 pounds frozen or fresh sliced okra
½ cup unbleached flour
1 medium-sized red bell pepper, cut into medium dice
1 28-ounce can plum tomatoes
1¼ cups finely chopped yellow onions (2 large)
¾ cup finely chopped celery (3 large stalks)
1 large green bell pepper, coarsely chopped
2 dried red chiles, crumbled
3 plump garlic cloves, minced
1 tablespoon freshly ground black pepper
1 tablespoon freshly ground white pepper
1 tablespoon kosher salt
2 teaspoons dried oregano
2 teaspoons dried thyme
2 bay leaves
4 boneless, skinless chicken breasts, cut into 1-inch cubes
2 cups fresh or frozen yellow corn kernels
   Tabasco sauce

> 1 cup finely sliced scallions
>
> 4 cups cooked jasmine rice (from 1½ cups raw;
>   see Sources, page 335)

To prepare shrimp: Combine onion, bay leaves, peppercorns, cayenne, dry mustard, cloves and garlic in a large pot. Stir in 4 quarts (16 cups) water and bring to a boil over high heat. Simmer until liquid is reduced by half, about 1 hour.

Bring reduced mixture to a boil. Add shrimp and cook for 2 minutes. Remove shrimp from pot with a skimmer or slotted spoon and cool in a bowl of ice water. Strain; set aside 8 cups cooking liquid. Peel and devein shrimp. Cover with plastic wrap and refrigerate.

To make gumbo: Heat ¼ cup oil in a large cast-iron skillet. Stir in okra and cook over low heat, stirring often, until seeds appear and okra softens, about 45 minutes for frozen or 1 to 2 hours for fresh.

Meanwhile, make a roux: Heat ¼ cup oil in a small cast-iron skillet over medium heat. Whisk in flour. Stir over medium-high heat until roux is dark walnut brown, 5 to 10 minutes. Remove skillet from heat. Stir in red pepper; set aside.

When okra is done, add tomatoes and juice. Cook, covered, for 15 minutes; set aside.

In a large, heavy nonreactive pot, heat remaining 3 tablespoons oil over medium heat. Add onions, celery, green pepper, chiles and garlic. Cover and cook over low heat until onions soften, 6 to 8 minutes. Stir in black and white peppers, salt, oregano, thyme and bay leaves. Cover and cook for 5 minutes.

Blend in okra mixture and reserved cooking liquid. Bring to a boil over high heat; stir in roux, and continue to cook, stirring, until mixture thickens slightly. Add chicken. Tightly cover pot, reduce heat to low and simmer for 15 minutes.

Add shrimp and corn. Cover and cook for 5 minutes. Add Tabasco to taste. Stir in scallions.

Divide rice among large heated soup plates. Ladle generous portions of gumbo into each and serve.

Wine: ZD Wines Chardonnay (California), Sanford Winery Chardonnay (California: Santa Barbara County) or another barrel-fermented Chardonnay from Santa Barbara County

Nana's Chicken Fricassee

Serves 6

EVERYONE LOVES THIS LUSCIOUS STEW of chicken and meatballs slowly simmered in dark, rich gravy—especially when it is served over mashed potatoes. As a child, Linda used to beg her grandmother to make this for her. Now Linda's sons ask their grandmother to make it for them. It is even better when prepared a day before serving.

Chicken

1½	frying chickens (4½-5 pounds total)
2	tablespoons hot Hungarian paprika
1	teaspoon freshly ground black pepper
1	teaspoon kosher salt
2	tablespoons vegetable oil
1	large yellow onion, finely diced
2	plump garlic cloves, minced

Meatballs

1	pound ground veal
½	cup coarse fresh bread crumbs
1	large egg
1	small yellow onion, minced
1	plump garlic clove, minced
1	tablespoon mixed dried herbs (parsley, oregano, sage, thyme)
1	teaspoon kosher salt, plus more to taste
1	teaspoon freshly ground black pepper, plus more to taste

Gravy

2	cups chicken stock (page 325)
¼	cup vegetable oil
¼	cup unbleached flour
	Minced fresh flat-leaf parsley, for garnish

To prepare chicken: Cut each wing into 2 pieces. Cut breast halves into 2 or 3 pieces, depending on size. Cut thighs into 2 pieces. Combine paprika, pepper and salt in a large bowl. Add chicken pieces and toss well to coat.

Pour oil into a large, deep skillet or sauté pan and heat over medium heat. Add onion and garlic and cook, stirring, for 2 minutes. Add chicken and sauté until golden on all sides, 5 to 8 minutes.

Cover skillet, reduce heat to low and cook, stirring occasionally, for 30 minutes.

Meanwhile, make meatballs: Preheat oven to 500 degrees F.

Combine veal, bread crumbs, egg, onion, garlic, herbs, 1 teaspoon salt and 1 teaspoon pepper and ⅓ cup water, and beat with an electric mixer until light and fluffy, or mix vigorously with hands. Form into walnut-sized balls, placing them on a large baking sheet with shallow sides.

Roast meatballs until they are brown on top, about 10 minutes. When chicken has cooked for 30 minutes, gently transfer meatballs to skillet with a slotted spoon. Remove from heat and keep covered.

To make gravy: Pour stock into a small saucepan and heat until hot. Meanwhile, make a roux: Heat oil in a small cast-iron skillet over high heat. Whisk in flour and keep whisking over medium-high heat until roux is a rich dark brown, 5 to 7 minutes. Gradually stir roux into hot stock; whisk until evenly blended. Slowly simmer gravy for 10 minutes to remove floury taste.

Add gravy to chicken and meatballs and stir gently to blend. Cover skillet and cook over low heat, stirring from time to time, for another 30 minutes.

Skim off any surface fat. Taste and adjust seasonings, adding salt and pepper to taste. Sprinkle with parsley.

Wine: Truchard Vineyard Syrah Carneros (California: Carneros) or another complex Syrah

Peppered Chicken with Curried Onion & Mustard Sauce

Serves 4

W E OFTEN FIND OURSELVES adding a spoonful or two of curry powder to dishes that include more than an average amount of pepper. The spice blend adds a deep, rich flavor to a peppery dish. While serious fans of Indian cooking might eschew commercially blended curry powder, preferring to mix their own as they use it, we find that a good-quality commercial powder is quite satisfying.

3	tablespoons canola oil
2	chicken breasts, skinned and split
1	large Spanish onion, finely diced
3	plump garlic cloves, minced
2	teaspoons curry powder
4	tablespoons Dijon mustard
2	teaspoons finely ground black pepper
1	teaspoon finely ground white pepper
½	cup chicken stock (page 325), plus more if needed
½	cup dry white wine
	Kosher salt
⅓	cup low-fat sour cream
⅔	cup fresh or frozen green peas
3	scallions, trimmed to include 1 inch of green, minced

Preheat oven to 375 degrees F.

In a large cast-iron skillet with a tight-fitting lid, heat oil over high heat. Place chicken breasts, top side down, in skillet and cook until browned, about 5 minutes. Turn and brown undersides, about 5 minutes. Remove chicken to a warm platter. Pour off all but 1 tablespoon oil.

Evenly distribute onion and garlic in skillet. Sprinkle evenly with 1 teaspoon curry powder. Place chicken breasts, top side up, on onion. Coat chicken breasts with 3 tablespoons mustard. Sprinkle evenly with black and white peppers and remaining 1 teaspoon curry powder. Pour stock and wine around prepared breasts. Sprinkle generously with salt.

Tightly cover and bake, basting several times with onion and pan juices and adding chicken stock if pan appears to be too dry, until chicken is tender when pierced with a knife, about 1 hour.

Gently transfer chicken breasts to heated plates. Put skillet over high heat. Scrape and stir until sauce comes to a boil. Boil vigorously for 1 minute to reduce and thicken sauce. Blend in remaining 1 tablespoon mustard and sour cream; stir in peas. Cook until heated through; do not boil. Spoon sauce over chicken and sprinkle with scallions.

Wine: De Loach Vineyards Zinfandel Russian River Valley O.F.S. (California: Sonoma County) or any peppery Zinfandel

Casserole of Spanish-Style Chicken & Brown Rice

(*Arroz con Pollo*)

Serves 4

PICY CHICKEN AND RICE are cooked in a tomato sauce warmly laced with a subtle suggestion of saffron. While the dish is traditionally made with white rice, we prefer the richer, nutty flavor of brown rice, and it's especially good with Lowell Farms' brown jasmine rice (see Sources, page 335.) Some recipes for this dish call for chunks of spicy *chorizo* sausage. Others call for cumin instead of saffron, or artichoke hearts in addition to peas. Have fun and experiment.

4	tablespoons olive oil
2	medium-sized yellow onions, finely diced
2	plump garlic cloves, minced
1	jalapeño chile, minced
1	cup raw brown rice
1	3½-to-4-pound chicken, quartered
1	28-ounce can whole tomatoes, with juice drained and reserved
	Up to 1 cup chicken stock (page 325) or water
⅛	teaspoon saffron threads
	Kosher salt and freshly ground black pepper
2⅓	cups sliced pimiento-stuffed green olives
⅓	cup fresh or frozen green peas
¼	cup minced fresh flat-leaf parsley

Preheat oven to 350 degrees F. Lightly oil a 3-quart ovenproof casserole.

Heat 2 tablespoons oil in a medium skillet. When hot, add onions and stir until softened, 2 to 3 minutes. Add garlic and jalapeño; stir over medium heat for 1 minute. Add rice and stir until well coated with oil, about 1 minute. Transfer rice mixture to casserole and keep warm.

Pour remaining 2 tablespoons oil into a large nonreactive skillet; heat until hot. Add chicken pieces and cook until well browned on each side, 6 to 7 minutes per side. Place chicken, skin side up, over rice. Drain fat from skillet.

Add enough chicken stock or water to reserved tomato juice to measure 2½ cups. Combine saffron with 2 tablespoons boiling water and stir to dissolve; add to tomato juice. Add juice mixture to skillet and stir over high heat until all browned particles loosen and liquid boils. Pour over chicken and rice.

Working quickly, use your fingers to break tomatoes into pieces; scatter over chicken. Season generously with salt and pepper.

Tightly cover casserole with a lid or foil and bake for 1 hour 10 minutes.

Uncover casserole, add olives and peas. Carefully stir rice underneath chicken. Cover and bake for 20 minutes more, or until heated through.

Divide among heated plates and sprinkle generously with fresh parsley.

Wine: Harpersfield Vineyard Pinot Gris (Ohio: Lake Erie) or St.-Marc Estate Barrel Fermented Chardonnay (Spain) or a complex white Rioja from Spain

Old Kentucky Curried Chicken

Serves 4

Lettice Bryan's recipe for "A Curry of Chickens" in *The Kentucky Housewife*, first published in 1839, sounded too good to ignore. In this recipe, the chicken is browned for extra flavor before being stewed in a curry sauce until tender. The generous splash of lemon we added makes a light, bright sauce, indeed. Otherwise, this spicy and wonderfully fragrant dish isn't too far from the original, and amazingly convenient.

Curry appeared in Kentucky as early as 1839. Ships sailing from India, laden with exotic spices, commonly docked at Southern ports. The spices moved inland with the peddlers and were carried up the Mississippi to Ohio on trading boats.

1	3½-to-4½-pound chicken, cut into 8 pieces, or 2 chicken breasts, split
	Kosher salt and freshly ground black pepper
¼	cup unbleached flour
¼	cup canola oil, plus more if needed
4	medium-sized yellow onions, finely chopped
3	plump garlic cloves, minced
1½	teaspoons turmeric
1½	teaspoons curry powder
1	teaspoon ground ginger
½	teaspoon ground mace
¼	teaspoon cayenne pepper
¼	teaspoon freshly grated nutmeg
1½	cups chicken stock (page 325)
	Juice of 1 lemon
2	cups cooked jasmine rice (from ¾ cup raw; see Sources, page 335)
1	bunch scallions, trimmed to include 1 inch of green, minced

Rub chicken pieces with salt and pepper and flour.

Heat ¼ cup oil in a heavy, large sauté pan over high heat. Add chicken, skin side down, and fry until golden on both sides, 10 to 12 minutes total. Transfer chicken to a platter. Measure oil in pan; you should have 3 tablespoons.

Add onions to hot pan; stir over high heat until onions begin to brown, about 10 minutes.

Stir in garlic, spices, 1 teaspoon salt and 1 teaspoon black pepper. Cook, stirring constantly, for 2 minutes. Add stock and cook, stirring, until liquid begins to bubble. Add chicken to sauté pan; spoon some of sauce over each piece.

Cover pan and reduce heat to low. Cook until chicken is fork-tender, about 45 minutes.

Stir in lemon juice. Flavors seem to improve upon standing; if time permits, let stand for about 30 minutes and reheat until hot, about 10 minutes.

Spoon chicken and sauce over hot rice. Sprinkle with scallions.

Wine: Husch Vineyards Gewürztraminer (California: Anderson Valley) or another Gewürztraminer

Chicken Stew with Virginia Ham, Mushrooms, Peas & Cornmeal Dumplings

Serves 6-8

THIS CREAMY CHICKEN STEW has its roots in a host of old Southern cookbooks in which mace and poultry were often paired. Bites of red peppers and smoked ham combine with fresh peas and mushrooms in a yellow sauce. Tasty cornmeal dumplings are steamed right in the sauce.

3	tablespoons unsalted butter
1	pound large-bulbed green onions, trimmed to include 1 inch of green, or 1 pound white onions, finely chopped
3	celery stalks, finely diced
¼	pound mushrooms, thinly sliced
1	red bell pepper, seeded and cut into medium dice
3	plump garlic cloves, minced
½	rounded teaspoon ground mace
¼	cup unbleached flour
4	cups chicken stock (page 325)
1	cup dry white wine
1	cup slivered smoked ham, preferably from Virginia
1	pint pearl onions, blanched and peeled
4	medium carrots, cut into 2-inch lengths
1	teaspoon minced fresh rosemary or ½ teaspoon dried
3	boneless, skinless chicken breasts, cut into 1-inch cubes
	Kosher salt and freshly ground white pepper
1	teaspoon fresh thyme leaves or ½ teaspoon dried

Dumplings

1½	cups yellow cornmeal
¼	cup unbleached flour
2	teaspoons baking powder
	Generous pinch of ground mace
2	tablespoons minced scallions

1	teaspoon kosher salt
2	teaspoons solid shortening
¾	cup chicken stock or water, heated to boiling

¼	teaspoon Tabasco sauce, plus more if desired
1	cup frozen peas
¼	cup minced fresh flat-leaf parsley
¼	cup thinly sliced scallions, trimmed to include 1 inch of green

In a wide, heavy-bottomed, nonreactive 6-quart pot, melt butter over medium heat. Add finely chopped onions, celery, mushrooms, red pepper and garlic. Cover, reduce heat to low, and cook until onions soften, 4 to 5 minutes.

Stir in mace. Add flour and stir over medium heat until flour loses its whiteness, 2 to 3 minutes. Stir in stock and wine; blend thoroughly. Cook over medium heat until liquid begins to bubble. Add ham, pearl onions, carrots and rosemary. Reduce heat to low, cover and cook for 15 minutes.

Add chicken, salt and white pepper and thyme. Cover and simmer for 15 minutes.

Meanwhile, make dumplings: In a large mixing bowl, combine cornmeal, flour, baking powder, mace, scallions and salt; blend well. Lightly cut in shortening with your fingers; stir in boiling stock or water. Mix briskly, just until dough holds together. Pat dough into a ¾-inch-thick rectangle. Cut into 1½-inch squares (makes 10 to 12). Place dumplings on a flat plate and chill until needed

After stew has cooked for 30 minutes, taste and adjust seasonings, adding more salt and white pepper if needed. Stir in Tabasco and peas; arrange dumplings over surface of simmering stew. Cover and cook until dumplings have a shiny surface and are cooked through, 12 to 14 minutes.

Ladle stew and dumplings into heated soup plates. Sprinkle with parsley and scallions.

Wine: Lewis Cellars Chardonnay (California: Napa Valley) or another spicy, medium-bodied Chardonnay

Silky Slow-Cooked Stew of Chicken, Beans, Garlic & Herbs

Serves 8-10

SLOW COOKING AT A LOW TEMPERATURE yields remarkably silky beans. This dish is a much-simplified *cassoulet*, the celebrated dish of beans, preserved duck and lamb that originated in the southwest of France. It is inspired by a recipe called "North Woods Chicken and Beans" in the Louisville, Kentucky, *Courier-Journal & Times Cookbook*, published in 1971. The beans are baked in a slow oven until they become soft and garlicky, and then they are uncovered and baked until a crust forms on top. The result is a fine-textured, fragrant dish, perfect for a special covered-dish supper when you're expecting company.

2	pounds dried navy beans
⅓	pound salt pork, cut into matchsticks
4	plump garlic cloves, minced
½	cup minced fresh flat-leaf parsley
1	tablespoon fresh thyme leaves or 1½ teaspoons dried
2	large yellow onions
4	whole cloves
1	6-to-7-pound roasting chicken or capon, cut into 16 pieces
	Kosher salt and freshly ground black pepper
1	teaspoon confit seasonings (page 332; optional)
1	teaspoon dry mustard
1	bay leaf
	About 12 cups (3 quarts) boiling chicken stock (page 325)
1	cup fine dry bread crumbs
4	tablespoons (½ stick) unsalted butter, melted

Early in the morning, place beans in a large saucepan and cover with several inches of water. Bring to a boil. Remove from heat and let stand for 1½ hours. Drain well.

Preheat oven to 275 degrees F.

Place one-third of beans in a large 6- or 7-quart cast-iron Dutch oven or stoneware casserole. Sprinkle with half of salt pork, garlic, parsley and thyme. Stud each onion with 2 cloves; place 1 onion over seasonings. Cover with half of remaining beans and add remaining salt pork, garlic, parsley and thyme. Distribute chicken pieces and remaining clove-studded onion over beans. Sprinkle generously with salt and pepper. Cover with remaining beans. Sprinkle with confit seasonings (if using), dry mustard and more salt and pepper. Place bay leaf in center.

Pour 7 to 9 cups hot stock over beans until top is covered. Cover casserole and bake until beans are just tender, 3½ to 4½ hours. Add more stock if mixture becomes dry.

Increase heat to 375 degrees. Remove casserole from oven. Discard bay leaf and onions. Skim off surface fat. Carefully lift out chicken pieces. Remove meat from bones in large pieces; discard skin and bones. Return meat to beans, burying pieces under beans. There should be enough liquid to bubble around edges of pan; if not, add more stock.

Combine bread crumbs and melted butter. Sprinkle mixture evenly over beans. Bake, uncovered, until crumbs are golden and liquid bubbles around edges, about 1 hour.

If you wish to prepare this 1 day ahead, cook it up to the point of adding the bread-crumb topping. Cool and refrigerate. The next day, bring to room temperature. Cook, covered, for 30 minutes in a 350-degree oven. Increase temperature to 375 degrees and sprinkle with bread-crumb mixture. Bake until top is golden and liquid bubbles around sides, 1 hour more.

Serve hot.

Wine: Alban Vineyards Viognier (California: St. Luis Obispo), another California Viognier or a Condrieu (France)

Deviled Turkey Legs with Olive Pan Sauce

Serves 6-8

HERE IS A MEAL for those who rush to the holiday table to secure a drumstick or thigh. The turkey legs are dipped in a dressing of lemony Dijon mustard and rolled in herbed bread crumbs. After a quick browning, they are braised on a bed of red onions, carrots and celery with red wine, herbs and Kalamata olives and served with pasta mixed with the delicious onion and olive sauce.

4	celery stalks, finely chopped
4	medium-large carrots, finely chopped
2	large red onions, finely chopped
3	plump garlic cloves, minced
1	cup Dijon mustard
5	tablespoons olive oil, plus more if needed
	Juice of 1 lemon
1½	cups fine dry bread crumbs
2	teaspoons kosher salt, plus more to taste
1	teaspoon freshly ground black pepper, plus more to taste
2	teaspoons herbes de Provence or mixture of dried rosemary, savory, thyme, basil and crumbled bay leaf
4	turkey legs and thighs (8 pieces total; about 6 pounds)
⅔	cup chicken stock (page 325)
1	cup dry red wine, plus more if needed
1	cup pitted Kalamata olives, coarsely chopped
⅓	cup minced fresh flat-leaf parsley
2	pounds farfalle or farfallette pasta (little bow ties)
2	bunches scallions, trimmed to include 1 inch of green, minced

Preheat oven to 375 degrees F.

Combine celery, carrots, onions and garlic in a large, heavy, nonreactive roasting pan. Set aside.

In a small bowl, blend together mustard, 2 tablespoons oil and lemon juice. Pour onto a large plate. On another large plate, blend bread crumbs, 2 teaspoons salt, 1 teaspoon pepper and herbes de Provence.

Heat 3 tablespoons oil in a large cast-iron skillet over medium-high heat. Coat turkey parts in mustard mixture and then in bread crumbs. Add in batches to heated skillet and brown on all sides, about 5 minutes per side; do not crowd. Transfer browned turkey parts to roasting pan, placing them in a single layer over vegetables. Repeat until all parts are browned.

Pour stock and wine around turkey pieces. Season generously with more salt and pepper. Sprinkle evenly with olives and parsley. Cover roasting pan with a lid or foil and braise turkey, basting several times, until fork-tender, about 2 hours.

About 15 minutes before turkey is done, fill a large pot with salted water and bring to a boil. Cook pasta until tender but firm to the bite, 10 to 12 minutes. Drain thoroughly.

Place turkey parts around outside of a large, heated serving platter. Skim any fat off sauce; toss pasta with pan sauce and scallions. Transfer to center of platter. Let guests serve themselves.

Wine: Château Routas Luc Sorin Côteaux Varois (France) or an intensely fruity Australian Cabernet-Shiraz blend

Chili of Smoked Turkey & Peppers

Serves 6-8

OUR FRIEND SANFORD HERSKOVITZ, whose life is one perpetual diet, was really, really hungry when he proposed that we consider making a chili out of smoked turkey legs. He even sent some over, just to make certain that we obliged. This smoky, richly flavored dish is perfect on a snowy day when you are tired of winter and need something hearty to warm and cheer you. Add some tasty corn bread and a big salad for a perfect in-front-of-the-fire supper.

3	tablespoons olive oil
1	jumbo Spanish onion, coarsely diced
2	plump leeks, trimmed, well washed and thinly sliced
2	medium-sized red or yellow bell peppers, cut into medium dice
¾	pound mixed sweet peppers (bell or Anaheim), seeded and thinly sliced
3	fresh hot chiles, seeded and thinly sliced
3	plump garlic cloves, minced
1	tablespoon ground cumin
1	tablespoon medium-hot chile powder
2	teaspoons crumbled dried oregano
⅓	cup unbleached flour
5	cups chicken stock (page 325)
1	cup dry white wine
5	pounds smoked turkey thighs and legs or smoked turkey breast, skinned, boned and cubed
3	cups cooked black-eyed peas
	Kosher salt and freshly ground white pepper
¼	cup minced fresh cilantro
	Sour cream, grated sharp Cheddar cheese and chopped scallions, for garnish

In a wide, heavy-bottomed, nonreactive 6-quart pot, heat oil over medium heat. Add onion, leeks and all peppers and chiles. Cover, reduce heat and braise until soft, about 5 minutes. Add garlic, cumin, chile powder and oregano and cook, stirring often, for 5 minutes more.

Sprinkle flour over onion mixture, increase heat to medium and stir until flour loses its whiteness, 2 to 3 minutes. Stir in stock, wine and turkey. Increase heat to high and cook, stirring often, until liquid simmers. Reduce heat to low, cover and cook for 40 minutes.

Add black-eyed peas, cover and cook for 15 minutes more. Season with salt and white pepper. Stir in cilantro.

Ladle chili into heated chili bowls and garnish with dollops of sour cream, cheese and scallions.

Wine: Santa Rita Cabernet Sauvignon Medalla Real (Chile: Maipo Valley) or another complex Cabernet Sauvignon

Casserole of Ducks with Carrots, Onions & Turnips

Serves 6-8

DUCKS AND TURNIPS are a classic French combination. In this dish, marinated duck quarters are combined with carrots, onions and turnips in a dark stew. A last-minute addition of grated nutmeg, fresh chives and parsley give a pleasing fresh accent to this dish. We like to serve it with mashed potatoes, but it is equally good with buttered noodles.

1½	pounds yellow onions, coarsely chopped
2	teaspoons dried thyme
2	bay leaves
1	tablespoon coarsely ground black pepper, plus more to taste
1	750-ml bottle dry red wine
2	3-to-4-pound ducks, quartered and trimmed of excess fat
1¼	cups unbleached flour
3	thick slices bacon, preferably smoked, cut into matchsticks
2	cups duck or chicken stock (page 326 or 325)
16	boiling onions, blanched and peeled
6	medium turnips, scrubbed and quartered
3	carrots, cut into 2-inch chunks
2	plump garlic cloves, minced
	Kosher salt
2	generous pinches of freshly grated nutmeg
⅔	cup minced fresh flat-leaf parsley and chives, for garnish

Combine coarsely chopped onions, 1 teaspoon thyme, 1 bay leaf, 1 tablespoon pepper and wine in a large bowl. Add ducks and turn to coat with marinade. Cover with plastic wrap and refrigerate for 16 to 20 hours. Turn duck quarters several times.

Remove duck quarters from marinade and pat dry. Pour marinade through a strainer into a bowl; reserve liquid and discard solids. Dredge duck pieces in ¾ cup flour and set aside on a rack.

Place bacon in a large Dutch oven and cook, stirring, over medium heat just to render fat. Remove bacon with a slotted spoon and reserve. Cook duck pieces in bacon fat until nicely crisped on both sides, 4 to 5 minutes per side. As pieces brown, place them on a large platter.

Drain off all but ⅓ cup fat. Over medium-high heat, whisk together reserved fat and ½ cup flour until mixture is dark brown, 5 to 10 minutes. Slowly add reserved marinade, whisking vigorously for 2 minutes. Add stock, whisking well to blend. Return duck quarters to sauce. Add bacon, boiling onions, turnips, carrots, garlic, remaining bay leaf, remaining 1 teaspoon thyme and salt and pepper to taste. Cover and simmer over low heat until duck is very tender, about 1½ hours.

With a slotted spoon or skimmer, remove duck, boiling onions, turnips and carrots and keep warm. Over medium heat, bring sauce to a simmer, uncovered. Spoon off fat and froth until surface is defatted, 10 to 20 minutes. Stir in nutmeg.

Return duck and vegetables to simmering sauce and heat through over medium-low heat for 5 minutes.

Serve duck on heated plates and garnish with vegetables. Spoon over gravy and sprinkle generously with parsley and chives.

Wine: Franus Zinfandel Hendry Vineyard (California: Napa Valley) or a fruity, not too tannic Zinfandel

Duck & Wild Rice Casserole

Serves 4

L UCKY ARE THE FOLKS invited to a waterfowl dinner at the Cleveland home of Kathy and Tom Roulston—especially when one of the many courses is this creamy combination of duck and wild rice. While the Roulstons usually prepare this with wild ducks, it's equally delicious with domestic ducks. You will, however, need 2 wild ducks to get 3 cups of cooked meat. This makes a perfect brunch dish.

1	5-to-6-pound duck, quartered, all visible fat removed
3	celery stalks
1	large yellow onion, cut in half, plus 1⅓ cups finely diced
1	bay leaf
1	teaspoon *each* kosher salt and freshly ground black pepper, plus more to taste
1	cup wild rice
8	tablespoons (1 stick) unsalted butter, plus more for buttering casserole
½	pound mushrooms, thinly sliced
¼	cup unbleached flour
1½	cups half-and-half or whole milk
1	tablespoon minced fresh flat-leaf parsley
1	tablespoon minced mixed fresh herbs (thyme, tarragon, rosemary, flat-leaf parsley) or 2 teaspoons dried
⅛	teaspoon freshly grated nutmeg
½	cup slivered almonds, lightly toasted

In a large pot, combine duck with celery, halved onion, bay leaf and 1 teaspoon each salt and pepper. Cover with cold water; bring to a boil over high heat. Cover and simmer until duck is tender, about 1 hour. Remove duck pieces from pot and let cool. Pour stock into a large bowl and chill.

Meanwhile, combine wild rice and 3 cups water in a saucepan. Cover and bring to a boil. Reduce heat to low and simmer until rice absorbs water, about 20 minutes. Set aside.

When duck is cool, remove and discard skin and cut meat into ¾-inch cubes; you will have about 3 cups total. Set aside.

Thoroughly butter a 2½-quart casserole. Preheat oven to 350 degrees F.

Melt 4 tablespoons butter in a large skillet over medium heat. Add mushrooms, cover and cook until liquid is released, 4 to 6 minutes. Transfer to a large bowl.

Melt remaining 4 tablespoons butter in skillet; add diced onions. Cover and cook, stirring often, over medium heat until tender, 4 to 6 minutes. Stir mushrooms into onions. Add flour and stir over medium heat to blend thoroughly. Stir in 1½ cups reserved duck stock and cook over medium heat until sauce thickens. Stir in half-and-half or milk and cook until hot. Remove skillet from heat and stir in rice, duck meat, parsley, herbs and nutmeg. Taste and adjust seasonings, adding salt and pepper if needed.

Spoon duck mixture into casserole. Sprinkle evenly with almonds. (Casserole can be prepared ahead to this point, covered and refrigerated for up to 6 hours.) Cover tightly with foil or a lid and bake for 25 minutes or, if casserole has been refrigerated, for 35 minutes.

Uncover and bake until almonds brown, about 10 minutes more. Serve at once.

Wine: Gary Farrell Pinot Noir Russian River Valley (California: Sonoma County) or another complex Pinot Noir

Duck Legs Braised with Baby Lettuces

Serves 4

THIS DISH HAS SOME OF THE MARVELOUS FLAVORS of the traditional French preserved duck known as *confit*—but without all the work. Rubbed with a variety of warm spices, it is also generously seasoned with garlic and shallots. Best of all, it contains no added fat. Duck legs can be special-ordered from many meat markets. Serve with Fred's Famous Fried Potatoes (page 291), garnished with a mixture of minced garlic and fresh parsley.

2½	tablespoons confit seasonings (page 332)
4	plump garlic cloves
1	plump shallot
½	cup chopped fresh flat-leaf parsley
2	teaspoons fresh thyme leaves or 1 teaspoon dried
2	teaspoons kosher salt
8	duck legs and thighs (about 4 pounds), trimmed of all excess fat
4	heads of Boston lettuce, trimmed and quartered
1	cup duck stock (page 326)
½	cup dry red wine, plus more if needed
3	medium carrots, grated
	Kosher salt
1	teaspoon coarsely ground black pepper
1	bay leaf
½	cup thinly sliced fresh scallions, trimmed to include 1 inch of green

Combine confit seasonings, garlic, shallot, parsley, thyme and salt in a mini-chopper; pulse to finely chop. To mix by hand, finely chop garlic and shallot and mix with confit seasonings, parsley, thyme and salt. Rub seasonings over duck pieces. Where possible, push some seasonings underneath skin. Place duck and extra seasonings in a large bowl and refrigerate for 4 to 8 hours. Bring to room temperature before cooking.

Preheat oven to 400 degrees F.

Arrange lettuce in an earthenware casserole large enough to hold duck pieces in a single layer; set aside.

Heat a large cast-iron skillet over medium-high heat. Shaking excess seasoning mixture back into bowl, place duck legs and thighs, skin side down, in skillet and brown thoroughly. Turn and brown on other side, about 8 minutes total. Place duck pieces, skin side up, over lettuce in casserole. Sprinkle with remaining seasoning mixture.

Pour out fat from skillet and discard. Add stock and ½ cup wine and whisk over high heat to loosen any browned particles adhering to the bottom. When liquid boils, pour over duck pieces. Sprinkle with carrots, salt and pepper. Add bay leaf and scatter scallions over. Cover casserole and bake until duck is fork-tender, about 1½ hours. Baste several times, adding more wine if casserole becomes too dry.

Divide duck among 4 heated dinner plates, serving 2 leg and thigh pieces to each person. Garnish with lettuce and sauce.

Wine: Sanford Winery Pinot Noir Barrel Select (California: Santa Barbara County) or another complex, full-bodied Pinot Noir

Pheasant Stuffed with Wild Rice, Leeks & Cabbage

Serves 4

WE FIND THAT PHEASANT always tastes better when cooked under cover in liquid. This type of oven-steaming results in a moister and more tender bird. We also often add juniper berries to our pheasant—historically, their aroma and slightly piney flavor have been considered natural complements to most game. Happily, they are now a regular part of the easily available Spice Islands lineup of seasonings found in supermarkets. This is a splendid marriage of hearty flavors—mushrooms, wild rice, buttery cabbage and mellow leeks—that seems to envelop the pheasant and enrich it. It's a winter dish for a special dinner.

8	tablespoons (1 stick) unsalted butter
2	plump shallots, minced
4-5	ounces shiitake or portobello mushrooms, thinly sliced
2	teaspoons soy sauce
1	tablespoon minced fresh tarragon or 2½ teaspoons dried
1½	cups cooked wild rice (from ½ cup raw)
	Kosher salt and freshly ground white pepper
2	pheasants, dressed and cleaned
2-3	tablespoons olive oil
2	plump leeks, well washed, trimmed to include 1 inch of green, finely diced
2½	cups coarsely chopped cabbage
6	thin slices bacon, cut in half
1	tablespoon juniper berries, lightly crushed
2	teaspoons whole black peppercorns
½	cup chicken stock (page 325), plus more if needed
¼	cup port wine
½	cup sour cream
¼	teaspoon freshly grated nutmeg
1	bunch watercress, for garnish

Preheat oven to 475 degrees F.

In a large nonstick skillet, melt 5 tablespoons butter over medium heat. Add shallots, tightly cover and reduce heat to low. Braise until shallots are softened, 3 to 5 minutes. Add mushrooms, soy sauce and 1½ teaspoons fresh tarragon or 1¼ teaspoons dried. Cover and cook, stirring occasionally, until mushrooms are tender and have released their juices, 6 to 8 minutes. Stir in wild rice, ½ teaspoon salt and white pepper and set aside.

Remove giblets from pheasants and set aside. Lightly season cavities. Heat oil in a Dutch oven just large enough to hold pheasants. When hot, quickly sear pheasants and giblets until browned, 1 to 2 minutes on each side; set aside. When cool, stuff each with half of rice mixture.

Pour off oil from Dutch oven; melt remaining 3 tablespoons butter over medium heat. Stir in leeks, cabbage and remaining 1½ teaspoons fresh tarragon or 1¼ teaspoons dried. Cook until leeks begin to soften, 3 to 4 minutes; remove from heat.

Place pheasants, breast side up, on leeks. Add giblets to pot, tucking them under cabbage mixture. Wrap legs and wings with bacon; arrange remaining slices over breasts.

In a spice grinder or with mortar and pestle, grind juniper berries and peppercorns with 1 teaspoon salt. Sprinkle birds and cabbage with seasoning mixture.

Pour in stock; add port. Cover and roast in oven until tender and juices run clear when thigh is pierced with a skewer, about 45 minutes.

Transfer pheasants to a carving board and keep warm. Place Dutch oven over high heat and bring to a boil. Skim off surface fat; remove and discard giblets. Reduce heat to low, whisk in sour cream and cook until sauce is heated through; do not boil. Add nutmeg and salt and pepper if needed.

Cut birds in half. Divide cabbage and leek mixture among 4 heated serving plates. Place a pheasant half with some stuffing on vegetables. Garnish with sauce and watercress.

Wine: Robert Sinskey Vineyards Pinot Noir Carneros Napa Valley (California: Carneros) or any medium-bodied, fruity Pinot Noir

Beef

Baked Steak 152

Flank Steak Deluxe 153

Flank Steak Stuffed with Corn & Herbs 154

Italian Potted Beef with Basil & Garlic 156

Sauerbraten 158

Garlic-Studded Brisket with Tomatoes, Red Wine & Onions 160

Corned Beef & Cabbage 162

Dutch-Oven Meat Loaf 163

Oven-Braised Chili 164

Simple Goulash (*Gulyás*) 166

Gascon Beef Daube with Onions, Prunes & Carrots 168

Short Ribs Stew with Caramelized Root Vegetable Sauce 170

Oklahoma-Style Breaded Short Ribs 172

Beer-Braised Short Ribs with Onions & Shallots 174

Mom's Cabbage Rolls 176

Fragrant Calcutta Meatball Curry (*Kofta*) 178

Baked Steak

Serves 6

THIS HUMBLE DISH comes from Fred's memories of countless meals at the MacFarland Lunch, his father's West Virginia restaurant. No fancy cut of meat is used here: Top round steak is coated in flour, browned over high heat and slowly braised until tender in a tasty onion beef stock gravy. Mashed potatoes are a must with this dish.

3	pounds 1½-to-2 inch-thick boneless top round
¼	cup unbleached flour
2	tablespoons vegetable oil
2½	cups beef or veal stock (page 328)
3	tablespoons Worcestershire sauce
	Kosher salt and freshly ground black pepper
1½	pounds Spanish onions, cut in half and thinly sliced

Preheat oven to 375 degrees F.

Pound meat evenly, preferably with a tenderizing mallet, until 1 inch thick. Sprinkle top evenly with 2 tablespoons flour. Rub meat thoroughly to coat well. Turn and repeat process on other side, using remaining 2 tablespoons flour.

Heat oil over high heat in a large cast-iron skillet. Brown meat on both sides, about 10 minutes total. Transfer to a platter. Add stock to skillet and cook, stirring, over high heat until browned particles are loosened and stock comes to a vigorous boil. Stir in Worcestershire and salt and pepper. Add half of onions. Remove from heat.

Place steak over onions; sprinkle evenly with remaining onions. Spoon some liquid over top. Tightly cover with heavy-duty foil and a lid or another piece of foil.

Bake steak, basting after 1 hour, until fork-tender, about 2 hours total. Transfer meat to a carving board. If gravy is too thick, thin with a small amount of water. Adjust seasonings.

Cut meat into serving portions. Serve on heated plates, spooning over gravy generously.

Wine: Viader Vineyards Red Table Wine (California: Napa Valley) or a complex Napa Valley Meritage

Flank Steak Deluxe

Serves 2-4

THIS RECIPE FOR FLANK STEAK, braised in a rich onion sauce seasoned with mustard, paprika, thyme and a splash of vinegar, is a takeoff on one Linda found in Natalie V. Scott's *200 Years of New Orleans Cooking*, published in 1931. As much a culinary oral history as a cookbook, the book is a fascinating glimpse into the homes of local gentry, where black cooks ruled the kitchens. "No fine cut of meat could taste better," writes Scott, noting that the onions add a "virile taste" to the sauce. Serve with mashed potatoes.

1	2-pound flank steak
3	tablespoons unbleached flour
3	tablespoons unsalted butter, plus more if needed
1	large yellow onion, finely diced
3	tablespoons red wine vinegar
1	teaspoon dry mustard
1	teaspoon hot Hungarian paprika
1	teaspoon dried thyme
1	teaspoon cayenne pepper
1	teaspoon kosher salt
1	teaspoon freshly ground black pepper

Cut flank steak into 4 portions. Sprinkle both sides of each piece with flour, using a total of 1 tablespoon; rub to coat. Set aside.

Melt 3 tablespoons butter in a large, heavy skillet over medium heat. Add onion and cook, stirring often, until golden, 5 to 7 minutes. Using a slotted spoon, transfer onions to a large bowl or platter and reserve.

Adding a little more butter to skillet if needed, quickly brown meat over medium-high heat. Transfer browned meat to platter with onions. Whisk remaining 2 tablespoons flour into butter left in skillet. Gradually whisk in 2 cups water, vinegar, dry mustard, paprika, thyme, cayenne, salt and pepper. Increase heat to high and cook, whisking, until mixture bubbles, 2 to 4 minutes.

Return meat and onions to sauce, cover, reduce heat and simmer until meat is tender, 30 to 45 minutes. Serve immediately.

Wine: Flora Springs Wine Co. Trilogy Red Table Wine (California: Napa Valley) or another complex Napa Valley Meritage

Flank Steak Stuffed with Corn & Herbs

Serves 4

THIS BEEF ROLL, STUFFED WITH CORN AND BREAD CRUMBS, roasts slowly in a succulent red wine and tomato sauce enriched by red onions. When the meat is sliced, each slice displays a center studded with bits of red bell pepper and basil. Leftovers—served at room temperature, thinly sliced, garnished with a dollop of salsa—make a great lunch.

4	tablespoons olive oil
1	dried red chile, crumbled
½	medium-sized red bell pepper, finely diced
3	plump scallions, trimmed to include
	1 inch of green, minced
2	plump garlic cloves, minced
1½	cups finely chopped red onions
¾	cup fine dry bread crumbs
½	cup fresh or frozen yellow corn kernels
1	tablespoon minced fresh basil
	Kosher salt and freshly ground black pepper
1	large egg, beaten
1	2-pound flank steak
1	tablespoon unbleached flour
¾	cup tomato puree (page 324) or canned crushed tomatoes
½	cup dry red wine
1	cup beef or veal stock (page 328)

Preheat oven to 350 degrees F.

Heat 2 tablespoons oil and chile in a nonstick skillet. Add red pepper, scallions, garlic and ½ cup onions. Stir over medium heat until onions soften, 2 to 3 minutes. Scrape mixture into a large bowl. Add bread crumbs, corn, basil, salt and pepper and egg to onion mixture. Mix together; set aside.

Place flank steak on a wooden board and pound with a mallet until it is ⅓ to ½ inch thick. Spread stuffing evenly down middle, leaving about 1 inch border along long sides.

Cut five 7-inch lengths of kitchen twine. Fold long sides together, overlapping them to cover stuffing. Tie with kitchen string at ends and in middle. Tie roll on either side in between. Rub with flour and season with salt and pepper.

Heat remaining 2 tablespoons oil in a deep, heavy, nonreactive skillet with a tight-fitting lid until hot. Add rolled meat and brown on all sides over medium-high heat, about 7 minutes. Carefully remove to a plate. Add remaining 1 cup onions to skillet, and stir over medium heat until softened, 2 to 4 minutes. Stir in tomato puree or crushed tomatoes, wine and stock; bring to a boil. Add steak, seam side up.

Cover and bake for 1 hour. Baste, cover again and reduce oven temperature to 325 degrees. Braise until meat is tender, about 1 hour more.

Transfer meat to a carving board. Carefully remove twine. Carve into ½-inch-thick slices and distribute among 4 heated plates. Spoon pan sauce over each portion and serve.

Wine: Shafer Vineyards Merlot (California: Napa Valley) or another complex Merlot

Italian Potted Beef with Basil & Garlic

Serves 6-8

THE BEST CUTS OF THE CHUCK are the middle, what is sometimes called the chuck roll. And the very best part of the roll is the eye, usually one continuous muscle, well trimmed, with relatively little connective tissue. In this preparation, we've studded the roast with small pieces of garlic and basil and put it into a tomato sauce flavored with carrots and caramelized onions. Serve it with Creamy Polenta with Mascarpone (page 254) and lots of sauce.

1	4-to-4½-pound chuck roast, preferably eye of chuck, rolled and tied
4	plump garlic cloves, thinly sliced
6	fresh basil leaves, chopped, plus more for garnish
3	tablespoons unbleached flour
	Kosher salt and freshly ground black pepper
3	tablespoons olive oil, plus more if needed
4	large carrots, coarsely chopped
1	large red onion, coarsely chopped
1	cup dry red wine
1	28-ounce can crushed tomatoes
¼	cup tomato paste
⅓	cup minced fresh flat-leaf parsley, plus more for garnish
2	teaspoons dried oregano
1	bay leaf

Preheat oven to 325 degrees F.

With a sharp knife, carefully make 30 to 40 small slits all over beef. Push a garlic slice and a piece of basil into each slit. Rub meat with flour; season with salt and pepper.

In a 5-quart cast-iron Dutch oven, heat 3 tablespoons oil over medium heat until hot. Add beef and slowly brown on all sides, about 15 minutes. Transfer roast to a large platter.

Stir carrots and onion into pot. Cook over medium heat, stirring often, until onion begins to caramelize, about 10 minutes. Increase heat to high and add wine; cook, stirring, until pot is thoroughly deglazed and all browned bits adhering to the bottom are loosened. Remove pot from heat.

Stir in tomatoes, tomato paste, parsley and oregano. Place chuck roast in center of pot; add bay leaf.

Over high heat, bring liquid just to a boil. Baste meat with sauce. Tightly cover pot and braise in oven, basting several times during cooking, until fork-tender, 2½ to 3 hours.

Transfer roast to a carving board. Bring sauce to a boil over medium heat. Skim off surface fat.

Carve roast into thin slices. Serve on heated plates, topped with some sauce. Sprinkle generously with basil and parsley.

Wine: Moccagatta Dolcetto d'Alba (Italy: Piedmont) or another soft, fruity Dolcetto

Sauerbraten

Serves 6

SAUERBRATEN IS A FULL-FLAVORED, SPICY, SWEET-AND-SOUR BEEF that is first marinated, or pickled, in a fragrant mixture of herbs, spices, wine and vinegar. Some people like a lightly flavored sauerbraten, so they marinate the meat for only 24 hours. We prefer ours to have more personality, so we opt for the traditional marinating time of 4 days. Most old recipes thicken the gravy with flour. We like to use crushed gingersnaps—they not only thicken but add sweetness and spice too.

Beef and Marinade

2½	cups dry red wine
½	cup red wine vinegar
2	medium-sized yellow onions, thinly sliced
2	plump garlic cloves, thinly sliced
1	lemon, thinly sliced
¼	cup packed dark brown sugar
2	teaspoons black peppercorns
1	teaspoon yellow mustard seeds
8	juniper berries, lightly bruised
6	whole cloves
1	bay leaf
1	4-pound beef brisket (the flat; see page 160)
¼	cup unbleached flour
	Kosher salt and freshly ground black pepper
3	tablespoons vegetable oil
⅓	cup crushed gingersnaps, plus more if needed

To marinate beef: In a medium nonreactive saucepan, combine wine, vinegar, onions, garlic, lemon, brown sugar, peppercorns, mustard seeds, juniper berries, cloves and bay leaf. Bring to a boil and cook for 2 minutes. Meanwhile, place meat in a large glass or ceramic bowl. Pour hot marinade over meat and let stand until cool. Carefully transfer meat and marinade to a large reclosable plastic bag. Seal and refrigerate for 2 to 4 days, turning several times a day.

To cook sauerbraten: Strain marinade, reserving both liquid and solids; pat meat dry. Thoroughly rub with flour and season with salt and pepper.

Preheat oven to 325 degrees F.

In a large nonreactive skillet with a tight-fitting lid, heat oil until hot. Add beef and brown on both sides, 10 to 15 minutes.

Remove and discard lemon slices from onion mixture. Spread remaining solids over meat. Add enough marinade to reach halfway up sides of meat. Cover and transfer to oven.

Braise meat, basting from time to time and gradually adding remaining marinade, until meat is fork-tender, about 3 hours.

Place meat on a heated platter and keep warm. Carefully place skillet over medium heat and bring gravy to a vigorous simmer. Add ⅓ cup gingersnaps and stir until gravy thickens, adding more crumbs if needed. Adjust seasonings and remove from heat.

Slice meat across grain and serve on heated plates, spooning over gravy generously.

Wine: Harpersfield Vineyard Gewürztraminer (Ohio: Lake Erie), Hugel Gewürztraminer Réserve Personnelle Jubilée (France: Alsace) or another Alsatian Gewürztraminer

Garlic-Studded Brisket with Tomatoes, Red Wine & Onions

Serves 8-10

THIS BRISKET is for a cold winter's night. The slivers of garlic melt into the meat, and braised onions are pureed into the red wine and tomato sauce to make a mellow meal. We roast the meat uncovered for a short while just to get a bit of browning; but if you prefer, start it covered right from the beginning.

A whole brisket, which is the chest of a steer, consists of the "point" and the "flat." The point refers to the fat-covered top; the flat is the bottom part. While some people prefer to cook only the flat, which is leaner, we find it dries out too much for our tastes. Cooking the whole brisket is best for flavor, texture and tenderness.

We prepare our brisket a day ahead, chilling the meat separately from the gravy. Since a thoroughly chilled brisket won't fall apart during slicing, we can easily separate the point from the flat, removing all obvious remaining fat. Chilling also makes it easier to remove all of the congealed fat from the top of the gravy.

2½-3	pounds onions, thinly sliced
1	9-to-14-pound whole beef brisket, trimmed
3	plump garlic cloves, slivered
1	tablespoon freshly ground black pepper
1	tablespoon kosher salt
1	tablespoon herbes de Provence or mixture of dried rosemary, savory, thyme, basil and crumbled bay leaf
2	cups tomato puree (page 324) or canned crushed tomatoes
1	cup dry red wine

The day before serving, preheat oven to 325 degrees F.

Distribute three-fourths of onions in a large, heavy, nonreactive covered roaster.

Make small slits all over both sides of brisket; fill each with a sliver of garlic. Season meat on both sides with pepper and salt.

Place meat, fat side up, over onions. Sprinkle with herbes de Provence and remaining onions. Place roaster in oven and cook, uncovered, for 45 minutes.

Add tomato puree or crushed tomatoes and wine. Tightly cover and braise until thin part of brisket is fork-tender, 2½ to 3 hours. Remove pan from oven, uncover, and let sit until brisket is cool. Remove brisket from roasting pan and wrap thoroughly in foil.

With a slotted spoon, transfer onions to a food processor fitted with the metal blade; add some liquid as well. Pulse until pureed. Pour mixture into a large container along with remaining pan liquids; cover tightly. Chill meat and gravy for 8 to 24 hours. While amount of gravy varies with meat and onions, you will have at least 4 cups of gravy.

To carve, trim off and discard all excess fat from top of brisket. Carefully separate top piece (point) from bottom (flat) with a sharp knife. Carve top into thin slices, cutting across grain on a slight angle. Arrange overlapping slices in an ovenproof casserole. Carve bottom the same way; place bottom slices over top slices.

Preheat oven to 350 degrees.

Remove fat from gravy and discard. Pour gravy over meat. Tightly cover and braise until meat is very tender, 1 to 1½ hours. Serve with gravy.

Wine: Domaine le Sang des Cailloux Vacqueyras (France: Rhône) or a robust red wine from the southern Rhône

Corned Beef & Cabbage

Serves 8

W E LOVE TENDER, BOILED CORNED BEEF complemented by buttery potatoes, carrots and cabbage. The juniper berries add a slightly piney flavor to the cooking liquid. This recipe comes from Linda's mother, Gert LeVine. (See photograph, page 89.)

1	8-to-10-pound cured whole beef brisket
3	garlic cloves, peeled
2	tablespoons black peppercorns, bruised
1	tablespoon yellow mustard seeds
1	tablespoon juniper berries, lightly crushed
3	bay leaves
3	whole cloves
16	small red or Yukon gold potatoes, unpeeled
8	medium carrots
1	large cabbage head, cored and cut into eighths
	Freshly ground black pepper
6	tablespoons (¾ stick) unsalted butter, cut into small pieces
	Grated white horseradish and Dijon mustard, for garnish

In a large pot, combine brisket, garlic, peppercorns, mustard seeds, juniper berries, bay leaves and cloves. Add water to cover and place over high heat. Tightly cover pot and bring to a boil. Reduce heat to low and simmer until meat is fork-tender, 3½ to 4½ hours.

Carefully remove meat from pot and place on a carving board. Bring cooking liquid to a boil. Add potatoes and carrots; cover, reduce heat to medium and simmer briskly until nearly tender, about 20 minutes.

Increase heat to medium-high and add cabbage. Boil until vegetables are tender, about 10 minutes.

Meanwhile, trim all visible fat from top of meat. Carve meat across grain into thin slices. Overlap slices slightly at one end of a large, heated serving platter. Using a skimmer or slotted spoon, remove vegetables from pot and arrange attractively on same platter. Grind pepper over all and scatter on pieces of butter. Serve with bowls of horseradish and mustard on the side.

Wine: Domaines Schlumberger Riesling des Prince Abbés (France: Alsace) or another Alsatian Riesling

Dutch-Oven Meat Loaf

Serves 6

ROASTING THIS SAGE-FLAVORED MEAT LOAF under a cover for 2 hours makes it especially moist. It is just as good cold, thinly sliced in a sandwich, as it is hot, served with a splash of its tomato-based gravy. It evolved from a recipe in Marion Flexner's fascinating *Out of Kentucky Kitchens*, published in 1949.

1	pound lean ground beef
1	pound ground veal
1	medium-sized yellow onion, finely diced
2	plump garlic cloves, minced
2	celery stalks, finely chopped
1	large carrot, finely chopped
½	medium-sized green bell pepper, finely diced
1	cup fine dry bread crumbs
2	tablespoons minced fresh flat-leaf parsley
1	tablespoon Worcestershire sauce
1½	teaspoons kosher salt
1½	teaspoons dried crumbled sage
1	teaspoon finely ground black pepper
1½	cups canned tomato sauce
½	cup tomato juice, plus more if needed

Preheat oven to 375 degrees F.

In a large mixing bowl, thoroughly combine beef, veal, onion, garlic, celery, carrot, green pepper, bread crumbs, parsley, Worcestershire, salt, sage and pepper. Form into a firmly packed loaf, about 9 x 4½ inches. Place in a Dutch oven; pour 1 cup water around meat. Spoon a few tablespoons tomato sauce over meat; pour remaining sauce around it.

Tightly cover and bake until meat loaf is browned and firm to the touch, about 2 hours.

Using 2 spatulas, carefully transfer meat loaf to a heated platter or carving board. Place pot on stovetop. Stir in enough tomato juice to make a sauce; cook, stirring, over high heat until hot.

Slice meat loaf and serve with a generous splash of sauce.

Wine: Paul Janin Moulin-à-Vent Beaujolais (France: Burgundy) or another complex, fruity Beaujolais

Oven-Braised Chili

Serves 14-18

ECAUSE OF THE MEAT'S RICH FLAVOR and moist texture, we use brisket tops (the fattier part known as the "point," see page 160) for our chili. Instead of cutting the meat into cubes, we simply cut it into strips and braise it, eliminating the need for browning in lots of oil. When the meat is tender, we pull the strips apart with forks, just like Southern barbecue. This labor-saving and fat-saving method was suggested by Sanford Herskovitz, and it makes preparing chili a real breeze. We prefer to make our chili a day ahead—a practice that we feel enhances the complexity of the sauce. It's also easier to remove any excess fat.

Keep in mind that if you don't have access to a variety of chiles, this dish will still be good, though not as complex in flavor. Vary the amounts to suit your own palate. This freezes superbly. (All of the dried chiles are available through various mail-order sources, as well as in many supermarkets.)

2	dried pasilla chiles
2	dried mulato chiles
3	dried ancho chiles
2	tablespoons vegetable oil
6-7	pounds brisket tops (point), boneless flanken or boneless short ribs, trimmed of surface fat, cut into 4-inch-wide strips
1	pound mixed sweet fresh chiles (such as Hungarian or Anaheim), seeded and thinly sliced
2	red bell peppers, seeded, deribbed and coarsely diced
2	fresh jalapeño or serrano chiles, seeded and thinly sliced
2	jumbo white onions (2½ pounds), thinly sliced
3	plump garlic cloves, finely minced
2	tablespoons ground cumin
2	tablespoons chile powder, or more to taste
2	teaspoons ground oregano
1	teaspoon dried basil
6	whole cloves
1	bay leaf
1	tablespoon kosher salt, or more to taste
1	tablespoon freshly ground black pepper
2	teaspoons freshly ground white pepper

1   teaspoon cayenne pepper
4   ounces unsweetened baking chocolate, coarsely chopped
2   28-ounce cans crushed tomatoes
1   750-ml bottle dry red wine
4   cups canned black beans or pinto beans, drained and rinsed
    Low-fat sour cream, shredded Cheddar cheese and
        thinly sliced scallions, trimmed to include
        1 inch of green, for garnish

At least 1 day before serving, break dried chiles into pieces; discard stems and seeds. Place dried flesh in a small bowl, add 2 cups boiling water, and let stand until softened, about 20 minutes. Put softened chiles and 1 cup soaking liquid in a food processor fitted with the metal blade and puree. Set aside.

Place oven rack in middle and preheat oven to 350 degrees F. Thoroughly coat an 8-quart nonreactive Dutch oven or any heavy roasting pot with oil.

Evenly distribute meat in a Dutch oven. Add sweet chiles, red peppers, jalapeño or serrano chiles and onions, spreading them over meat. Add garlic, cumin, 2 tablespoons chile powder, oregano, basil, cloves, bay leaf, 1 tablespoon salt, black and white peppers, cayenne and chocolate. Add pureed dried chiles, crushed tomatoes and wine. Tightly cover, place in oven, and braise for 1 hour.

Stir chili thoroughly, cover, reduce heat to 325 degrees and cook, stirring twice, for 3 hours more.

Test meat for doneness; it should be so tender that it falls apart. Add beans, cover and continue to braise for 30 minutes more.

When meat is done, remove pot from oven. Holding a large fork in each hand, carefully pull brisket tops apart into small chunks. Skim off all surface fat. Or let chili cool, cover, and chill at least overnight.

To serve, remove surface fat from chili and reheat either in oven or on top of stove. Taste and adjust seasonings, adding more chile powder and salt to taste. Serve in heated bowls and garnish with sour cream, Cheddar cheese and scallions.

Wine: R.H. Phillips Alliance EXP (California: Dunnigan Hills) or a spicy Rhône-style red

Simple Goulash

(*Gulyás*)

Serves 6

ulyás, OR GOULASH, is technically a thick Hungarian soup. But at least in this country, people commonly think it to be a Hungarian word for stew. This *gulyás* is a simple, soupy stew of browned beef, with onions, green pepper, potato, carrots and green beans, flavored by good hot Hungarian paprika, marjoram and a bay leaf. We chop the vegetables together in the food processor so that the onions release extra moisture and cook into an especially flavorful gravy. Since Cleveland has historically been home to more Hungarians than any city outside of Budapest, there are many cooks here with a favorite *gulyás*. While this one has evolved over the years, it's not far from the recipe first given to Linda by Cleveland artist Ivy Goldhammer Stone.

1	large Spanish onion, quartered
1	medium-sized green bell pepper, seeded and cut into quarters
2	plump garlic cloves
⅔	cup unbleached flour
3	pounds boneless flanken or boneless short ribs, cut into 1½-inch cubes
¼	cup olive oil, plus more if needed
2	tablespoons hot Hungarian paprika
1	tablespoon kosher salt
1	teaspoon freshly ground black pepper
2	teaspoons dried marjoram
1	bay leaf
3	medium-sized white potatoes, cut into 1-inch cubes
4	carrots, cut into 1-inch lengths
6	ounces green beans, trimmed
⅓	cup minced fresh flat-leaf parsley, for garnish

In a food processor fitted with the metal blade, combine onion, green pepper and garlic. Pulse until finely chopped; set aside.

Place flour in a plastic bag. Working in batches, toss beef with flour to coat thoroughly.

Heat 2 tablespoons oil in a Dutch oven until hot. Add half of beef and sear, browning on all sides, 3 to 4 minutes. Transfer to a large bowl with a slotted spoon. Add 2 tablespoons oil if needed, and sear remaining beef; transfer to bowl.

Add more oil if needed, and stir in onion mixture. Stir over medium-high heat until onion softens, 3 to 4 minutes. Add paprika, salt and pepper and cook for 1 minute. Add marjoram, bay leaf and 1 cup water. Cook, stirring, over high heat to loosen any browned particles adhering to pot. Add beef cubes and enough water to cover.

Tightly cover and cook over high heat until water comes to a boil. Reduce heat to low and simmer, stirring occasionally to scrape bottom well, for 1 hour. Stir in potatoes and carrots; cover and simmer for 30 minutes. Skim off surface fat. Stir in green beans, cover and cook until beans and other vegetables are tender, about 15 minutes more.

To serve, ladle into heated soup plates and sprinkle generously with fresh parsley.

Wine: Limerick Lane Zinfandel (California: Sonoma County) or a fruity and peppery red Zinfandel

Gascon Beef Daube with Onions, Prunes & Carrots

Serves 4-6

THIS IS A SIMPLE-TO-MAKE BUT COMPLEXLY FLAVORED stew of beef, onions, carrots and red wine. Prunes add a mellow sweetness to the gravy. We first sampled this dish many years ago in the home of Yves and Marie-Hélène Pochat, in the village of Bourg-de-Visa in southwestern France—not far from Agen, the prune center of France. A sensational cook, Marie-Hélène generously shared recipes with anyone staying in their lovely guesthouse.

4	tablespoons (½ stick) unsalted butter
3	tablespoons olive oil
3	pounds boneless flanken or boneless short ribs, cut into 2-inch pieces
1½	cups coarsely chopped yellow onions
6	large carrots, cut into 1-inch lengths
¼	cup sugar
1	tablespoon dried thyme
1	teaspoon dried marjoram
1	bay leaf
	Kosher salt and freshly ground black pepper
1	750-ml bottle dry red wine, plus more if needed
2	cups pitted prunes (12-ounce package)

Thickening (optional)

3	tablespoons unsalted butter, softened
3	tablespoons unbleached flour
⅓	cup minced fresh flat-leaf parsley

Preheat oven to 325 degrees F.

Combine butter and oil in a 5-quart nonreactive Dutch oven and heat over medium-high heat until hot. Add meat in small batches and brown on all sides. Transfer browned meat to a large bowl and continue browning until all is done.

Add onions and carrots to butter-oil mixture and cook, stirring, until onions soften, about 2 minutes. Return meat to pot, sprinkle with sugar, and cook, stirring, over high heat until sugar melts and begins to caramelize. Add thyme, marjoram, bay leaf, salt and pepper and wine. If meat is not covered with liquid, add more wine or water. Bring liquid to a boil. Tightly cover, place in oven and braise for 1 hour.

Add prunes, cover and continue to braise until meat is fork-tender, ½ hour more.

Skim off any surface fat and adjust seasonings. If you want a thicker gravy, thoroughly blend softened butter with flour. Place pot on medium heat and add flour mixture, a bit at a time, stirring it into simmering stew.

Serve sprinkled generously with parsley.

Wine: Seavey Vineyard Cabernet Sauvignon (California: Napa Valley) or an earthy Côtes du Rhône

Short Ribs Stew with Caramelized Root Vegetable Sauce

Serves 6

THESE RICH AND HUMBLE SHORT RIBS are cooked until the moist meat is ready to fall from the bone. The dark gravy is thickened with a puree of caramelized root vegetables. Ask your butcher for generic (ungraded) beef short ribs cut from the plate. Have them cut crosswise into 2-inch pieces.

½	cup unbleached flour
5-6	pounds beef short ribs, excess fat removed
5	tablespoons olive oil, plus more as needed
2	large carrots, finely diced, plus 2 medium carrots, cut into quarters
1	large Spanish onion, finely diced
3	garlic cloves, minced
1	cup dry red wine
3	cups veal or beef stock (page 328) or chicken stock (page 325)
1	bouquet garni (page 331)
	Kosher salt and freshly ground black pepper
1	large parsnip, cut into ½-inch-thick strips
1	large turnip, cut into ½-inch-thick strips
4	plump shallots, cut in half
¼	cup minced fresh herbs (chives, flat-leaf parsley, thyme, basil), plus more for garnish

Preheat oven to 325 degrees F.

Place flour on a large plate. Carefully coat short ribs with flour; set aside on a rack.

Heat 3 tablespoons oil in a large nonreactive Dutch oven until hot. Working in batches and adding more oil if needed, brown short ribs on all sides over medium-high heat, 10 to 15 minutes. As they are browned, transfer ribs to a large platter.

When all ribs are browned, add diced carrots, onion and garlic to pot; cook, stirring, until slightly browned, 3 to 4 minutes. Add wine and cook, stirring, until browned particles adhering to bottom are loosened. Stir in stock and cook until liquid begins to bubble. Add short ribs to pot; add bouquet garni and salt and pepper. Tightly cover pot.

Braise in oven, basting occasionally, until meat is fork-tender, about 2 hours. Discard bouquet garni. Set Dutch oven aside.

Increase oven temperature to 500 degrees. Line a large roasting pan with heavy foil. Scatter parsnip, turnip, quartered carrots and shallots over pan. Pour remaining 2 tablespoons oil over and toss with your fingers to coat well. Roast vegetables, stirring several times, until browned and tender, 18 to 22 minutes.

Transfer vegetables to a food processor fitted with the metal blade and pulse until finely chopped. Add about ½ cup hot gravy from short ribs and pulse thoroughly to make a finer puree.

Set Dutch oven over low heat. Skim off surface fat. Add vegetable puree and mix gently into sauce until blended. Stir in fresh herbs.

Divide short ribs among heated plates. Garnish lavishly with vegetable sauce and more herbs.

Wine: Havens Cellars Syrah (California: Napa Valley) or a robust red Côtes du Rhône

Oklahoma-Style Breaded Short Ribs

Serves 4

THIS IS A PERFECT EXAMPLE of humble thrift turned into a succulent two-course meal. The meal begins with a tasty consommé made from short ribs and root vegetables. Then the cooked meat is breaded, lightly moistened with some soup and baked. The pieces will be moist and tender, the crumb coating lightly browned. Some good horseradish or hot pepper jelly on the side is all you need. This very old recipe was a popular meal that our friend Wayne Marshall and his sister Marilyn Dabner enjoyed when they were children.

2	tablespoons olive oil
4-5	pounds lean, bone-in short ribs, excess fat removed, or 2½ pounds boneless flanken
1	large yellow onion, studded with 3 whole cloves
1	large turnip
1	whole carrot, plus 2 carrots, thinly sliced
1	celery stalk
3	whole allspice
2	teaspoons black peppercorns
1	bay leaf
	Kosher salt
1	cup grated dried bread crumbs, plus more if needed
1	cup dried fine egg noodles
	Horseradish, hot pepper jelly or another spicy condiment, for serving

Heat oil in a Dutch oven over medium heat. Working in batches, brown meat on all sides, 10 to 15 minutes.

Add 6 cups water, onion, turnip, whole carrot, celery, allspice, peppercorns, bay leaf and salt. Increase heat to high and bring to a boil. Reduce heat to low and simmer, skimming off froth, for 15 minutes.

Cover pot and simmer slowly until meat is very tender, about 2½ hours. Remove from heat, and let meat cool in the pot.

When meat is cool, remove from liquid. Carefully cut meat from bone, discarding any remaining fat. If using flanken, cut strips into 2-inch pieces.

Strain stock into a large bowl. Cover with plastic and chill until fat congeals. For quicker chilling, you can place this in the freezer for 1 to 2 hours.

Preheat oven to 375 degrees F. Lightly oil a large, shallow baking dish.

Skim off and reserve surface fat from stock. Spoon about ½ cup stock into baking dish.

Place bread crumbs in a shallow soup plate. Roll pieces of meat in crumbs to coat evenly on all sides. Place meat in a single layer in baking dish.

Carefully spoon about 1 tablespoon stock over each piece, taking care not to wash coating off meat. Place a pea-sized dab of reserved fat on top of each piece of meat. Bake until crumbs are browned, 40 to 45 minutes. Add more stock to baking dish if needed.

Meanwhile, pour stock into a medium saucepan and bring to a boil. Add sliced carrots, cover and simmer until carrots are tender, about 15 minutes.

Adjust seasonings in stock. About 5 minutes before serving, add noodles to stock and cook until tender.

Serve stock first, followed by the meat. Accompany meat with a tangy sauce, like horseradish or hot pepper jelly.

Wine: McDowell Valley Vineyards McDowell Valley Grenache Rosé (California: Mendocino County) or a rich rosé from Provence (France)

Beer-Braised Short Ribs with Onions & Shallots

Serves 4

THIS RECIPE IS OUR VERSION of the French *carbonade à la flamande*, a braised dish of beef and onions usually made with slices of chuck. The flavor and texture of the braised short ribs are outstanding, especially when accompanied by mashed potatoes for the gravy.

¾	cup unbleached flour
5	pounds beef short ribs cut from the plate
¼	cup plus 3 tablespoons vegetable oil
3	large yellow onions, cut into ¼-inch-thick slices
3	plump garlic cloves, minced
8-12	shallots
	Kosher salt and freshly ground black pepper
2	12-ounce bottles dark beer
2	teaspoons fresh thyme leaves or ½ teaspoon dried
1	teaspoon minced fresh marjoram or ½ teaspoon dried
1	teaspoon minced fresh tarragon or ½ teaspoon dried
1	bay leaf

Preheat oven to 325 degrees F.

Pour ½ cup flour into a soup plate. Carefully coat short ribs in flour; set aside on a rack.

Heat ¼ cup oil in a large cast-iron skillet until hot. Working in batches, brown short ribs on all sides over medium-high heat, about 5 minutes. Transfer to a large platter when browned.

Add onions and cook, stirring, over medium-low heat until they begin to soften, about 10 minutes. Add garlic and cook, stirring, until onions are golden, about 5 minutes more. Remove half of onions to another plate. Arrange beef on onions in skillet. Scatter shallots on top; sprinkle with remaining onions. Season generously with salt and pepper.

In a medium cast-iron skillet, whisk together remaining ¼ cup flour and remaining 3 tablespoons oil over medium-high heat until roux is dark brown. Reduce heat to low and slowly whisk in beer; cook for 5 minutes. Pour mixture over meat; sprinkle with herbs. Cover skillet tightly with foil, placing a lid over foil.

Braise in oven until meat is fork-tender, about 2 hours. Remove skillet from oven and carefully skim off surface fat before serving.

Wine: Étude Cabernet Sauvignon (California: Napa Valley) or another complex Cabernet Sauvignon

Mom's Cabbage Rolls

Serves 6-8

T HIS IS A RECIPE FROM Linda's childhood. While some versions—and there are scores of variations—have rice added to the meat as a filler, the tradition at her grandmother's house was to use well-seasoned ground beef with just a few bread crumbs to lighten it. Any cabbage will do, but the crinkly leaves of savoy cabbage make for a more interesting-looking result. The use of gingersnaps to thicken the gravy adds an unexpected and pleasing combination of piquancy and sweetness. Serve with buttered long-grain rice.

Cabbage Rolls

1	large savoy cabbage (2½-3 pounds)
2	pounds ground beef chuck
2	large eggs
⅔	cup fine dry bread crumbs
½	cup minced onion
2	plump garlic cloves, finely minced
2	tablespoons minced fresh flat-leaf parsley
2	teaspoons fresh thyme leaves or 1 teaspoon dried
1	tablespoon hot Hungarian paprika
1	tablespoon kosher salt
2	teaspoons freshly ground black pepper

Sauce

4	cups tomato puree (page 324) or canned tomato sauce
¼	cup tomato paste
⅔	cup packed dark brown sugar
⅔	cup gingersnap crumbs
1	large onion, finely diced
1	lemon, thinly sliced
1	tablespoon minced fresh ginger
1-2	tablespoons hot Hungarian paprika

To make cabbage rolls: Bring a large pot of salted water to a boil over high heat. Add cabbage, cover and reduce heat to medium and simmer briskly until cabbage softens, 10 to 15 minutes.

Drain cabbage and carefully separate leaves; there should be between 24 and 28. Chop any remaining cabbage and place it in a nonreactive Dutch oven or a 6-quart covered casserole.

In a large bowl, combine beef, eggs, bread crumbs, onion, garlic, parsley, thyme, paprika, salt and pepper and ½ cup water. Beat vigorously with an electric mixer for 2 minutes or by hand with a wooden spoon for about 5 minutes, until mixture is light.

Preheat oven to 350 degrees F.

Form meat into small rolls about 2 inches long and 1 inch in diameter; wrap in cabbage leaves. Place cabbage rolls, seam side down, close together in prepared pot.

To make sauce: Stir together tomato puree or sauce, tomato paste, brown sugar, gingersnaps, onion, lemon and ginger in a large mixing bowl. Blend thoroughly. Pour sauce over prepared rolls. Sprinkle generously with paprika.

Tightly cover casserole and bake for 1¾ hours. Remove cover and bake until tops are lightly browned, about 15 minutes more.

This is best when refrigerated overnight. Bring to room temperature several hours before reheating. Reheat at 325 degrees, covered, until sauce is bubbling, about 1¼ hours.

Serve hot, saucing generously.

Wine: Eberle Winery Zinfandel Paso Robles Sauret Vineyard (California: Paso Robles) or another full-bodied, complex Zinfandel

Fragrant Calcutta Meatball Curry

(*Kofta*)

Serves 6-8

OUR FRIEND MERV SOPHER, who was born and raised in Calcutta, India, shared this example of Sephardic Jewish cuisine. The meatballs are exceptionally tender. Adding the spices one by one makes for a particularly creamy result; place them on a plate so you can add them as you need them, just as you would for a stir-fry. This version is medium-hot. You can rev up the flavor by adding more chile powder. The meatballs are even better when made a day ahead. Serve with jasmine or basmati rice.

Meatballs

2	slices sturdy white bread
1	pound lean ground beef
1	pound ground veal
2	medium-sized yellow onions, finely chopped
4	plump garlic cloves, minced
¼	cup minced fresh cilantro
1	teaspoon ground turmeric
½	teaspoon ground ginger
1	large egg
	Kosher salt and freshly ground black pepper

Sauce

4	cardamom pods, slightly cracked by pressing on them
1	rounded tablespoon minced fresh ginger
1	rounded tablespoon ground coriander, plus more if desired
1	rounded tablespoon ground cumin
2	teaspoons turmeric
2	teaspoons chile powder, plus more if desired
1	teaspoon hot Hungarian paprika
1	teaspoon garam masala (available in Indian markets)
1	teaspoon kosher salt, or more to taste
½	cup vegetable oil

5   medium-sized yellow onions, finely chopped

3   plump garlic cloves, minced

2   bay leaves

2   large tomatoes, cut into medium dice

1   large russet potato, peeled and cut into ¾-inch cubes

3   tablespoons cider vinegar

⅓   cup minced fresh cilantro

To make meatballs: In a soup plate, combine bread with enough water to cover; soak for a few minutes to soften. Squeeze water from bread; place bread in a large mixing bowl. Add meats, onions, garlic, cilantro, turmeric, ginger, egg and salt and pepper. Mix vigorously with your hands to blend thoroughly. Form into walnut-sized balls, placing them on a large platter. Chill while you make sauce.

To make sauce: Arrange all spices and salt in separate mounds around a large plate and set aside. Place 4 cups water near stovetop.

In a large, deep, nonreactive skillet, heat oil over high heat. Stir in onions, garlic and bay leaves and cook over medium-high heat, stirring often, until onions begin to stick, 10 to 15 minutes.

Stir constantly until onions turn light gold and begin to brown, about 10 minutes more. (If onions begin to stick to pan too much, stir in ⅓ cup water.)

Add 1 spice at a time, stirring in ⅓ cup water after each spice is added. Stir vigorously for 30 seconds after each addition. When all spices have been incorporated, place lid slightly ajar on skillet. Reduce heat to low and cook, stirring occasionally, until raw smell of spices disappears and oil begins to separate from onion and spices, about 5 minutes.

Add tomatoes and potato. Tightly cover pot and cook over low heat until potato is just tender, about 20 minutes. Vigorously stir in vinegar and ⅓ cup more water. Cook until mixture begins to simmer again. If sauce is too thick, add up to ⅓ cup more water

Carefully slip meatballs into simmering sauce, tipping skillet from side to side to make room for meatballs and to distribute sauce around them. Make certain they are covered by sauce, but do not stir. Cover and simmer until meatballs are firm, 25 to 30 minutes. Remove pan from heat and let stand, covered, until cool. Refrigerate overnight for optimum flavor. Skim off surface fat before reheating.

Reheat over medium heat. Stir in cilantro and serve.

Wine: Alois Lageder Alto Adige Chardonnay (Italy: Alto Adige) or a spicy, full-bodied barrel-fermented Chardonnay from Santa Barbara County (California)

Veal

—

Spice-Rubbed Veal Brisket with Red Wine Sauce 182

Beer-Braised Veal Brisket with Onions & Parsnips 184

Veal Roast with Leek & Caramelized Onion Gravy 186

Blanquette of Veal 188

Mediterranean Veal Stew with Black Olives 190

Baked Veal Chops with Mushrooms 192

Joey's Osso Bucco Milanese 194

Lemon Veal Shanks with White Wine 196

Veal Shanks with Braised Lentils & Caramelized Onions 198

Spice-Rubbed Veal Brisket with Red Wine Sauce

Serves 6-8

VEAL BRISKET, THE BONED TIP OF THE VEAL BREAST, is tender and delicious when braised. And it's lower in fat than its beef counterpart. In this preparation, the meat is rubbed with a seasoning paste that includes brown sugar, coriander, curry powder and allspice, bound together with garlic and lime juice. The meat is then cooked with carrots, onions, tomato puree and red wine for a thick, mellow gravy. The meat and gravy are chilled separately before serving; the meat must be well chilled so it slices evenly. Chilling also makes it easy to skim the fat off the gravy.

2½-3	pounds Spanish onions, finely diced
3	medium carrots, finely diced
3	garlic cloves
1	tablespoon kosher salt
	Juice of 2 limes
¼	cup packed dark brown sugar
1	tablespoon curry powder
1	tablespoon hot Hungarian paprika
2	teaspoons ground coriander
2	teaspoons ground allspice
2	teaspoons freshly ground black pepper
1	teaspoon ground cinnamon
1	teaspoon dried thyme
2	veal briskets (about 5 pounds total)
1	cup dry red wine
1	cup tomato puree (page 324) or canned crushed tomatoes

The day before serving, combine half of onions with carrots and spread in a large, heavy, nonreactive roasting pan.

In a mini-chopper, or using mortar and pestle, mash together garlic, salt and lime juice. Blend in brown sugar, curry powder, paprika, coriander, allspice, pepper, cinnamon and thyme. Thoroughly rub seasoning mixture over both briskets. Place them, fat side up, over onions and carrots. Let marinate for 1 hour at room temperature.

About 20 minutes before you plan to cook briskets, preheat oven to 325 degrees F.

Distribute remaining onions over briskets. Add red wine and tomato puree or crushed tomatoes. Cover pan and roast, basting occasionally, until briskets are fork-tender, about 2½ hours.

Remove roasting pan from oven. Scraping onions from briskets, transfer briskets to a large container. When briskets are cool, wrap in foil and refrigerate for 5 to 24 hours. Pour onions and gravy into a container; cover and chill.

A few hours before serving, remove briskets from refrigerator and thinly slice across grain. Arrange slices in an ovenproof dish.

Preheat oven to 325 degrees.

Remove and discard congealed fat from surface of gravy. Pour gravy over sliced meat. Cover with foil or a lid and bake until hot, about 1 hour. Serve brisket on heated plates with a generous portion of sauce.

Wine: Cafaro Cellars Merlot (California: Napa Valley) or another Napa Valley Merlot

Beer-Braised Veal Brisket with Onions & Parsnips

Serves 6-8

V EAL BRISKET LENDS ITSELF to a variety of delicious preparations. It improves in flavor when made ahead and freezes well too. In this recipe, onions, parsnips, chili sauce and beer combine to make a full-flavored sauce with a tinge of spice and sweetness. This is a great dish for family gatherings. It's often served in our house at the Passover seder or Rosh Hashanah dinner. Any leftovers make delightful hot sandwiches.

2	jumbo Spanish onions, thinly sliced
2	medium parsnips, scrubbed and thinly sliced
2	veal briskets (about 5 pounds total)
	Kosher salt and freshly ground black pepper
1	teaspoon hot Hungarian paprika
1	teaspoon garlic powder
1	teaspoon dried thyme
1	12-ounce bottle Bennett's Chili Sauce
	or another spicy chili sauce
1	cup beer
2	bay leaves

Preheat oven to 325 degrees F.

Place half of onions and all of parsnips in a heavy, nonreactive roasting pan. Place briskets, fat side up, on onions. Rub evenly with salt and pepper, paprika, garlic powder and thyme. Scatter remaining onions over briskets; pour chili sauce and beer over briskets. Place a bay leaf on each brisket.

Cover pan with a lid or foil and roast, basting occasionally, until meat is fork-tender, about 2½ hours.

Remove from oven and place meat on a large platter to cool. Discard bay leaves, wrap briskets in foil and refrigerate. Spoon onions and parsnips into a food processor fitted with the metal blade; pulse to puree. Combine with remaining gravy and pour into a container. Cover and chill for 5 to 24 hours.

A few hours before serving, remove briskets from refrigerator and thinly slice across grain. Arrange slices in an ovenproof dish.

Preheat oven to 325 degrees F.

Remove and discard congealed fat from surface of gravy. Pour gravy over sliced meat. Cover with foil or a lid and bake until hot, about 1 hour. Serve brisket and sauce on heated plates.

Wine: A. Rafanelli Winery Zinfandel Dry Creek Valley (California: Sonoma County) or another complex, fruity Zinfandel

Veal Roast with Leek & Caramelized Onion Gravy

Serves 4-6

OVEN-CARAMELIZED ONIONS and sautéed leeks blend beautifully with cloves and allspice to make a deeply flavored gravy for this humble shoulder roast. This is inspired by a recipe in Marion Flexner's *Dixie Dishes*.

2 jumbo Spanish onions, quartered

6 tablespoons olive oil, plus more if needed

3-4 pounds trimmed and tied boneless veal shoulder
  or chuck roast

3 tablespoons unbleached flour
  Kosher salt and freshly ground black pepper

2 cups thinly sliced leeks, well washed,
  trimmed to include tender green parts

2 plump garlic cloves, minced

2 cups veal stock (page 328)

1 tablespoon Worcestershire sauce

4 whole cloves

2 whole allspice

1 bay leaf

1 tablespoon minced fresh flat-leaf parsley,
  plus more for garnish

Preheat oven to 500 degrees F.

Place onions in a large, shallow baking dish and toss with 1 tablespoon oil. Roast, stirring several times, until onions are darkly caramelized with charred edges, about 1 hour.

Scrape onions and any caramelized bits adhering to pan onto a chopping board. Let cool. Coarsely chop; set aside.

Reduce oven temperature to 325 degrees.

Evenly sprinkle veal with flour and rub to coat well; set aside excess flour. Sprinkle veal generously with salt and pepper. Heat 2 tablespoons oil in a large cast-iron skillet until hot. Brown veal on all sides over high heat, about 10 minutes. Transfer to a plate and set aside.

While veal is browning, pour remaining 3 tablespoons oil into a Dutch oven.

Heat over medium heat. Add leeks and garlic and cook, stirring often, until golden, about 10 minutes. Stir in reserved flour and blend thoroughly. Stir in veal stock. When liquid is bubbling, add reserved onions, Worcestershire, cloves, allspice, bay leaf and 1 tablespoon parsley. Place roast in center, spooning sauce over meat until top is coated with chopped onions. Tightly cover.

Braise in oven, basting occasionally, until meat is fork-tender, about 1½ to 2 hours.

Transfer roast to a carving board. Carefully skim surface fat off sauce. Adjust seasonings, adding salt and pepper if desired. Discard bay leaf.

Carve roast into medium-thick slices. Divide among heated serving plates and sauce generously. Sprinkle with parsley.

Wine: Joseph Phelps Vineyards Cabernet Sauvignon Backus Vineyard (California: Napa Valley) or another complex, full-bodied Napa Valley Cabernet Sauvignon

Blanquette of Veal

Serves 4

CHATTING ABOUT THIS PROJECT one evening with our good friend Chef Lucien Vendome, we were reminded about one of the most basic covered dishes in French home cuisine, the *blanquette de veau*. "As a child growing up in France, there was not a week without this dish," Lucien told us. "Every French housewife knew how to prepare it and made it often, because it was simple, inexpensive and so familiar. What could be easier than putting some cubes of meat into a pot with water or chicken stock and some seasonings?" While touches of lemon and nutmeg are essential to a true *blanquette*, carrots, onions and mushrooms are entirely optional additions. You will want to serve this with noodles or rice.

2	pounds veal shoulder, cut into 2-inch cubes
6	cups chicken stock (page 325) or water
1	whole clove
1	large yellow onion, unpeeled
2	teaspoons kosher salt
1	teaspoon freshly ground white pepper, plus more to taste
1	bouquet garni (page 331*)*
3	medium carrots, cut into thirds
8	small boiling onions, blanched and peeled
8	mushrooms (optional)
3	tablespoons unsalted butter
3	tablespoons unbleached flour
2	large egg yolks
1	tablespoon fresh lemon juice
¼	teaspoon freshly grated nutmeg
¼	cup chopped fresh flat-leaf parsley, for garnish

In a large saucepan, combine veal with stock or water and bring to a boil over high heat. Reduce heat to low and skim off froth until no more appears, 5 to 10 minutes.

Push clove into yellow onion and add to pot along with salt, white pepper and bouquet garni. Tightly cover and simmer for 1 hour.

Add carrots, boiling onions and mushrooms, if using; cover and simmer for 30 minutes more.

Discard onion with clove and bouquet garni. Carefully drain cooking liquid into a large measuring cup or pitcher and set aside; there should be at least 3 cups. Set saucepan aside.

In a medium, heavy saucepan, melt butter over medium heat. Whisk in flour, continuing to whisk just until flour loses its whiteness (do not brown). Gradually whisk in hot cooking liquid and simmer until sauce thickens. Place egg yolks in a small bowl and slowly add some of hot sauce to yolks, whisking well after each addition. Whisk egg mixture into remaining hot sauce, being careful not to let sauce boil and curdle. Stir in lemon juice and nutmeg. Pour sauce over meat and vegetables. Cook over low heat just until meat is heated through.

Adjust seasonings. Serve on heated plates with buttered noodles or rice. Sprinkle generously with parsley.

Wine: Staglin Family Vineyard Cabernet Sauvignon (California: Napa Valley) or another medium-bodied Napa Valley Cabernet with complex fruit flavors

Mediterranean Veal Stew with Black Olives

Serves 6

OMATOES, ONIONS, GARLIC, HERBS AND OLIVES—the building blocks of cuisines from the sunny Mediterranean—make a complex setting for this veal. Cooked together until the meat is tender, these ingredients meld into a luscious whole. An addition of anchovies near the end brings a note of richness.

½	cup unbleached flour
3½	pounds veal stew meat, cut into 2-inch cubes
	Up to ½ cup olive oil
1	cup dry red wine
1	large yellow onion, finely chopped
3	plump garlic cloves, minced
4	cups tomato puree (page 324) or canned crushed tomatoes
1	cup pitted Kalamata olives, minced
2	tablespoons minced fresh flat-leaf parsley
2	teaspoons minced fresh oregano or 1 teaspoon dried
1	teaspoon kosher salt
1	teaspoon freshly ground black pepper
1	2-ounce can oil-packed anchovy fillets, drained, rinsed and minced

Preheat oven to 325 degrees F.

Place flour in a plastic bag. Add meat and shake to coat evenly but lightly. Heat 3 tablespoons oil in a large cast-iron skillet over medium-high heat. Working in batches, add meat and brown on all sides, adding more oil as needed. Transfer browned veal to a nonreactive Dutch oven or covered casserole.

When veal is browned, add wine to skillet and whisk over high heat to loosen any browned particles adhering to bottom. Pour mixture over meat. Pat skillet dry with a paper towel.

Pour 2 tablespoons oil into skillet and heat over medium heat. Stir in onion and garlic, and cook, stirring often, until golden, 5 to 7 minutes. Stir in tomato puree or crushed tomatoes and olives. Cook over low heat for about 15 minutes.

Stir in herbs and salt and pepper. Pour sauce over veal. Cover casserole and bake for 1 hour.

Stir in anchovies. Continue to cook, covered, until meat is fork-tender, 1 hour more. Skim off any surface fat and adjust seasonings before serving.

Wine: Arrowood Vineyards Merlot (California: Sonoma County) or a robust Italian red

Baked Veal Chops
with Mushrooms

Serves 4

THERE'S A HINT OF TARRAGON in these melt-in-your-mouth chops. After they are browned in their tangy coating of sour cream and crumbs, they are cooked on braised mushrooms. It's a recipe adapted from one for chicken given long ago to Linda by her mother, Gert LeVine. While veal chops are usually broiled or grilled, this particular preparation gives them spectacular texture and flavor.

1	pound mushrooms, thinly sliced
1	medium-sized yellow onion, finely diced
½	cup fine dry bread crumbs
½	cup crushed corn flakes
¾	cup sour cream
1	teaspoon Worcestershire sauce
1	tablespoon fresh lemon juice
1	teaspoon dried tarragon
1	teaspoon kosher salt, plus more to taste
¼	teaspoon freshly ground white pepper, plus more to taste
4	1-inch-thick veal rib chops, trimmed
2	tablespoons unsalted butter

In a medium saucepan, combine mushrooms and 1 cup water. Bring to a boil over high heat. Tightly cover, reduce heat to low and simmer for 15 minutes. Add onion and cook for 15 minutes more. Set aside.

Meanwhile, combine bread crumbs and corn flakes in a shallow soup plate; set aside. In another shallow soup plate, blend together sour cream, Worcestershire, lemon juice, tarragon, 1 teaspoon salt and ¼ teaspoon white pepper. Carefully coat chops with sour cream mixture, then with crumbs. Place chops on a sheet of wax paper.

Melt butter in a large cast-iron skillet over high heat. Quickly brown chops on both sides, 6 to 8 minutes. Transfer chops to a platter.

Preheat oven to 375 degrees F.

Using a slotted spoon, transfer mushroom mixture to a buttered casserole just large enough to hold chops in a single layer; reserve liquid. Season with salt and white pepper if needed.

Place chops over mushrooms. Sprinkle each with 1 scant tablespoon mushroom liquid remaining in bottom of saucepan. Tightly cover and bake until meat is fork-tender, about 1¼ hours.

Divide chops among 4 heated serving plates, spooning some mushroom pan sauce over each chop.

Wine: Ferrari-Carano Vineyards Merlot Alexander Valley (California: Napa Valley) or another medium-bodied fruity Merlot

Joey's Osso Bucco Milanese

Serves 6-8

BROWNED THICK, MEATY VEAL SHANKS are slowly simmered in a fragrant, garlicky tomato and wine sauce studded with onions, carrots and mushrooms. The moist meat almost falls off the marrow-filled bone. Joey Santosuosso keeps this dish on the lunch menu of his acclaimed Johnny's Downtown all winter. Cleveland's cognoscenti never tire of it, and we know why. Serve it as Joey does—with Homey Creamed Spinach (page 290). See photograph, page 86.

6-8	1½-inch-thick veal shanks, about 5½ pounds total
	Kosher salt and freshly ground black pepper
⅔	cup unbleached flour
¼	cup olive oil
1	cup finely diced yellow onion
1	cup finely diced carrots
½	cup finely diced celery
2	cups peeled, seeded, finely diced tomatoes
1	cup sliced mushrooms, preferably shiitake
1	cup dry white wine
2	tablespoons minced garlic
2	bay leaves
1	tablespoon minced fresh rosemary or 1½ teaspoons dried
¼	cup minced fresh flat-leaf parsley, for garnish

Preheat oven to 350 degrees F.

Season each shank with salt and pepper. Place flour in a shallow soup plate and thoroughly coat shanks. Shake off excess flour.

Heat oil in a 12-inch nonreactive skillet or any deep, heavy pan large enough to hold shanks in a single layer. Over medium-low heat, brown shanks on all sides, 15 to 20 minutes.

Add onion, carrots and celery; cook, stirring, until soft, about 5 minutes. Stir in tomatoes, mushrooms, wine, garlic, bay leaves and rosemary. Cover with a lid or foil and reduce heat to low. When liquid bubbles, transfer covered skillet to oven. Braise until meat is fork-tender, 1½ to 2 hours.

Divide shanks among 6 heated serving plates. Spoon on pan sauce generously and sprinkle with parsley.

Wine: Flora Springs Wine Co. Sangiovese (California: Napa Valley) or a rich Tuscan red (Italy)

Lemon Veal Shanks with White Wine

Serves 4

T HESE SUCCULENT VEAL SHANKS are prepared in a white wine sauce that incorporates the piquancy of lemon and the mellowness of anchovies. It's a simple preparation that will inspire raves from all who taste it. Our hats are off to our friend Marcella Hazan, whose many lemon-sauced recipes have inspired our cooking for years.

5	tablespoons extra-virgin olive oil
1	large yellow onion, finely diced
3	plump garlic cloves, minced
⅓	cup unbleached flour
4	2½-to-3-inch-thick veal shanks
1¼	cups dry white wine
½	cup chicken stock (page 325), plus more if needed
½	cup minced fresh flat-leaf parsley
1	teaspoon fresh thyme leaves or ½ teaspoon dried
	Kosher salt and freshly ground black pepper
	Minced zest and juice of 1 lemon
1	2-ounce can oil-packed anchovies, drained, rinsed and minced
1	bay leaf

Preheat oven to 350 degrees F.

In a small nonstick skillet, heat 2 tablespoons oil over low heat. Add onion and garlic, cover and cook until onion softens, about 5 minutes. Turn off heat, but keep skillet covered while you brown veal.

Heat remaining 3 tablespoons oil in a large, heavy, nonreactive sauté pan over medium heat. At the same time, pour flour into a soup plate; carefully coat shanks in flour. Brown shanks on all sides in hot oil, 15 to 20 minutes. Transfer shanks to a large plate.

Drain fat from sauté pan. Place pan over medium heat and add wine. Whisk over high heat to loosen browned particles adhering to bottom. Add ½ cup stock, parsley, thyme, salt and pepper, lemon zest and juice and anchovies. Whisk together over medium-high heat until liquid is bubbling.

Return browned shanks in a single layer to sauté pan. Spoon onion mixture over shanks; baste shanks with pan sauce. Add bay leaf and tightly cover.

Place in oven, and braise, basting several times, until shanks are fork-tender, 1½ to 2 hours. Remove bay leaf.

Serve 1 shank per person on a heated plate. Spoon sauce over and around the shank.

Wine: Peter Michael Winery Chardonnay Sonoma County Mon Plaisir (California: Sonoma County) or another complex Chardonnay

Veal Shanks with Braised Lentils & Caramelized Onions

Serves 4

CARAMELIZED ONIONS BLENDED WITH CURRY FLAVORS make a splendid base for a tomato and red wine sauce. The lentils and veal absorb these lusty seasonings, making a tender and moist combination when the cooking is finished. Le Puy lentils, dark green in color, are commonly imported from France. We like them because of their firmer texture; they do not become as mushy as ordinary brown lentils.

⅓	cup unbleached flour
4	2½-inch-thick veal shanks
¼	cup olive oil
2	cups dry red wine
3	tablespoons unsalted butter
1	jumbo sweet onion, finely chopped
3	plump garlic cloves, minced
1	tablespoon curry powder
2	teaspoons ground ginger
1	teaspoon cayenne pepper
½	teaspoon ground cinnamon
½	teaspoon ground cardamom
1	cup tomato puree (page 324) or canned crushed tomatoes
1	tablespoon fresh lemon juice
	Kosher salt and freshly ground black pepper
1½	cups chicken stock (page 325), plus more if needed
1¼	cups (about 8 ounces) lentils, preferably French Le Puy brand, sorted and rinsed
1	bay leaf

Preheat oven to 350 degrees F.

Place flour in a shallow soup plate; carefully coat shanks in flour. Heat oil in a large cast-iron skillet. Add shanks and cook until browned on all sides, 15 to 20 minutes. Transfer shanks to a large platter. Deglaze pan by pouring wine into skillet and whisking over high heat until browned particles are loosened; set aside.

Melt butter in a large, heavy, nonreactive skillet with a tight-fitting lid. Stir in onion and garlic and stir over medium heat until onion caramelizes, 15 to 20 minutes.

Stir in curry powder, ginger, cayenne, cinnamon and cardamom. Cook, stirring, to release flavors, 2 to 3 minutes. Add wine from skillet, tomato puree or crushed tomatoes, lemon juice, salt and pepper and 1½ cups stock. Increase heat and cook until liquid is bubbling. Stir in lentils.

Return shanks to skillet by making little "nests" for them. Place bay leaf on top. Tightly cover and cook until liquid is bubbling. Transfer pan to oven and braise, basting occasionally and adding more stock if lentils become too dry, until meat is fork-tender and lentils are soft, 1½ to 2 hours.

Discard bay leaf. Serve 1 shank per person on a heated plate, spooning lentils and sauce around it.

Wine: Duckhorn Vineyards Merlot (California: Napa Valley) or another complex Merlot

Lamb

Leg of Lamb with Potatoes & Onions 202

Savory Leg of Lamb with Shallots, Turnips & Carrots 203

Leg of Lamb with White Wine, Prosciutto, Coriander & Rosemary 204

Stuffed Boneless Leg of Lamb with Sweet Potatoes 206

Springtime Stew of Lamb (*Printanier Navarin*) 208

Ragout of Lamb with Mushrooms, Onions & Red Wine 210

Indian-Style Spicy Braised Lamb with Okra 212

Rosemary Lamb Shanks with White Wine, Leeks & Shallots 214

Spiced Lamb Shanks in Red Wine 216

Lamb with Green Beans 218

Braised Eggplant Stuffed with Lamb, Pine Nuts & Mint 220

Leg of Lamb
with Potatoes & Onions

Serves 8-10

CELEBRATED ARTIST JOSEPH O'SICKEY's glorious color-filled paintings have lit up our lives for decades. Another cherished aspect of our friendship has been the many lamb dinners prepared for us by Joe and his wife Algesa. Cooked to perfection, this leg of lamb is accompanied by roasted potatoes and onions. At the O'Sickeys', this dish is served with a green vegetable and a salad of orange slices and purple onions.

1	7-to-9-pound leg of lamb, shank trimmed to fit roaster
3	plump garlic cloves, thinly sliced
1	heaping tablespoon unbleached flour
	Kosher salt and freshly ground black pepper
12	boiling onions, peeled
3½	pounds small red potatoes, peeled

Preheat oven to 375 degrees F.

Trim excess fat from top of lamb. With a sharp knife, make about 30 small slits all over meat. Insert garlic slices into slits. Place meat in a large roaster. Rub top with flour. Season generously with salt and pepper. If using a conventional meat thermometer, insert into thickest part of meat, taking care to avoid touching bone. Tightly cover.

Roast for 30 minutes. Scatter onions and potatoes around roast, turning to coat them well with pan drippings. Cover and roast for 30 to 35 minutes for rare or 40 to 45 minutes for medium to well-done, or until a meat thermometer or an instant-read thermometer reads 125 to 130 degrees for rare and 135 or more for medium to well-done.

Uncover pan and skim off obvious fat. Transfer lamb to a carving board and let rest. (Meat will continue to cook as it rests.) Return roaster, uncovered, to oven. Increase oven temperature to 450 degrees. Roast potatoes and onions, basting often, until lightly browned and tender, 10 to 15 minutes.

Carve lamb and arrange on a heated platter. Spoon potatoes and onions into heated serving bowls. Stir any meat juices back from carving board into pan; season with salt and pepper. Pour into a gravy boat.

Wine: Spottswoode Winery Cabernet Sauvignon (California: Napa Valley) or another full-bodied Cabernet Sauvignon

Savory Leg of Lamb with Shallots, Turnips & Carrots

Serves 6-8

THE PINEY FLAVOR OF WINTER SAVORY is well suited to lamb. The lamb melts into its oniony pan sauce, which is punctuated with garlic and tomato.

3	tablespoons olive oil
1	large Spanish onion, finely diced
3	large leeks, well washed and trimmed, finely sliced
3	rounded tablespoons whole fresh winter savory leaves, thyme or summer savory or 1 tablespoon dried
1	6-to-7-pound leg of lamb, pelvic bone removed
3	plump garlic cloves, thinly sliced
	Kosher salt and freshly ground black pepper
4	medium turnips, quartered
4	carrots, cut into 2-inch chunks
12	shallots
2	cups dry red wine
⅔	cup tomato puree (page 324) or canned crushed tomatoes

Preheat oven to 450 degrees F.

Place 1 tablespoon oil in a large, heavy, nonreactive roaster with a lid. Place onion and leeks in center; sprinkle with half of savory or thyme. With a sharp knife, make about 20 slits all over lamb. Insert a garlic slice into each. Rub lamb with 1 tablespoon oil. Season well with salt and pepper. Place lamb, fat side up, on onions. Sprinkle with remaining savory or thyme. Scatter turnips, carrots and shallots around lamb. Drizzle with remaining 1 tablespoon oil.

Place lamb in oven and roast, uncovered, until top is browned, about 20 minutes. Stir vegetables, add wine and tomato puree or crushed tomatoes; tightly cover. Reduce heat to 325 degrees. Braise, basting occasionally, until lamb is fork-tender, about 3 hours.

Transfer lamb to a carving board. Skim surface fat from remaining vegetables and sauce; adjust seasonings. Carve into thin slices; serve on heated plates garnished generously with pan sauce and accompanied by vegetables.

Wine: Leonetti Cellar Merlot Washington (Washington State), St. Clement Vineyards Merlot Napa Valley (California: Napa Valley) or a full-bodied Merlot

Leg of Lamb with White Wine, Prosciutto, Coriander & Rosemary

Serves 8-10

THIS TENDER LAMB gets its flavor from prosciutto and a garlic, coriander and rosemary paste. Spoon over the delicate pan sauce of onions, white wine and Dijon mustard and accompany it with Pureed White Beans (page 264).

3	garlic cloves
¼	cup loosely packed fresh flat-leaf parsley
1	tablespoon ground coriander
1	tablespoon fresh rosemary leaves or 1½ teaspoons dried, plus 2 fresh rosemary branches or ½ teaspoon dried
4	tablespoons olive oil
1	6-to-7-pound leg of lamb, boned and tied, bones reserved
2	ounces prosciutto ham, thinly sliced and cut into 30 strips, each 1 x ½ inches
2	large red onions, finely chopped
2	carrots, finely chopped
	Kosher salt and freshly ground black pepper
3	cups dry white wine
¼	cup Dijon mustard

Preheat oven to 450 degrees F.

In a food processor fitted with the metal blade, combine garlic, parsley, coriander, rosemary leaves or 1½ teaspoons dried and 1 tablespoon oil. Pulse until mixture is finely chopped; set aside.

With a sharp paring knife, cut 30 slits, each at least ½ inch deep, all over both sides of lamb. Put about ¼ teaspoon of garlic-herb mixture on each piece of prosciutto, fold into a small package and stuff into a slit. Continue until all slits are packed. (Reserve any unused garlic mixture.) Rub lamb with 1 tablespoon oil and set aside. Rub any bones and shank with a bit of oil as well.

Thoroughly coat a large, heavy roaster with remaining 2 tablespoons oil. Place onions in center; scatter carrots on top. Add rosemary branches or ½ teaspoon dried and any remaining garlic-herb mixture. Season underside of lamb with salt and pepper; place lamb, fat side up, on onions and carrots. Generously season top with salt and pepper. Season bones and shank and place them in roaster.

Roast, uncovered, until top is browned, about 20 minutes. Add wine, tightly cover with a lid or foil, and reduce heat to 325 degrees. Braise, basting from time to time, for 3 hours.

Transfer lamb to a carving board. Place pan over high heat and bring mixture to a boil. Carefully remove surface fat; whisk in mustard. Simmer briskly for 2 to 3 minutes to thicken sauce slightly. Adjust seasonings and remove from heat.

Slice lamb and serve on heated plates with sauce. Serve more sauce on the side.

Wine: Kistler Vineyards Sonoma Valley Kistler Estate Chardonnay (California: Sonoma County), Kistler Vineyards Russian River Valley Cuvée Catherine Pinot Noir (California: Sonoma County) or a full-bodied red or white Burgundy (France)

Stuffed Boneless Leg of Lamb with Sweet Potatoes

Serves 6-8

THIS BUTTERFLIED LEG OF LAMB is stuffed with smoked ham and mushrooms seasoned with sage and mace and is braised on a bed of sweet potatoes. It was inspired by a recipe in *The Kentucky Housewife*, by Lettice Bryan, published in 1839.

3	tablespoons unsalted butter
½	pound shiitake or portobello mushrooms, thinly sliced
3	garlic cloves, thinly sliced
¼	teaspoon ground mace
1	5-to-6-pound boneless leg of lamb, prepared for stuffing
	Kosher salt and freshly ground black pepper
½	pound smoked ham, very thinly sliced
5	fresh sage leaves, minced
¼	cup minced fresh flat-leaf parsley
5	tablespoons canola oil
3	medium-sized yellow onions, minced
1	cup finely chopped celery
2	cups white wine
3	sweet potatoes, peeled and sliced ½ inch thick
3	tablespoons unbleached flour

Melt butter in a medium nonstick skillet over medium heat. Add mushrooms and garlic, cover and cook, shaking skillet several times, until liquid is released, 5 to 10 minutes. Stir in mace. Set aside.

Preheat oven to 325 degrees F.

On a work surface, open up leg of lamb. Generously season meat with salt and pepper. Arrange ham slices over meat. Spread mushroom mixture over ham. Scatter sage leaves on top. Sprinkle evenly with parsley.

Tightly roll up lamb and tie in 4 or 5 places with kitchen twine.

Pour 2 tablespoons oil in a large cast-iron skillet and heat over high heat. Carefully brown lamb on all sides, 6 to 10 minutes.

Scatter onions and celery in a large nonreactive roasting pan. Place browned lamb, seam side down, over vegetables. Season with salt and pepper. Pour wine and 2 cups water around lamb. Cover roasting pan with a lid or foil. Braise meat for 1 hour.

Gently lift lamb out of roaster. Arrange sweet potato slices in roasting pan. Return meat to pan, placing it over potatoes and basting with pan juices. Cover and braise, basting several times, until meat is fork-tender, about 2 hours more.

Meanwhile, combine remaining 3 tablespoons oil with flour in a small skillet. Whisk together over high heat until dark brown, 3 to 5 minutes. Remove from heat and whisk until cool. Reserve.

Transfer lamb to a carving board. Place roasting pan over medium-high heat and skim surface fat from bubbling juices. Add browned flour mixture and cook, stirring, to thicken. Season with salt and pepper.

Carve roast into ½-inch-thick slices. Serve on heated plates with some sweet potato slices. Spoon over sauce.

Wine: Patz & Hall Wine Co. Russian River Pinot Noir (California: Sonoma County) or another medium-bodied Pinot Noir

Springtime Stew of Lamb

(*Printanier Navarin*)

Serves 6

I n French cooking, a *navarin* is a stew. This is a splendid and delicate stew of spring lamb and tender spring vegetables—freshly shelled peas, young green beans and baby turnips simmered in a light sauce. It is pleasing in any season. (See photograph, page 85.)

3	tablespoons olive oil, plus more if needed
3	pounds boneless leg of lamb, cut into 2-inch cubes
1½	tablespoons sugar
¼	cup unbleached flour
3½	cups vegetable or chicken stock (page 330 or 325)
1	cup finely chopped yellow onions
2	plump garlic cloves, minced
1	cup tomato puree (page 324) or canned crushed tomatoes
1	teaspoon fresh thyme leaves or ½ teaspoon dried
2	teaspoons fresh rosemary leaves or 1 teaspoon dried
1	bay leaf
	Kosher salt and freshly ground black pepper
12	small red potatoes, scrubbed
6	small boiling onions, blanched and peeled
4	medium carrots, cut into 2-inch pieces
3	small turnips, cleaned and cut in half
¼	pound green beans, trimmed and cut into 1-inch pieces
1	cup freshly shelled peas (about 1¼ pounds pods)
¼	cup minced fresh flat-leaf parsley, for garnish

Preheat oven to 350 degrees F.

Heat 2 tablespoons oil in a large cast-iron skillet over medium-high heat. Add one-third of lamb cubes and brown on all sides. Transfer browned cubes to a large bowl and repeat until all are browned; add oil if needed. When browning is complete, increase heat to high and return all meat to skillet. Sprinkle evenly with sugar and stir vigorously until sugar melts and caramelizes, 2 to 4 minutes. Evenly sprinkle flour over meat and stir until flour begins to brown, 1 to 3 minutes more. Stir in 2 cups stock and cook over low heat to heat through.

Meanwhile, lightly coat a Dutch oven with remaining 1 tablespoon oil; heat over medium heat. Add chopped onions and garlic and cook, stirring, until softened, 3 to 5 minutes. Add lamb mixture, remaining 1½ cups stock and tomato puree or crushed tomatoes. Increase heat to high and bring liquid to a boil. Add herbs and salt and pepper. Cover and place in oven. Braise for 30 minutes.

Add potatoes, boiling onions, carrots and turnips. Cover and cook for 1¼ hours.

Stir in green beans and peas. Cover and cook until beans and peas are tender, about 15 minutes more.

Remove pot from oven; adjust seasonings. Ladle meat and vegetables into heated soup plates. Sprinkle with parsley and serve.

Wine: Beaux Frères Pinot Noir (Oregon: Willamette Valley) or a complex red Burgundy (France)

Ragout of Lamb with Mushrooms, Onions & Red Wine

Serves 6

THIS FRAGRANT LAMB STEW has a red wine gravy that blends the mellow richness of mushrooms with the piquancy of black olives. It's perfect served over creamy mashed potatoes.

1	ounce dried porcini or cèpes
3	tablespoons unsalted butter
¾	pound fresh mushrooms, preferably portobello, thinly sliced
2	teaspoons soy sauce
2	medium carrots, finely chopped
2	plump garlic cloves, minced
2	plump shallots, minced
1	tablespoon minced fresh tarragon or 1½ teaspoons dried
2	thick slices bacon, cut into matchsticks
½	cup unbleached flour
3	pounds boneless leg of lamb, trimmed and cut into 2-inch cubes
	Olive oil if needed
3	cups dry red wine, preferably Rhône
⅔	cup pitted Niçoise olives
	Kosher salt and freshly ground black pepper
12	boiling onions, blanched and peeled
¼	cup minced fresh chives, for garnish

Preheat oven to 350 degrees F.

Soak porcini or cèpes in 1 cup boiling water for at least 20 minutes to soften.

Melt butter in a large cast-iron skillet over medium heat. Stir in fresh mushrooms, soy sauce, carrots, garlic and shallots. Cover and cook, stirring several times, until mushrooms soften, 10 to 15 minutes. Set aside.

Meanwhile, squeeze liquid from soaked dried mushrooms; finely chop dried mushrooms. Strain soaking liquid through a coffee filter and set aside.

Stir dried mushrooms into mushroom-vegetable mixture. Add tarragon and cook, stirring, over medium heat for 2 minutes. Transfer to a bowl and set aside.

Place bacon in skillet in which you cooked mushrooms. Cook over medium-high heat until fat is rendered and bacon is nearly crisp. Remove with a slotted spoon and add to mushroom mixture; leave fat in skillet.

Pour flour into a plastic bag. Add lamb cubes and shake well to coat lightly but evenly.

Working in batches, brown lamb cubes in bacon fat. As meat is browned, transfer it to a Dutch oven or covered earthenware casserole. If there is not enough fat from bacon, add oil. When all meat is browned, pour off any remaining fat from skillet. Add 1 cup wine and whisk over high heat to loosen any browned particles adhering to skillet. Add reserved mushroom liquid and remaining 2 cups wine. Bring to a rolling boil.

Add mushroom mixture to meat. Pour in hot wine mixture. Stir in olives. Season with salt and pepper. Cover tightly and place in oven. Braise for 1 hour. Stir in boiling onions. Cover and braise until meat is very tender and sauce is thick, about 1½ hours more.

Remove from oven. Skim off any surface fat. Sprinkle with minced chives and serve.

Wine: August Clape Cornas (France: Rhône) or another full-bodied earthy red wine from the southern Rhône

Indian-Style Spicy Braised Lamb with Okra

Serves 8-10

THIS LAMB STEW WITH POTATOES AND SWEET POTATOES is cooked in a rich sauce of onions, tomatoes and okra enlivened by ginger, cardamom and turmeric. Splashes of lemon juice and red wine vinegar are added. If you make this the day before serving, the flavors will intensify and mellow delightfully. Serve over rice.

5-6	tablespoons vegetable oil, plus more if needed
3	pounds boneless leg of lamb, cut into 2-inch cubes
1½	cups finely chopped yellow onions
2½	cups thickly sliced okra
4	dried red chiles, crumbled
3	plump garlic cloves, minced
1	tablespoon minced fresh ginger
4	green cardamom pods, cracked
4	whole cloves
2	teaspoons curry powder
1	teaspoon ground cinnamon
1	teaspoon ground turmeric
2	cups drained canned plum tomatoes (35-ounce can)
2	tablespoons red wine vinegar
1	tablespoon fresh lemon juice
2	large russet potatoes, peeled and cut into 1-inch cubes
1	large sweet potato, peeled and cut into 1-inch cubes
	Kosher salt and freshly ground black pepper
¼	cup minced fresh cilantro, for garnish

Heat 2 tablespoons oil over high heat in a large nonreactive Dutch oven. When hot, add meat in batches and quickly brown on all sides, transferring to a large bowl and adding more oil if needed, 15 to 20 minutes total.

Reduce heat to medium. Adding more oil as needed, sauté onions and okra. Cook, stirring often, until onions are browned, 10 to 15 minutes.

Add chiles, garlic, ginger, cardamom, cloves, curry powder, cinnamon and turmeric. Cook, stirring, for 2 minutes to release flavors. Stir in tomatoes, vinegar, lemon juice and 1 cup water. When liquid is bubbling, stir in lamb.

Tightly cover and bring to a boil. Reduce heat to low and simmer, stirring occasionally, for 45 minutes.

Add potatoes and sweet potato and season with salt and pepper. If mixture is too dry, add more water. Cover and cook until meat and potatoes are fork-tender, about 30 minutes more.

Serve stew in heated soup plates, sprinkled with cilantro.

Wine: Quivera Vineyard Zinfandel Dry Creek Valley (California: Sonoma County) or another full-bodied Zinfandel

Rosemary Lamb Shanks with White Wine, Leeks & Shallots

Serves 4

SLOW-COOKING MAKES THESE SHANKS BUTTERY-TENDER. The sauce, seasoned with rosemary, has a sweetness from the leeks and shallots.

2	cups chicken stock (page 325)
¼	cup unbleached flour
4	¾-to-1-pound lamb shanks
3	tablespoons olive oil, plus more if needed
4	large leeks, well washed, split and finely diced
3	plump garlic cloves, minced
4	plump shallots, whole
1	cup dry white wine
2	teaspoons minced fresh rosemary leaves or 1 teaspoon dried, plus fresh rosemary branches, for garnish
1	teaspoon kosher salt
1	scant teaspoon freshly ground black pepper, plus more to taste

Preheat oven to 325 degrees F.

Pour stock into a large saucepan and bring to a boil. Cook over high heat until reduced by half, 8 to 10 minutes. Set aside.

Place flour in a shallow soup plate and dredge shanks to coat evenly. Pour 3 tablespoons oil into a 10-inch cast-iron or other ovenproof skillet; heat over medium-high heat. Quickly sear shanks, browning on all sides, 6 to 8 minutes. Transfer to a plate and set aside.

Add more oil to skillet if needed, and add leeks. Stir over medium heat until leeks soften, about 4 minutes. Add garlic and shallots and stir over medium heat until garlic softens and shallots are slightly cooked, 4 to 5 minutes. Stir in wine and reduced stock, scraping skillet to loosen any browned particles that adhere. Bring sauce to a boil.

Return shanks to skillet. Sprinkle with minced or dried rosemary, salt and pepper. Baste shanks with sauce; cover with a tight-fitting lid. Place in oven and braise shanks until very tender, about 2¼ hours.

Uncover and baste shanks with pan sauce. Preheat broiler, with a rack 3 inches from heat source. Broil shanks until glazed, 3 to 5 minutes.

Carefully remove skillet from oven and place on stove. Transfer shanks to heated plates. Bring sauce to a rolling boil over high heat. Cook, stirring constantly, until sauce reduces slightly and thickens, 1 to 3 minutes.

Spoon sauce over each and garnish with a shallot. Sprinkle with a few grindings of pepper. Garnish each serving with a rosemary branch.

Wine: Laurel Glen Cabernet Sauvignon Sonoma Mountain (California: Sonoma County) or another full-bodied Cabernet Sauvignon

Spiced Lamb Shanks in Red Wine

Serves 4

THESE SLOWLY BRAISED SHANKS are coated with a fragrant spice mixture that includes cloves, fennel seeds, ginger and cinnamon. Finely chopped carrots, onions and garlic not only add more flavor to the meat but thicken the red wine, making an exceptionally rich gravy for the finished shanks. Serve with Fred's Famous Fried Potatoes (page 291) sprinkled with a mixture of minced fresh garlic and parsley.

4	juniper berries (optional)
2	whole cloves
1	teaspoon fennel seeds
1	1-inch cinnamon stick
1	whole allspice
¼	teaspoon freshly grated nutmeg
¼	teaspoon ground ginger
¼	teaspoon ground cardamom
¼	teaspoon ground coriander
¼	cup unbleached flour
4	¾-to-1-pound lamb shanks
3	tablespoons olive oil, plus more if needed
4	medium carrots, finely diced
2	cups finely chopped yellow onions
3	plump garlic cloves, minced
	Kosher salt and freshly ground white pepper
¼	cup Cognac or brandy
1	cup dry red wine
1	cup chicken stock (page 325)
	Peel of ½ orange, in 2 large pieces
1	bay leaf
¼	cup minced fresh flat-leaf parsley, for garnish

Preheat oven to 325 degrees F.

In a spice mill or with a mortar and pestle, combine juniper berries (if using), cloves, fennel seeds, cinnamon stick and allspice. Pulse until finely ground. In a small bowl, combine with nutmeg, ginger, cardamom and coriander. Rub lamb shanks with spice mixture and let stand at room temperature for 1 hour.

Place flour in a shallow soup plate. Dredge lamb shanks with flour.

Heat oil over medium-high heat in a large cast-iron or other heavy, deep ovenproof skillet or Dutch oven. Brown shanks on all sides, 6 to 10 minutes. Remove shanks to a warm platter.

Adding more oil if needed, add carrots and onions to skillet. Cook, stirring often, until onions soften, 3 to 4 minutes. Stir in garlic and cook for 2 minutes. Return lamb shanks to skillet; season with salt and white pepper. Add Cognac or brandy and carefully ignite, spooning mixture over lamb. When flames have died out, add wine, stock, orange peel and bay leaf. Tightly cover. Braise in oven, basting once or twice, until fork-tender, about 2¼ hours.

Preheat broiler. Uncover skillet and baste shanks. Place under hot broiler for 2 minutes to glaze.

Remove shanks to heated dinner plates. Carefully place skillet over high heat and boil sauce to reduce and thicken slightly. Remove any surface fat while sauce is bubbling. Discard bay leaf.

Spoon sauce over lamb shanks and serve, sprinkled with parsley.

Wine: Domaine de la Gautière Buis-les-Baronnies (France: Provence) or an earthy, medium-bodied Côtes du Rhône

Lamb with Green Beans

Serves 4

OUR FRIENDS WEDAD AND HELEN SHAHEEN, keepers of a rich tradition of Syrian cooking, slowly simmer this simple stew of lamb and green beans in a flavorful tomato sauce. While the stew is cooking, they brown some orzo and rice and cook it together with beef stock. The stew is served over the slightly toasty rice mixture. All together, this is a satisfying but delicate dish—well suited to summer, when green beans are in season.

Up to 4 tablespoons olive oil
1   pound lamb shoulder, cut into 1-inch cubes
2   medium-sized yellow onions, finely chopped
2   plump garlic cloves, minced
¼   rounded teaspoon ground allspice
     Kosher salt and freshly ground black pepper
2   pounds green beans, trimmed and cut into 1-inch pieces
1   8-ounce can tomato sauce or 2 large fresh tomatoes, chopped

Orzo and Rice
4   tablespoons (½ stick) unsalted butter
1   cup orzo
2   cups long-grained white rice
4   cups beef or veal stock (page 328), heated to boiling

Heat 2 tablespoons oil in a large nonreactive skillet over medium-high heat. Add lamb and stir until browned on all sides, about 10 minutes. Add more oil as needed. Add onions, garlic, allspice and salt and pepper. Cook, stirring, until onions are tender, 3 to 5 minutes. Add ¼ cup water, reduce heat to medium and simmer for 10 minutes.

Stir in beans and tomato sauce or tomatoes. Add enough water to reach halfway up pan. Increase heat to high until liquid bubbles. Cover, reduce heat to medium and cook, stirring occasionally, until lamb is tender, 20 to 30 minutes.

To cook orzo and rice: In a large saucepan, melt butter over medium-high heat. Add orzo and stir until browned, 10 to 12 minutes.

Add rice and stir until grains are well coated. Add hot stock. When mixture is bubbling, reduce heat to low, cover and simmer until rice absorbs all liquid, about 30 minutes.

Spoon generous amounts of rice into heated soup plates. Ladle stew over rice.

Wine: Château Musar Red Table Wine (Lebanon) or a medium-bodied fruity Merlot

Braised Eggplant Stuffed with Lamb, Pine Nuts & Mint

Serves 4-6

Leftover leg of lamb combined with fresh mint, shallots, garlic and pine nuts becomes a tasty stuffing for eggplants, which are then braised in olive oil and stock. This versatile dish can be served hot, cold or at room temperature. The inspiration for this recipe came from Elizabeth David's *Summer Cooking*.

4	medium-small (10-12 ounces each) eggplants
	Kosher salt
1	cup cubed cooked lamb (about ½ pound)
2	plump garlic cloves
1	plump shallot
3	tablespoons pine nuts
8	fresh mint leaves or 4 fresh basil leaves, plus 2 tablespoons minced fresh, for garnish
4	tablespoons olive oil
	Freshly ground black pepper
1	cup chicken or vegetable stock (page 325 or 330)
½	cup plain yogurt

Place eggplants on a work surface. With a sharp knife, cut a V-shaped wedge, ¾ inch deep, in top of each eggplant. (Discard or save for another dish.) Rub some salt into each eggplant and invert over several layers of paper towels. Let drain for 1 to 2 hours. Rinse and pat dry.

In a food processor fitted with the metal blade, combine lamb, garlic, shallot, pine nuts and mint or basil leaves. Pulse until finely chopped. Add 2 tablespoons oil and salt and pepper; pulse until well blended. Divide among eggplants, thoroughly stuffing each opening.

Pour 2 tablespoons oil into a deep, nonreactive skillet large enough to hold eggplants. Add eggplants, stuffed sides up. Pour stock around eggplants. Tightly cover and cook over medium heat until liquid bubbles, about 5 minutes.

Reduce heat to low and simmer until eggplants are very tender, 30 to 40 minutes.

Carefully remove eggplants with a large spatula or tongs. Place them on a heated platter. With a sharp knife, remove stem ends. Slice each eggplant on an angle into 3 pieces. Serve with a dollop of yogurt and minced fresh mint or basil.

Wine: Jean-Marc Aujoux Fleurie Beaujolais (France: Burgundy) or another fruity Beaujolais

Pork

Roast Loin of Pork with
Black-Eyed Peas, Plum Tomatoes & Rosemary 224

Fennel-Braised Pork Roast with Apples, Endive & Herbs 226

Gingered Pork Loin with Sweet Potatoes & Prunes 228

Braised Pork Chops & Mushrooms in Mustard Cream Sauce 230

Pork Chops Braised with Apples & Cabbage 232

Pork Chops in Savory Plum Sauce 234

Mushroom-Stuffed Pork Chops with Escarole & Onion Sauce 236

Chianti-Braised Pork Chops
Stuffed with Sun-Dried Tomatoes & Ham 238

Choucroute Garni (Braised Alsatian Sauerkraut & Pork) 240

Spicy Pork Stew with Hubbard Squash & Escarole 242

Roast Loin of Pork with Black-Eyed Peas, Plum Tomatoes & Rosemary

Serves 8

THIS PORK LOIN, richly seasoned with fresh rosemary and roasted in foil with tomatoes and black-eyed peas, has solid roots in Southern cooking. It comes from Marcel Desaulniers, chef of The Trellis, a restaurant in Williamsburg, Virginia. Marcel says, "For a final Southern touch, serve some greens steamed with a splash of water and balsamic vinegar as an accompaniment." A special cooking note: Pork loins vary significantly in diameter, so the roasting time varies as well. An instant-read thermometer is essential for this dish, since the cut is not thick enough to accommodate a regular meat thermometer.

1	5-to-6-pound whole boneless pork loin, silverskin and fat removed
4	tablespoons olive oil
	Kosher salt and coarsely ground black pepper
4	cups cooked black-eyed peas
8	whole plum tomatoes, halved lengthwise
2	cups finely chopped yellow onions
1½	cups chicken stock (page 325)
3-4	fresh rosemary sprigs, leaves removed and chopped

Preheat oven to 325 degrees F.

Cut pork loin into 2 equal-sized pieces. Coat each piece with 1 tablespoon oil; season generously with salt and pepper.

Line a shallow baking dish with a large sheet of foil; cover bottom with parchment. Brush parchment with 1 tablespoon oil.

Place pork loin pieces in center of parchment, leaving space between them. Spoon black-eyed peas around pork. Distribute tomatoes and onions evenly over black-eyed peas. Carefully pour stock over all. Sprinkle evenly with rosemary. Season vegetables with more salt and pepper.

Brush another parchment sheet with remaining 1 tablespoon oil. Place, oiled side down, over meat and vegetables. Cover everything with another large sheet of foil and crimp edges around dish to seal.

Bake for 1 hour 10 minutes. Check temperature by inserting an instant-read thermometer directly through foil into center of pork. (Cover hole with another piece of foil.) When pork reaches an internal temperature of 140 degrees, remove from oven.

Let stand, still sealed, at room temperature, for 10 to 15 minutes for pink (145-to-150-degree internal temperature). For medium well-done (160-degree internal temperature), let stand for 20 to 25 minutes. (Pork will stay warm, in its wrapper, for up to 1 hour after removal from oven.)

Remove pork from foil and parchment and slice. Serve pork slices along with some tomato and black-eyed pea mixture.

Wine: Robert Biale Vineyards Zinfandel Napa Valley Aldo's Vineyard (California: Napa Valley) or another complex Zinfandel

Fennel-Braised Pork Roast with Apples, Endive & Herbs

Serves 4-6

THESE SUCCULENT SLICES OF PORK, with their attached ribs, are moist and tender. The sauce, made from onions, endive, apples and fennel, gets a creamy finish from sour cream. This fresh-flavored pork roast is light enough to serve at any time of year.

1	4½-to-5-pound bone-in pork roast from rib end, chine bone removed
2	plump garlic cloves, slivered
2	tablespoons unbleached flour
	Kosher salt and freshly ground black pepper
3	tablespoons olive oil
2	medium-large yellow onions, finely chopped
2	Belgian endives, thinly sliced
2	large apples, peeled, cored and finely chopped
1	large fennel bulb, trimmed and finely chopped, fronds minced
1	tablespoon minced fresh herbs (rosemary, thyme, tarragon)
1	teaspoon ground coriander
½	teaspoon fennel seeds, crushed
¼	teaspoon cayenne pepper
½	cup apple cider
½	cup dry white wine
1	tablespoon packed dark brown sugar
⅔	cup sour cream

Preheat oven to 325 degrees F.

With a sharp knife, make 18 to 20 small slits in pork. Stuff each slit with a sliver of garlic. Place roast on a large sheet of wax paper. Sprinkle flour evenly over meat and rub to coat well. Season generously with salt and pepper. Heat oil in a large cast-iron skillet over high heat. Reserving any seasoned flour that falls from roast, transfer meat to skillet and brown well on all sides, 10 to 14 minutes.

While roast is browning, scatter onions in a large nonreactive Dutch oven or casserole. Add endives, apples and chopped fennel. Toss with reserved seasoned flour.

Place browned roast, bone side down, in casserole. Sprinkle evenly with minced fennel fronds, fresh herbs, coriander, fennel seeds, cayenne and more salt and pepper.

Discard fat from skillet used to brown pork. Add apple cider and wine; cook over high heat until browned particles adhering to skillet are loosened. Pour hot cider mixture around roast.

Tightly cover and braise in oven, basting several times, until internal temperature is 150 degrees on an instant-read thermometer, about 1 hour 20 minutes.

Transfer roast to a carving platter. While roast is resting, finish sauce: Carefully place Dutch oven on stovetop. (If you used a ceramic casserole, transfer apple mixture and juices to a saucepan.) Bring to a boil over high heat. Stir in brown sugar and cook for 4 minutes to reduce somewhat and thicken pan juices. Stir in sour cream and blend; do not allow to boil. Adjust seasonings, adding salt and pepper as needed.

Slice roast and serve with sauce.

Wine: Fiddlehead Cellars Pinot Noir (California: Santa Maria Valley) or a medium-bodied Pinot Noir

Gingered Pork Loin with Sweet Potatoes & Prunes

Serves 6-8

THE COMBINATION OF PORK AND PRUNES is tried and true. We decided to go one step further and roast our pork on a bed of sweet potatoes, another timeless accompaniment for pork roast, and add some ginger, cloves and sage.

Pork and Marinade

1	4-to-5-pound boneless pork loin, silverskin removed
2	cups pitted prunes (12-ounce package)
2	cups dry white wine
½	cup applejack or Calvados
1	large yellow onion, finely diced
2	garlic cloves, minced
1	tablespoon grated fresh ginger
2	whole fresh sage leaves or ¼ teaspoon dried
¼	teaspoon ground cloves

3	large sweet potatoes, peeled and cut into ½-inch-thick slices
¼	cup minced fresh flat-leaf parsley
2	teaspoons minced fresh sage or 1 teaspoon dried
1	teaspoon minced fresh ginger
¼	teaspoon cayenne pepper
2	plump shallots, minced
2	tablespoons olive oil
	Kosher salt and freshly ground white pepper
	Up to 1 cup chicken stock (page 325)

To marinate pork: Place pork and prunes in a nonreactive baking dish or large resealable plastic bag. Add wine and applejack or Calvados; sprinkle evenly with onion, garlic, ginger, sage and cloves. Cover or seal and marinate in refrigerator, turning several times, for 3 to 6 hours.

To prepare roast: Preheat oven to 325 degrees F. Lightly oil a Dutch oven or roasting pan just large enough to hold meat and potatoes.

Fill a large saucepan with salted water and bring to a boil over high heat. Add sweet potatoes; parboil for 5 minutes. Drain thoroughly. Arrange sweet potatoes in pan.

Remove pork from marinade and pat dry; reserve marinade. Place pork, fattier side up, on a work surface. With a very sharp knife, slice evenly halfway into center so that meat opens like a book.

Using a slotted spoon, transfer prunes to a mixing bowl. Blend with parsley, sage, ginger, cayenne and shallots. Evenly stuff roast with mixture. Close roast with a few skewers and use kitchen twine to tie roast together at 3-inch intervals.

Heat oil in a large nonreactive skillet or sauté pan over high heat. Carefully sear pork on all sides, about 10 minutes total.

Place meat, slit side up, over sweet potatoes. Pour marinade over meat. Season generously with salt and white pepper. Add ½ cup stock. Tightly cover and roast until a thermometer inserted into center reads 140 degrees, about 1¼ hours.

Transfer meat to a carving platter and keep warm until internal temperature reaches 150 degrees (pork will be juicy and slightly pink), about 10 minutes. Keep sweet potatoes covered to retain heat, adding more chicken stock if pan juices have evaporated.

Slice pork into ½-inch-thick slices and serve on heated plates with sweet potatoes and pan juices.

Wine: Christom Vineyards Pinot Gris (Oregon: Willamette Valley) or a Tokay Pinot Gris from Alsace

Braised Pork Chops & Mushrooms in Mustard Cream Sauce

Serves 2

THIS LITTLE DISH TAKES FIVE MINUTES to prepare for braising, so it's one of our favorite cold-weather dinners when we're pressed for time but want something nourishing. Pork chops and mushrooms are braised in a fragrant mixture of stock and herbs. The pan juices are made into a tangy sauce with Dijon mustard and sour cream added.

2	1½-to-2-inch-thick loin pork chops
2	tablespoons unbleached flour
3	tablespoons olive oil, plus more if needed
4-5	ounces cremini or portobello mushrooms, thinly sliced
1	plump shallot, minced
1	plump garlic clove, minced
1	cup beef or veal stock (page 328)
1	teaspoon minced fresh rosemary or ½ teaspoon dried
	Kosher salt and freshly ground black pepper
¼	cup low-fat sour cream
1	rounded tablespoon Dijon mustard

Preheat oven to 325 degrees F.

Evenly sprinkle one side of pork chops with 1 tablespoon flour. Rub to coat; repeat on second side, using remaining 1 tablespoon flour.

Heat 3 tablespoons oil in a medium-sized ovenproof skillet over high heat. Brown chops on both sides, 3 to 4 minutes. Transfer to a plate.

Reduce heat to medium and add more oil if needed. Add mushrooms, shallot and garlic to skillet, cover and cook over medium heat until mushrooms release their liquid, 3 to 4 minutes. Stir in stock, rosemary and salt and pepper. When liquid begins to bubble, add pork chops and baste well.

Cover skillet with a tight-fitting lid or foil. Braise in oven until chops are tender, about 1¼ hours. Transfer chops to a heated plate and keep warm. Carefully return skillet to stove-top. Stir in sour cream and mustard. Whisk over medium heat until sauce is blended and hot; do not boil. Add more pepper, if you wish.

Divide chops among heated plates and spoon over sauce.

Wine: Storrs Winery Chardonnay Santa Cruz Mountains Meyley Vineyard (California: Santa Cruz Mountains) or a medium-bodied, fruity Chardonnay from California or France

Pork Chops Braised with Apples & Cabbage

Serves 4

IN THIS VARIATION ON A CLASSIC PREPARATION, pork, apples and cabbage are slowly braised together in applejack and chicken stock with a touch of ginger. A final finish of sour cream and mustard with a little nutmeg creates a thick, delicious sauce for the tender chops. Add some buttered noodles for a complete meal. (See photograph, page 94.)

¼	cup unbleached flour
4	1½-to-2-inch-thick center-cut loin pork chops
3	tablespoons vegetable oil, plus more if needed
1	medium-sized yellow onion, finely chopped
2	plump garlic cloves, minced
2	tart apples, cored and thinly sliced
3	cups finely chopped cabbage
1	teaspoon dried tarragon
½	teaspoon ground ginger
	Kosher salt and freshly ground black pepper
⅓	cup applejack or Calvados
1	cup chicken stock (page 325)
¼	cup sour cream
1	tablespoon Dijon mustard
⅛	teaspoon freshly grated nutmeg

Preheat oven to 325 degrees F.

Pour flour into a shallow soup plate. Carefully coat chops in flour; set aside on a rack.

Pour 3 tablespoons oil into a large, heavy skillet with a tight-fitting lid and heat over medium-high heat. Add pork chops and brown on both sides, 3 to 4 minutes. Transfer pork chops to a plate.

Pour in more oil if needed; add onion and garlic and cook over low heat, stirring occasionally, to soften, about 2 minutes. Add apples and increase heat to high. Cook, stirring, just until apples lose their whiteness, 1 to 2 minutes. Add cabbage, tarragon, ginger and salt and pepper. Stir together for 1 minute.

Add applejack or Calvados and stir to loosen any browned bits adhering to skillet. Add stock and cook until mixture begins to bubble. Place pork chops over cabbage mixture, spooning some liquid and cabbage over chops. Tightly cover.

Place skillet in oven and braise, basting from time to time, until chops are fork-tender, about 1¼ hours.

Remove skillet from oven. Place chops on heated plates.

Whisk sour cream, mustard and nutmeg into cabbage and apple mixture; heat until hot, but do not boil. Adjust seasonings. Serve with chops.

Wine: Domaine Zind-Humbrecht Gewürztraminer Alsace Herrenweg Turckheim (France: Alsace) or a complex Gewürztraminer from France

Pork Chops in Savory Plum Sauce

Serves 4

THICK PORK CHOPS ARE BRAISED in a sparkling sauce of dark plums and applesauce with nuances of nutmeg, cinnamon, cloves, cider vinegar and horseradish. This delicious dish is adapted from *John Schumacher's New Prague Hotel Cookbook*. John's exceptional Minnesota inn has fed us remarkably well over the years.

1	cup unsweetened applesauce
¼	teaspoon freshly grated nutmeg
¼	teaspoon ground cinnamon
¼	teaspoon ground cloves
1	tablespoon cider vinegar
1	tablespoon fresh orange juice
2	teaspoons fresh lemon juice
1	tablespoon honey
1	teaspoon prepared horseradish
1	cup thinly sliced dark, ripe plums
4	2-inch-thick center-cut pork chops
	Kosher salt and freshly ground black pepper
2	tablespoons canola oil, plus more if needed

Preheat oven to 350 degrees F.

In a medium bowl, blend together applesauce and spices. Add vinegar, juices, honey, horseradish and plums. Blend well and set aside.

Thoroughly season pork chops with salt and pepper. Heat 2 tablespoons oil in a large nonreactive skillet over high heat. Brown chops well on both sides in batches, adding more oil as needed, 4 to 6 minutes. Transfer chops to a baking dish just large enough to hold them in a single layer.

Add 1 cup water to skillet and deglaze over high heat, scraping up any browned particles. Boil until water is reduced by half, 3 to 5 minutes. Add applesauce mixture and stir until sauce comes to a boil. Pour evenly over chops.

Tightly cover. Bake until chops are fork-tender, about 1¼ hours.

Divide chops among heated plates. Spoon generous amounts of sauce over each.

Wine: Ridge Petite Sirah Napa County York Creek (California: Napa Valley) or a tannic, full-bodied, peppery Syrah

Mushroom-Stuffed Pork Chops with Escarole & Onion Sauce

Serves 4

THESE THICK CHOPS are stuffed with our variation on the traditional French *duxelles*, or mushroom, stuffing. Carrots and herbs add color and flavor. The chops are then braised with onions, escarole and chicken stock. Serve with mashed potatoes and as-paragus for a satisfying supper.

4	1½-to-2-inch-thick center-cut loin pork chops
4	tablespoons olive oil, plus more as needed
1¾	cups finely chopped mushrooms, such as portobello, shiitake and cremini
2	medium carrots, finely chopped
1	plump garlic clove, minced
1	plump shallot, minced
1	dried red chile
2	teaspoons soy sauce
¼	cup fine dry bread crumbs
1	tablespoon unsalted butter
2	tablespoons minced fresh flat-leaf parsley
1	tablespoon minced fresh tarragon or 1½ teaspoons dried
1	tablespoon minced fresh chives
	Kosher salt and freshly ground black pepper
¼	cup unbleached flour
2	cups chicken stock (page 325)
1½	cups finely diced yellow onions
1	bay leaf
1	whole clove
2½	cups torn escarole

Preheat oven to 325 degrees F.

To make a pocket, cut through each chop so as to almost butterfly large, meaty part.

Pour 2 tablespoons oil in a medium nonstick skillet and heat until hot. Stir in mushrooms, carrots, garlic, shallot, chile and soy sauce. Cover and cook over medium-low heat until mushrooms are soft and release their juices, 3 to 4 minutes. Stir in bread crumbs, butter, parsley, tarragon, chives and salt and pepper. Remove skillet from heat; let stuffing cool.

Divide stuffing among chops, firmly packing it into each pocket. Pour flour into a shallow soup plate. Carefully coat chops in flour, keeping one hand on the pocket opening to hold in stuffing. Set chops aside on a rack.

Lightly coat a cast-iron skillet with remaining 2 tablespoons oil; heat over medium-high heat. Brown chops on both sides, 3 to 4 minutes. Quickly remove to a large platter. Add stock and cook over high heat until bubbling. Stir in onions. Return chops to skillet and baste with sauce. Sprinkle generously with salt and pepper; add bay leaf and clove. Cover skillet with a tight-fitting lid and place in oven.

Braise for 45 minutes.

Stir in escarole and cook until pork is fork-tender, about 30 minutes more.

Transfer chops to heated plates. Place skillet over high heat and cook for 1 to 2 minutes to reduce and somewhat thicken sauce. Remove bay leaf. Adjust seasonings and garnish chops generously with sauce.

Wine: Bernadus Winery Chardonnay (California: Monterey County) or another complex Chardonnay

Chianti-Braised Pork Chops Stuffed with Sun-Dried Tomatoes & Ham

Serves 4

LOTS OF HERBS, sun-dried tomatoes and smoked ham combine in a distinctive stuffing for these chops. After we braise the pork chops in red wine, we finish the sauce with a touch of tomato.

4	1½-to-2-inch-thick center-cut loin pork chops
4	tablespoons olive oil, plus more as needed
2	large oil-packed sun-dried tomatoes, minced
1	dried red chile, crumbled
1	plump garlic clove, minced
1	plump shallot, minced
⅓	cup finely diced smoked ham or prosciutto
1	tablespoon unsalted butter
2	tablespoons minced fresh flat-leaf parsley
1	tablespoon minced fresh basil
1	teaspoon minced fresh oregano or ½ teaspoon dried
½	cup fine dry bread crumbs
	Kosher salt and freshly ground black pepper
⅓	cup unbleached flour
1	750-ml bottle Chianti or other red wine
1	rounded tablespoon tomato paste

Preheat oven to 325 degrees F.

To make a pocket, cut through each chop so as to almost butterfly large, meaty part.

Heat 2 tablespoons oil in a large cast-iron skillet until hot. Add sun-dried tomatoes, chile, garlic and shallot. Cook, stirring, over medium heat until shallot softens, 2 to 3 minutes. Add ham or prosciutto, butter, parsley, basil and oregano; stir together until butter melts. Remove skillet from heat.

Scrape sun-dried tomato mixture from skillet into a bowl and mix with bread crumbs. Season with salt and pepper. Divide stuffing among chops, pushing stuffing into each pocket.

Pour flour into a soup plate. Carefully coat chops in flour; set aside on a rack.

Add 2 tablespoons oil to skillet in which sun-dried tomato mixture was cooked and heat over medium-high heat. Brown chops on both sides, about 2 minutes, adding more oil if needed.

Add 2½ cups wine to skillet and cook over high heat until bubbling. Cover skillet with a tight-fitting lid and place in oven. Braise, basting occasionally and adding more wine if needed, until chops are fork-tender, about 1¼ hours.

Transfer chops to heated plates. Carefully place skillet over high heat and whisk in tomato paste. Simmer briskly for 2 minutes, just to thicken slightly. Adjust seasonings. Spoon sauce over chops.

Wine: Isole E Olena Chianti Classico (Italy: Tuscany) or another rich Tuscan Chianti Classico

Choucroute Garni

(Braised Alsatian Sauerkraut & Pork)

Serves 8-10

Choucroute garni, or sauerkraut accompanied by meats, can be an extraordinary dish, especially when it's prepared with a smoked pork loin and a wide variety of other parts of the pig. This recipe simplifies things, utilizing meats that are easier to obtain. But the essential succulent flavors are all there. Some good Dijon mustard and chilled Alsatian Riesling to accompany it are all you need. (See photograph, page 90.)

6	cups sauerkraut
3	tablespoons unsalted butter
1	4-pound boneless pork loin, silverskin removed
	Kosher salt and freshly ground black pepper
2	pounds smoked sausage, such as kielbasa, cut into 3-inch lengths
⅔	pound bacon, diced
2	yellow onions, finely chopped
2	plump garlic cloves, minced
2	teaspoons caraway seeds
1	teaspoon dried thyme
¼	teaspoon ground coriander
1	750-ml bottle Alsatian Riesling
1	cup chicken stock (page 325), plus more if needed
1	tablespoon juniper berries, crushed
1	bay leaf
6	large white potatoes, peeled, thickly sliced, boiled and buttered
	Dijon mustard, for serving

Preheat oven to 350 degrees F.

Place sauerkraut in a colander and rinse thoroughly for several minutes. Squeeze dry and reserve.

Melt butter in a large cast-iron skillet over high heat. Add pork loin and sear quickly, browning on all sides, about 5 minutes. Transfer to a large plate and season with salt and pepper. Sear smoked sausage in same fashion and set aside. Reserve pan drippings.

In a Dutch oven over low heat, cook bacon until fat is partially rendered; bacon will still be limp. Stir in onions, garlic, caraway, thyme, coriander and 2 teaspoons black pepper. Cover and cook over low heat until onions are tender, 10 to 15 minutes.

Add reserved sauerkraut, 2 cups wine, stock, juniper berries and bay leaf. Cover and cook over medium heat until liquid bubbles, 5 to 10 minutes. Remove from heat.

Place pork loin and sausage on sauerkraut. Spoon some of reserved pan drippings over meat. Carefully move some of sauerkraut mixture over meat. Add remaining wine to sauerkraut.

Tightly cover and bake for 1¼ hours.

Add more stock if sauerkraut is dry. Continue baking until pork is fork-tender, 20 to 30 minutes more.

To serve, arrange slices of pork and sausages on a heated platter. Garnish with sauerkraut and potatoes. Serve with Dijon mustard on the side.

Wine: Pierre Sparr Riesling Alsace Carte d'Or (France: Alsace) or another rich Riesling from Alsace

Spicy Pork Stew with Hubbard Squash & Escarole

Serves 6-8

THIS PORK STEW WITH CUBES OF WINTER SQUASH has many of the flavors common to Southwestern cooking—garlic, cumin and chiles, along with oregano and a dash of clove. This tomato-sauced dish is handsome when served over either rice or black beans.

½	cup unbleached flour
3	pounds boneless pork shoulder, cut into 2-inch cubes
	Up to 4 tablespoons vegetable oil, plus more if needed
1	cup finely diced yellow onions
1	large green bell pepper, coarsely diced
2	plump garlic cloves, minced
2	dried red chiles, crumbled
1	teaspoon ground oregano
1	teaspoon ground cardamom
½	teaspoon ground cumin
2	whole cloves
1	28-ounce can crushed tomatoes
2	tablespoons red wine vinegar
	Kosher salt and freshly ground white pepper
2½	pounds Hubbard or butternut squash, seeded, peeled and cut into 1½-inch cubes
3	cups coarsely chopped escarole
	Tabasco sauce
1	bunch scallions, trimmed to include 1 inch of green, chopped
⅓	cup minced fresh cilantro

Preheat oven to 350 degrees F.

Combine flour and pork cubes in a paper bag and toss until meat is lightly coated. Heat 2 tablespoons oil in a large nonreactive Dutch oven over medium-high heat. Working in batches, brown meat on all sides, transferring it to a large platter or bowl as you go along. Add more oil as you need it.

When meat is browned, add onions, green pepper, garlic and chiles to pan. Cook, stirring, over medium heat until onions soften, 3 to 5 minutes. Add herbs and spices and stir for 1 minute to release flavors. Return meat and meat juices to pot. Add tomatoes and enough water to bring liquid to top of meat. Add vinegar. Season generously with salt and white pepper. Bring liquid to a boil.

Tightly cover pot and bake for 1 hour.

Stir in squash. Cover and cook for 50 minutes.

Add escarole and cook until meat and squash are fork-tender, about 25 minutes more.

Remove pot from oven. Stir in Tabasco to taste. Add scallions and cilantro and serve in soup plates.

Wine: Silverado Vineyards Cabernet Sauvignon (California: Napa Valley) or another complex, moderately tannic Cabernet Sauvignon

Grains, Beans & Breads

Covered Risotto with Wild Mushrooms & Radicchio 246

Covered Risotto with Spicy Sausage, Sun-Dried Tomatoes & Escarole 248

Covered Green Risotto 250

Casserole of Brown Rice in Spanish Sauce 251

Steamed Spicy Grits Pudding 252

Creamy Polenta with Mascarpone 254

Lentils on Rice (*Im-Jud' Dara*) 255

Red Beans with Spicy Sausage 256

Five-Bean Chili 258

Slow-Baked Barbecued Beans 260

Stew of Dried Lima Beans & Tomatoes with Sage, Basil & Garlic 262

Braised Flageolets with Herbs, Shallots & Lemon 263

Pureed White Beans 264

Silky Farfel with Peas & Carrots 265

Daufuskie Island Brown Bread 266

Under-Cover Corn Bread 267

Lydie's *Pain de Mie* (Pullman Bread) 268

Covered Risotto with Wild Mushrooms & Radicchio

Serves 8

AWAY WITH THE TEDIUM of constant stirring! You can make delightfully creamy risotto in a covered casserole right in the oven. Radicchio adds a pleasing counterpoint to the woodland flavors of mushrooms. We thank Patricia Wells, who alerted us to the possibilities of baking risotto in her book, *Trattoria* (William Morrow, 1993). See photograph, page 88.

1½	ounces dried porcini mushrooms, rinsed
5	cups chicken stock (page 325), plus more if needed, heated to a simmer
4	tablespoons (½ stick) unsalted butter
¼	pound fresh shiitake, portobello or any cultivated exotic mushrooms, thinly sliced
2	teaspoons minced fresh tarragon or 1 teaspoon dried
1	plump shallot, minced
2	tablespoons olive oil
1½	cups Arborio rice
1¼	cups coarsely shredded radicchio
½	teaspoon kosher salt
½	teaspoon freshly ground white pepper
¾	cup freshly grated Parmesan cheese, plus more for passing at table
¼	teaspoon freshly grated nutmeg

Preheat oven to 400 degrees F. Thoroughly oil a 2-quart baking dish.

Combine dried mushrooms with 5 cups stock in a small saucepan and let stand, covered, for 20 minutes.

Using a strainer, scoop up softened mushrooms and press their liquid back into pan. Coarsely chop mushrooms and reserve. Strain mushroom stock through a triple thickness of dampened cheesecloth to remove sand. Measure liquid, adding enough stock to measure 5 cups. Set aside and keep warm.

Melt butter in a large skillet over medium heat. Add fresh mushrooms, tarragon and shallot; cover and cook over low heat until mushrooms are tender, about 5 minutes. Stir in chopped dried mushrooms and cook, uncovered, for 2 minutes. Set aside.

Heat oil in a large saucepan over medium heat. Add rice and cook, stirring well, for 2 minutes. Add stock mixture and cook over high heat for 3 to 4 minutes. Remove from heat, stir in mushroom mixture, radicchio, salt, white pepper and half of cheese.

Pour mixture into baking dish; sprinkle evenly with remaining cheese and nutmeg. Tightly cover and bake until rice is cooked through and has absorbed most of liquid, 30 to 40 minutes; risotto should be creamy.

Serve in heated bowls with more cheese.

Wine: Flora Springs Wine Co. Sangiovese (California: Napa Valley) or another rich Sangiovese from California or Tuscany

Covered Risotto with Spicy Sausage, Sun-Dried Tomatoes & Escarole

Serves 4 for a main dish, 8 as a first course

THIS COLORFUL CASSEROLE IS A MEAL IN ITSELF. The sausage-flavored rice is given color by bitter escarole and sun-dried tomatoes.

3	tablespoons olive oil
1	pound hot Italian sausage, cut into ¾-inch-thick slices
6	oil-packed sun-dried tomatoes, drained and finely diced
1	small yellow onion, finely diced
1½	cups Arborio rice
5	cups chicken stock (page 325), plus more if needed, heated to a simmer
1	cup coarsely chopped escarole
½	teaspoon kosher salt
½	teaspoon freshly ground white pepper
1	cup freshly grated Parmesan cheese, plus more for passing at table
¼	teaspoon freshly grated nutmeg
	Fresh basil, shredded, for garnish

Preheat oven to 400 degrees F. Thoroughly oil a 2-quart baking dish.

Heat 1 tablespoon oil in a large cast-iron skillet, add sausage and cook, stirring, over medium heat until browned. Using a slotted spoon, remove sausage and place in a small bowl. Add sun-dried tomatoes to sausage and set aside.

Heat 2 tablespoons oil in a heavy saucepan, add onion and cook, stirring, over medium heat until onion begins to soften, 3 to 5 minutes. Add rice and cook, stirring, for 2 minutes. Add 5 cups hot stock and cook over high heat until mixture begins to boil, 3 to 4 minutes. Remove from heat, stir in sausage mixture, escarole, salt, white pepper and ½ cup cheese.

Pour mixture into prepared baking dish; sprinkle evenly with remaining ½ cup cheese and nutmeg. Tightly cover with foil and bake until rice is cooked through and absorbs most of liquid, 30 to 40 minutes; risotto should be creamy.

Serve in heated soup plates with more cheese and a sprinkling of basil.

Wine: T-Vine Cellars Zinfandel (California: Napa Valley) or Giuseppe Cortese Barbaresco Rabajà (Italy: Piedmont) or a medium-light, fruity Zinfandel

Covered Green Risotto

Serves 6 to 8

FRESH HERBS AND GREENS GIVE GREAT COLOR and flavor to this delicious risotto. We like to serve this as a first course or as a main dish.

1	cup minced fresh flat-leaf parsley
1	cup minced fresh mixed herbs (tarragon, basil, thyme, chives)
1	cup finely chopped arugula and escarole
1	cup finely chopped chard and kale
5	cups chicken or vegetable stock (page 325 or 330)
2	tablespoons olive oil
1	dried red chile, crumbled
1	plump shallot, minced
1½	cups Arborio rice
½	teaspoon kosher salt
½	teaspoon freshly ground white pepper
1	cup freshly grated Parmesan cheese, plus more for garnish
¼	teaspoon freshly grated nutmeg

Preheat oven to 400 degrees F. Thoroughly oil a 2-quart baking dish.

Combine herbs and greens in a large bowl. Mix well and set aside.

Pour stock into a medium saucepan and bring to a boil.

Meanwhile, heat oil in a heavy saucepan over medium heat. Stir in chile, shallot and rice; cook, stirring, for 2 minutes to soften shallot. Add boiling stock to rice, stir and cook until mixture boils again. Remove from heat and stir in herb mixture, salt, white pepper and ½ cup cheese. Pour into baking dish; sprinkle evenly with remaining ½ cup cheese and nutmeg.

Tightly cover and bake until rice absorbs liquid and is cooked through, 30 to 40 minutes; rice should be creamy.

Serve in heated bowls with more cheese.

Wine: Bonny Doon Vineyard Le Sophiste Santa Cruz Mountains (California: Santa Cruz Mountains) or a complex white wine from the Rhône (France)

Casserole of Brown Rice in Spanish Sauce

Serves 6-8

THIS RICE DISH COMBINES TWO OF OUR FAVORITES—brown rice and an oniony tomato sauce. A suggestion of cumin melds beautifully with the flavors of the green olives.

2	medium-sized sweet onions, quartered
3	scallions, trimmed to include 1 inch of green, cut in half
2	plump garlic cloves, peeled
3	tablespoons olive oil
1	dried red chile
1	tablespoon hot Hungarian paprika
2	teaspoons ground cumin
1½	cups brown rice, preferably jasmine (see Sources, page 335)
1½	cups tomato puree (page 324) or canned crushed tomatoes
1	teaspoon herbes de Provence or mixture of dried rosemary, savory, thyme, basil and crumbled bay leaf
¼	cup chopped fresh flat-leaf parsley
½	cup sliced pimiento-stuffed green olives
	Kosher salt and freshly ground black pepper

Combine onions, scallions and garlic in a food processor fitted with the metal blade; pulse until finely chopped.

In a medium-sized heavy saucepan, heat oil over medium heat. Add chile, paprika, cumin and onion mixture; cook, stirring often, until onions soften, about 5 minutes. Stir in rice; stir in tomato puree or crushed tomatoes, herbes de Provence and 2½ cups water. Bring to a boil. Tightly cover, reduce heat to low, and simmer for 45 minutes.

Stir rice, adding ½ cup more water if rice is dry. Continue to cook for 10 minutes.

If rice appears dry, add ¼ cup more water. Turn heat off and let rice stand for 10 minutes more.

Stir in parsley, olives and salt and pepper. Serve immediately.

Wine: Millbrook Winery Chardonnay (New York: Hudson River) or a medium-bodied, fruity red wine from Spain

Steamed Spicy Grits Pudding

Serves 6

THIS SAVORY RING-SHAPED steamed pudding is a big hit whenever we serve it. The grits are made rich-tasting by the addition of onions, peppers and cheese. We like to use yellow grits from The Fowler's Milling Company (page 335), but white grits are fine too.

3	tablespoons vegetable oil
½	cup finely diced red onion
⅓	cup finely diced red bell pepper
1	fresh jalapeño chile, minced
1	tablespoon chile powder
½	teaspoon freshly ground white pepper
4	cups chicken or vegetable stock (page 325 or 330)
1	teaspoon kosher salt
1	cup grits
1	cup grated jalapeño jack cheese
4	large eggs
2	tablespoons minced fresh cilantro
1	cup store-bought salsa, for garnish

Thoroughly butter an 8-inch springform pan with a tube insert or a 6-cup ring mold. Set a steaming rack or basket into a wide pot. Fill pot with water to reach just to bottom of rack.

Heat oil in a medium skillet. Add onion, red pepper and jalapeño; cook, stirring, over medium heat until softened, 2 to 4 minutes. Stir in chile powder and white pepper; cook, stirring constantly, for 1 minute. Remove from heat and set aside.

In a medium saucepan, bring stock and salt to a rolling boil over high heat. Reduce heat to medium-low, and very slowly stir in grits; cook until mixture begins to bubble. Cover, reduce heat and cook, stirring from time to time, for 10 to 12 minutes.

Remove cover and stir grits thoroughly, taking care to scrape bottom and sides of pot. Add cheese and stir vigorously until melted. Beat in eggs, one at a time. Stir in cilantro and onion mixture.

Scrape mixture into pan or mold. Cover tightly with foil, allowing center hole to remain exposed. (You can refrigerate pudding for up to 6 hours at this point; bring to room temperature for 1 hour before cooking.)

Place pudding on rack in pot and tightly cover. Bring to a boil over high heat. When you see some steam escaping, reduce heat to low. Steam pudding until a skewer inserted into center comes out clean, about 1¼ hours. When pudding is done, remove from pot and cool, uncovered, on a rack for 15 minutes.

To serve, loosen sides and carefully lift pudding from ring. Or you can invert a large serving plate over pudding. Protecting your hands with oven mitts, hold both together and tip upside down. If pudding does not come out, run a sharp knife around it and invert again. Serve in large wedges, garnished with salsa.

Wine: Lorinon Tempranillo (Spain: Rioja) or another medium-bodied, fruity red wine from Spain

Creamy Polenta with Mascarpone

Serves 6

WHEN OUR JANUARY/FEBRUARY 1995 issue of *Cook's Illustrated* arrived, we had already been experimenting with the covered cooking of polenta, a cornmeal pudding that is traditionally made by boiling the cornmeal and stirring it constantly until it becomes creamy and smooth. In the magazine was Sarah Fritschner's excellent article on making polenta in a double boiler. Aha! Our problem was that we weren't cooking it long enough. Now we prepare splendid, creamy polenta with relatively little time spent stirring. You can serve it with creamy mascarpone, as we do here. Or you might wish to serve it without the mascarpone, generously covered with Ragout of Mushrooms, Shallots & Herbs (page 280) or dusted with freshly grated Parmesan.

6	cups chicken or vegetable stock (page 325 or 330), heated to boiling
1	teaspoon kosher salt, plus more to taste
⅛	teaspoon freshly ground white pepper, plus more to taste
1⅔	cups cornmeal (not finely ground)
2	tablespoons unsalted butter
⅔	cup mascarpone cheese
2	tablespoons minced fresh basil or chives, for garnish

Fill bottom of a double boiler with water close to but not touching top pan. Bring to a boil over high heat. Reduce heat to low so that water simmers very slowly. Pour boiling stock and 1 teaspoon salt and ⅛ teaspoon white pepper into top of double boiler. Slowly add cornmeal, whisking vigorously to avoid lumps. Tightly cover and cook, whisking vigorously every 10 minutes, until polenta is very creamy and tender, 1 to 1¼ hours. Stir in butter. Taste and adjust seasonings, adding salt and white pepper if needed.

Divide polenta among heated soup plates. Spoon mascarpone over center of each, dividing evenly, sprinkle with basil or chives and serve.

Wine: Massolino Vigna Rionda Barolo (Italy: Piedmont)

Lentils on Rice

(Im-Jud ' Dara)

Serves 4-6

OUR FRIENDS HELEN AND WEDAD SHAHEEN have been preparing this simple Syrian stew of lentils, rice and onions for more than 50 years. What was once served to save money is now chic and stylish—even politically correct. Warm or cold, this dish is best with a generous helping of yogurt and a lavish sprinkling of cilantro. To make a soup from it, brown cubes of lamb and add the leftover lentils and rice to some chicken stock.

½ cup olive or vegetable oil
1 large yellow onion, finely chopped
1 cup brown or green lentils, rinsed
1 cup long-grain white rice
Kosher salt and freshly ground black pepper
Minced fresh cilantro and mint and
good-quality yogurt, for garnish

Heat oil in a small skillet over medium heat. Add onion and sauté, stirring often, until light gold, 12 to 18 minutes. Set aside.

Combine lentils and 4 cups water in a large saucepan; bring to a boil over high heat. Reduce heat to medium-low, cover and simmer briskly for 10 minutes.

Stir in rice and onions with their cooking oil; stir in salt and pepper. Cover and cook over low heat, stirring occasionally and adding more water if needed, until rice and lentils are very tender, 25 to 30 minutes.

Serve hot, at room temperature or cold. If serving at room temperature, we place a doubled-over clean dish towel under the lid to absorb moisture as rice and lentils cool.

Garnish with herbs and yogurt.

Wine: Joseph Phelps Vineyards Grenache Rosé California Vin du Mistral (California: Napa Valley) or a full-bodied rosé from Provence

Red Beans with Spicy Sausage

Serves 6-8

THIS SPICY STEW OF RED BEANS, smoked ham and hot sausage is easy to prepare. There's just a hint of tomato in the sauce. If you prefer the dish to be soupy, monitor the water content while it cooks, adding more liquid if the stew becomes too dry. Serve with buttered jasmine rice and Under-Cover Corn Bread (page 267) on the side.

½ pound dried red kidney beans
4 tablespoons vegetable oil
1 cup finely diced onions
½ cup chopped celery
1 cup finely diced green bell pepper
4 plump garlic cloves, minced
2 dried red chiles, crumbled
1 1½-pound smoked ham hock
2 cups tomato puree (page 324) or canned crushed tomatoes
2 bay leaves
2 teaspoons fresh thyme or 1 teaspoon dried
1 teaspoon freshly ground white pepper
½ teaspoon freshly ground black pepper
1 pound andouille or other smoked sausage, cut into ½-inch-thick slices
1 teaspoon Tabasco sauce, plus more to taste
Kosher salt
4 scallions, trimmed to include 1 inch of green
¼ cup minced fresh flat-leaf parsley, plus more for garnish

The night before, cover beans with water in a large bowl. Soak overnight; drain and rinse.

Pour 3 tablespoons oil in a Dutch oven and heat until hot. Add onions, celery, green pepper, garlic and chiles. Cook, stirring, over medium heat until nearly tender, 8 to 10 minutes.

Add beans, ham hock, tomato puree or crushed tomatoes, bay leaves, thyme and white and black peppers; stir in 3 cups water. Bring to a boil. Reduce heat to low, cover and simmer for 1 hour, adding more water as needed.

Meanwhile, heat remaining 1 tablespoon oil over medium heat. Add sausage slices and cook until lightly browned. Add sausage to bean mixture; stir in 1 teaspoon Tabasco and salt. Continue cooking until hock and beans are tender, about 1 hour more. Adjust seasonings, adding more Tabasco and salt if desired.

Remove ham hock from beans and slice meat. Return meat to beans and stir in scallions and ¼ cup parsley. Remove and discard bay leaves. Garnish with more parsley.

Wine: Georges Duboeuf Régnié Beaujolais (France: Burgundy) or Carchello Mourvèdre (Spain: Jumilla) or a full-bodied Côtes du Rhône (France)

Five-Bean Chili

Serves 8

WHAT COULD BE HEARTIER AND MORE COLORFUL than a blend of black, red, purple and yellow dried beans cooked together with a variety of fresh sweet and hot peppers? We've piqued our tomato-based sauce with a generous addition of cumin and blended chili powder to give it a Southwestern touch. Serve this with a big salad and some toothsome bread. If you aren't feeding a crowd, rest assured that leftovers freeze beautifully.

1	cup dried black beans
½	cup dried kidney beans
½	cup dried pinto beans
½	cup dried black-eyed peas
½	cup dried Anasazi or Jacob's cattle beans
3	tablespoons olive oil
1	large green bell pepper, seeded, deribbed and diced
1	large red bell pepper, seeded, deribbed and diced
3-4	fresh hot chiles, seeded and thinly sliced
1	jumbo Spanish onion, coarsely diced
1	large red onion, coarsely diced
2	carrots, thinly sliced
2	celery stalks, thinly sliced
2	plump garlic cloves, minced
2	teaspoons blended chili powder
2	teaspoons ground cumin
½	teaspoon dried oregano
½	teaspoon freshly ground white pepper
½	teaspoon freshly ground black pepper
1	bay leaf
4	cups vegetable stock (page 330) or water, plus more if needed
1	28-ounce can crushed tomatoes
	Kosher salt and freshly ground black pepper
	Chopped fresh cilantro, chopped red onion, sour cream and grated Cheddar cheese, for garnish

Rinse all beans, discarding any damaged ones. In a large saucepan, combine beans and water to cover; place over high heat until water comes to a rolling boil. Cover, remove from heat and let stand for 1 hour. Drain and set aside.

In a 5-quart Dutch oven, heat oil over low heat. Stir in green and red peppers, chiles, onions, carrots, celery and garlic. Cover and cook, stirring from time to time, over medium heat until peppers begin to soften and vegetable juices begin to bubble, about 10 minutes. Stir in chili powder, cumin, oregano, white and black peppers and bay leaf. Add beans, 4 cups stock or water and tomatoes. Increase heat to high and cook until liquid begins to bubble.

Cover tightly, reduce heat to low and simmer, stirring from time to time, until beans are very tender, about 1 hour. If chili appears to be drying out, add more stock or water as necessary.

Season with salt and pepper; discard bay leaf.

Serve chili in heated bowls garnished with cilantro, red onion, sour cream and Cheddar cheese.

Wine: Oxford Landing Merlot (southern Australia) or Mitchelton Shiraz (Australia: Victoria) or another rich Shiraz from Australia

Slow-Baked Barbecued Beans

Serves 12-16

THESE BEANS SIMMER EVER SO SLOWLY in a thick, zesty sauce that has a hint of smoke and a touch of heat. The dish is especially good for a buffet party. To make it, you need a pot that holds about 6 quarts. If you have a large bean pot with a tight-fitting cover, use it. Leftovers freeze beautifully.

2	pounds Great Northern beans
3-4	pounds smoked ham hocks
2½	cups finely diced yellow onions (about 4 medium)
3	plump garlic cloves, minced
1	tablespoon kosher salt
1	tablespoon dry mustard
1	tablespoon ground medium-hot chile powder
2	teaspoons dried thyme
2	teaspoons coarsely ground black pepper
1	teaspoon freshly ground white pepper
1	teaspoon ground allspice
4	cups tomato puree (page 324) or canned crushed tomatoes
2	tablespoons tomato paste
1	cup maple syrup
1	cup packed dark brown sugar
⅔	cup dark molasses
2	bay leaves

Place beans in a large soup pot; add water to cover beans by at least 3 inches. Add ham hocks, tightly cover and bring to a boil over high heat. Reduce heat to low and simmer, adding water as needed to keep beans covered, until beans are tender but not mushy, 1½ to 2½ hours.

Remove ham hocks and set aside. Drain cooked beans, reserving cooking liquid. When ham hocks are cool enough to handle, carefully remove meat from bones and dice into small pieces.

Preheat oven to 275 degrees F. Thoroughly oil a 6-quart bean pot or Dutch oven fitted with a tight lid.

Place one-fourth of beans in pot; scatter some of onions, garlic and diced ham on top. Repeat until all of beans are in pot, ending with onions and ham on top layer.

In a large bowl, blend together salt, mustard, chile powder, thyme, black and white peppers and allspice. Whisk in tomato puree or crushed tomatoes, tomato paste, maple syrup, brown sugar, molasses and 1 cup reserved bean liquid. Pour mixture over beans. Place bay leaves on top. Cover pot and bake for 6½ hours. Add some of remaining bean liquid as needed, if beans look too dry.

Increase oven temperature to 375 degrees. Remove cover, discard bay leaves and cook beans, uncovered, until bubbling, about 30 minutes. Serve hot.

Wine: Luigi Coppo Dolcetto d'Alba (Italy: Piedmont), served slightly chilled, or another medium-bodied, fruity Dolcetto from Piedmont

Stew of Dried Lima Beans & Tomatoes with Sage, Basil & Garlic

Serves 4-6

STEWED LIMA BEANS AND TOMATOES, seasoned with garlic, basil and lemon, makes a great dish on its own or a side dish for lamb or roasted chicken.

1	whole clove
1	large yellow onion
1	pound dried lima beans, rinsed
3	tablespoons olive oil
1	large Spanish onion, finely chopped
3	plump garlic cloves, minced
1½	teaspoons ground sage
2	teaspoons fresh lemon juice
1	28-ounce can plum tomatoes with their juices
	Kosher salt and freshly ground black pepper
⅓	cup minced fresh flat-leaf parsley
¼	cup shredded fresh basil

Push clove into onion. In a large nonreactive saucepan, combine whole onion and lima beans. Add enough cold water to cover by 2 inches. Cover, bring to a boil, reduce heat and simmer until beans are not quite tender, 40 to 50 minutes. Drain and discard onion; set beans aside.

In same saucepan, heat oil over medium heat. Add chopped onion, garlic and sage; stir until onion softens, 3 to 4 minutes. Stir in beans and lemon juice; add tomatoes and juices, crushing tomatoes with your fingers as you add them to pot. Cover and simmer over low heat until beans are tender, 15 to 20 minutes.

Season with salt and pepper and parsley and basil. Serve in small heated bowls.

Wine: Carmen Cabernet Sauvignon (Chile) or a fresh, medium-bodied Cabernet Sauvignon

Braised Flageolets with Herbs, Shallots & Lemon

Serves 6-8

WE'VE ALWAYS LIKED FLAGEOLETS, a pale green dried French bean that is low in starch. With their delicate flavor, flageolets lend themselves to buttery herb preparations like this one. This is an excellent accompaniment to salmon as well as lamb. Should you wish, you can prepare this recipe with dried baby lima beans, instead of flageolets.

1⅓	cups (about 12 ounces) dried French flageolets
1	yellow onion, unpeeled
1	teaspoon dried thyme
4	tablespoons (½ stick) unsalted butter
1	tablespoon fresh lemon juice
1	teaspoon herbes de Provence or mixture of dried rosemary, savory, thyme, basil and crumbled bay leaf
4	plump shallots, finely minced
1	plump garlic clove, minced
1	teaspoon minced fresh sage or ¼ teaspoon dried
	Kosher salt and freshly ground white pepper

Combine flageolets and enough water to cover in a large, heavy saucepan. Cover and cook over high heat until water comes to a rolling boil. Drain beans and return to saucepan.

Slice top off onion and add to pot. Add thyme and 8 cups water; cover and bring to a boil over high heat. Reduce heat to low and simmer until beans are tender and skins plump up, 30 to 40 minutes.

Discard onion, drain beans and refresh in cold water to stop cooking. Drain again and set aside.

In a large skillet, melt butter over low heat. Stir in lemon juice, herbs, shallots, garlic and sage. Tightly cover and cook until shallots are translucent, about 5 minutes.

Add flageolets and salt and white pepper. Cover and cook, stirring from time to time, until beans are piping hot, about 10 minutes. Serve hot.

Pureed White Beans

Serves 8-10

IT'S HARD TO BEAT the taste of simple white beans that have been simmered with herbs and an onion and then pureed and mixed with a touch of chicken stock and butter. This is a versatile dish: it is perfect with lamb, but it can be a main dish, with a big salad and bread and cheese, or it can be served, liberally garnished with minced fresh herbs, as a dip with toasted pita.

1	pound dried Great Northern beans, rinsed
1	large yellow onion
10	fresh flat-leaf parsley sprigs
3	fresh thyme sprigs or ½ teaspoon dried
1	bay leaf
1	whole allspice
1	lemon verbena branch or two 1-inch strips lemon peel
⅓	cup chicken stock (page 325), warmed
8	tablespoons (1 stick) unsalted butter, melted
2	teaspoons kosher salt
1	teaspoon freshly ground white pepper
3	tablespoons sour cream
⅓	cup minced fresh chives, for garnish

In a large saucepan, combine beans with enough water to cover by 1 inch. Cover and bring to a boil over high heat. Remove from heat and let stand for 1 hour; drain.

Add 2 quarts (8 cups) water, onion, parsley, thyme, bay leaf, allspice and lemon verbena or lemon peel. Cover and cook over high heat until water begins to boil. Reduce heat and cook until beans are very tender, about 1 hour.

Remove pan from heat; reserve ¼ cup cooking liquid. Drain beans and discard allspice, lemon verbena or peel, bay leaf, thyme sprigs and parsley.

Combine bean mixture, stock and butter in a food processor fitted with the metal blade. Pulse to blend. Add salt and white pepper; scrape down sides. Add reserved cooking liquid and sour cream. Process until beans are smoothly pureed, stopping to scrape sides once more.

Serve beans as a side dish or in heated soup plates; generously garnish with chives.

Wine: Bodegas Angel Rodriguez Martinsancho Verdejo (Spain: Rueda) or another crisp, dry white wine

Silky Farfel with Peas & Carrots

Serves 6-8

FARFEL, JEWISH SOUL FOOD, is one of the world's most satisfying dishes. Cooked with seasonings and liquid, the small, dried pellets of egg noodles absorb moisture and flavor, becoming tender and tasty. A dish of farfel is sublime served on its own or with roasted or grilled chicken, meat loaf, brisket or just about anything else. This version is studded with bits of onions, carrots and peas. Covered cooking makes it almost creamy. While there are many farfels on the market, the best comes from Canada. Thankfully, Toronto's Best Kosher Haimishe Farfel is now available countrywide.

¼	cup olive oil
2	large carrots, finely diced
1	large Spanish onion, finely diced
1	tablespoon hot Hungarian paprika
1	tablespoon kosher salt, plus more to taste
2	teaspoons coarsely ground black pepper, plus more to taste
2	7-ounce packages Haimishe farfel
9-10	cups hot chicken or vegetable stock (page 325 or 330)
⅔	cup frozen or fresh green peas

Heat oil in a large, heavy skillet over medium heat until hot. Add carrots and onion and cook, stirring often, until slightly softened, 3 to 4 minutes. Add paprika, 1 tablespoon salt, pepper and farfel. Cook, stirring, over high heat for several minutes to release flavor of paprika. Stir in 5 cups stock; cover and bring to a boil. Reduce heat to low and simmer, stirring once, for 10 minutes.

Stir in 3 cups stock. Cover and simmer for 20 minutes, stirring twice.

Add 1 cup stock and stir thoroughly. Cover and cook for 15 minutes.

If farfel is not tender and liquid is almost totally absorbed, add remaining 1 cup stock and cook for 10 minutes more, or until farfel is tender.

Stir in peas and cook until hot, 2 to 3 minutes. Season with more salt and pepper.

Wine: Château St. Jean Fumé Blanc Sonoma County (California: Sonoma County) or Zamò & Palazzolo Tocai Friuliano (Italy: Friuli) or another Tocai from Friuli

Daufuskie Island Brown Bread

Makes 1 loaf

A DAPTED FROM A RECIPE in Billie Burn's *Stirrin' the Pots on Daufuskie*, this is a dark, dense cornmeal and whole wheat bread with the barest suggestion of sweetness. It's a Southern specialty from an island located off the coast of South Carolina and is similar to northern Boston brown bread. Perfect with soups and stews, it is an excellent accompaniment to barbecue and baked beans. Traditionally, this bread was made in old coffee cans. We make it in our much-used pudding mold—the one sold for plum puddings.

1	cup yellow cornmeal
2	cups whole wheat flour
1	teaspoon kosher salt
1	teaspoon baking soda
⅔	cup dark molasses
1	cup milk

Set a steaming rack or basket in a wide pot. Fill pot with water to reach just to bottom of rack. Set aside.

Generously butter or oil an 8-to-12-cup pudding mold.

In a large mixing bowl, combine cornmeal, flour and salt. Dissolve baking soda in 1 cup hot water; mix into cornmeal mixture. Stir in molasses and milk.

Pour batter into mold, cover and place on rack. Bring water to a rolling boil. Cover pot, reduce heat to medium-low and steam, checking water and replenishing as needed, until sides of bread pull slightly away from mold and a skewer inserted into center comes out clean, about 2½ hours.

Transfer mold to a cooling rack and let stand, uncovered, for 30 minutes. Invert mold on rack to release bread. Serve warm, with lots of butter.

Under-Cover Corn Bread

Makes a 10-inch loaf

OUR EARLY SETTLERS AND COVERED-WAGON PIONEERS made corn bread by placing a cast-iron Dutch oven directly in the fire and covering the lid with hot coals. Not only does this covered baking intensify the hearty flavor of the cornmeal, it creates a steamy atmosphere for the baking bread, resulting in an exceptionally tender, moist texture. We buy whole-grain cornmeal that is stone-ground, which has a fuller, sweeter taste than the commercial roller-ground mass-produced kind. A cast-iron Dutch oven is best for this bread, but a heavy, cast-aluminum one will do, although the bread may take 5 to 8 minutes longer to bake.

2	cups stone-ground yellow cornmeal
1¼	cups unbleached flour
2	tablespoons sugar
1	tablespoon plus 1 teaspoon baking powder
1	teaspoon kosher salt
½	teaspoon baking soda
2	cups buttermilk
3	large eggs, beaten
6	tablespoons (¾ stick) unsalted butter, melted and cooled
¼	cup vegetable oil

Preheat oven to 400 degrees F.

Thoroughly coat a 5-quart cast-iron Dutch oven with oil. As soon as you have assembled ingredients and are ready to mix corn bread, place covered Dutch oven in oven to preheat.

Combine dry ingredients and sift into a large mixing bowl. With an electric mixer, combine buttermilk, eggs, butter and oil in another mixing bowl. With motor running on low, add buttermilk mixture to dry ingredients and mix well. Scrape sides of bowl once and mix again briefly. Let batter rest for 15 minutes.

Carefully transfer heated Dutch oven to top of stove. Blend batter well and pour into Dutch oven. Cover and bake for 30 minutes without lifting lid. Test with a toothpick inserted into middle of corn bread. When toothpick comes out dry, corn bread is done.

Transfer Dutch oven to a rack. Uncover and let stand for 15 minutes. Place another rack over top and carefully invert pot to unmold. Let bread cool slightly before serving.

Lydie's Pain de Mie

(Pullman Bread)

Makes 1 loaf

P AIN DE MIE, known in this country as Pullman Bread, is a French bread made in a special rectangular loaf pan that has a top on it. Because it is baked covered, the bread develops only the lightest, thinnest crust, yielding a fine, firm yet tender, very white bread that is perfect for canapés as well as sandwiches. It makes exceptional breakfast toast. Because of its shape, each slice from the loaf is the same dimension as every other. This intriguing recipe was given to us by cookbook author Lydie Marshall. The covered Pullman bread pan is available through King Arthur Flour (see Sources, page 336). You can also bake the bread in an ordinary loaf pan wrapped with foil and weighted down with a larger oven-proof pan.

Sponge

1	tablespoon active dry yeast
¾	cup lukewarm milk
1	teaspoon sugar
1½	cups unbleached flour

2½	cups unbleached flour, plus more as needed
2	teaspoons kosher salt
6	tablespoons (¾ stick) unsalted butter, cut into small pieces
1	cup lukewarm milk

To make sponge: In a medium bowl, mix yeast with milk and sugar. Gradually incorporate flour to make a soft dough. Cover with plastic wrap and set aside until doubled in bulk, 1 to 2 hours.

To make bread: On a work surface, combine 2½ cups flour with salt. Make a 12-inch-wide well. Place butter pieces and ¼ cup milk in center. Using your fingers, start to incorporate flour into milk and butter. Gradually add remaining ¾ cup milk, stirring it in with your fingers and using a pastry scraper with your free hand to scrape up dough.

When dough is thoroughly mixed, pat it into a rectangle about 1 inch thick. Scrape sponge from bowl and place it on top of dough. Gather up ends of dough and bury sponge inside. Generously sprinkle work surface with flour and begin to knead, stretching mixture into a long sausage; twist together and repeat, stretching into a sausage and twisting. Use your pastry scraper to assist you. Lightly sprinkle work surface with flour only when dough becomes too sticky. Keep kneading and stretching dough until very smooth and just slightly tacky, 12 to 15 minutes. Transfer dough to a lightly greased bowl, cover with plastic and let rise in a warm place until doubled, 1 to 2 hours.

Preheat oven to 425 degrees F. Grease a Pullman or 13-x-4-x-4-inch (12-cup) loaf pan.

Punch down dough. Knead for a few minutes. Pat and stretch dough to fit pan. Let rise to just below top of pan, about 1 hour.

Cover tightly with lid. Or, if you do not have a Pullman pan, wrap with foil and weight down with bricks or a heavy, larger pan. Bake for 40 minutes.

Remove from oven and place on a rack for 2 to 3 minutes. Keeping your face averted, remove cover; top of bread will be golden brown. If it is not, return to oven, uncovered, until browned. Remove loaf from pan and let cool for at least 2 hours before cutting into slices.

Vegetables

Entrées

Autumn Vegetable Stew 272

Ragout of Curried Lima Beans & Mushrooms 274

Mélange of Root Vegetables 276

Melt-in-Your-Mouth Cabbage, Leeks & Lima Beans 277

Scalloped Corn, Lima Beans & Tomatoes 278

Curried Vegetables with Ginger & Mint 279

Ragout of Mushrooms, Shallots & Herbs 280

Eggplant & Garbanzo Stew (*Im-Naz' Zalee*) 282

Summer Eggplant & Tomato Stew 283

Braised Kale with Caramelized Leeks 284

Side Dishes

Braised Snow Pea Pods with Lettuce & Butter 285

Braised Asparagus with Lemon-Egg Butter 286

Buttery Snap Beans with Herbs 287

Gingered Carrots with Lemon & Thyme 288

Braised Yellow Squash with Fresh Herbs 289

Homey Creamed Spinach 290

Fred's Famous Fried Potatoes 291

Garlic-Braised New Potatoes with Herbs 292

Mashed New Potatoes with Chicken Stock, Herbs & Scallions 293

Lemon-Braised Fennel & Endive 294

Piquant Rapini 295

Red Cabbage with Leeks & Apple Cider 296

Simple Spicy Cabbage 297

Red Onions & Sage 298

Glazed Brussels Sprouts with Black Walnut Butter 299

Autumn Vegetable Stew

Serves 12-14

FRAGRANT WITH AROMAS OF CINNAMON, CLOVES AND ALLSPICE, this squash and root-vegetable stew is one of the most popular winter dishes of Kookie Brock, a talented cook and caterer. A splendid main dish for a meatless dinner, it is also a fine side dish for a buffet supper. You can substitute your own combination of squashes; they should weigh about 7 pounds total.

1	small butternut squash, split and seeded
1	small acorn squash, split and seeded
1	small cooking pumpkin, top sliced off, seeds removed
3	turnips
2	sweet potatoes or yams
1	large parsnip
6	tablespoons (¾ stick) unsalted butter
1	large leek, trimmed to include tender green, well washed and cut into julienne
¼	cup unbleached flour
1	28-ounce can whole tomatoes, drained
2	teaspoons ground cinnamon
½	teaspoon ground cloves
½	teaspoon ground allspice
½	teaspoon ground mace
2	teaspoons kosher salt
1	teaspoon freshly ground white pepper
1½	cups apple cider
2	tart apples, peeled, cored, quartered and thinly sliced

Preheat oven to 350 degrees F.

Place squashes and pumpkin, cut sides up, on a baking sheet. Keeping in mind that some will be ready ahead of others, bake until almost tender, 45 to 60 minutes.

Remove from oven and let cool. Remove skin from flesh and cut flesh into ¾-inch cubes. Place in a large pot.

Meanwhile, peel turnips, sweet potatoes or yams and parsnip. Cut into ¾-inch cubes and place in a large saucepan. Cover with 2 quarts salted water and bring to a boil. Reduce heat and simmer, covered, until almost tender, about 15 minutes. Drain, reserving liquid. Add sweet potato mixture to squash.

Melt 2 tablespoons butter in a medium skillet. Add leek, cover and cook over very low heat until tender, about 10 minutes. Add to squash.

Melt remaining 4 tablespoons butter in a small cast-iron skillet, whisk in flour and cook over medium heat, whisking often, until roux is almost the color of butternut squash, 6 to 10 minutes. Add roux to vegetables; add 3 cups reserved sweet potato cooking liquid. With your hands, squish tomatoes to break them apart; add to vegetables.

Cover pot and cook over low heat, carefully stirring occasionally, until mixture is hot and roux is incorporated, 4 to 6 minutes.

Add spices, salt, white pepper, cider and apples. If stew is too thick, add more reserved sweet potato liquid. Cover and cook for 10 minutes more.

Taste and adjust seasonings. Ladle into a heated tureen or deep casserole.

Wine: Hidden Cellar Alchemy Mendocino County (California: Mendocino County) or Eberle Winery Côtes du Robles (California: Paso Robles) or a Rhône-style red wine from California

Ragout of Curried Lima Beans & Mushrooms

Serves 6-8

THE HEARTY FLAVOR AND TEXTURE OF LIMA BEANS make them particularly appealing in stews and ragouts. Mushrooms and onions are sautéed in a combination of Indian spices and a splash of dark brown sugar. A thick tomato puree and some sour cream finish the dish. Serve it as part of a vegetarian meal or as an accompaniment to roasted chicken or a grilled fish like mackerel.

1	pound frozen baby lima beans
6	ounces cremini mushrooms, cleaned and trimmed
1	large yellow onion, quartered
3	tablespoons olive oil
1	small dried red chile, crumbled
¼	cup packed dark brown sugar
1½	teaspoons curry powder
1	teaspoon ground cardamom
1	teaspoon ground coriander
1	teaspoon ground ginger
1	teaspoon kosher salt
1	teaspoon freshly ground black pepper
½	teaspoon turmeric
¼	teaspoon cayenne pepper
2	cups tomato puree (page 324) or canned crushed tomatoes
¼	cup sour cream

Preheat oven to 425 degrees F.

Combine limas and ½ cup water in a medium saucepan. Cover and bring to a boil. Reduce heat to low and simmer for 10 minutes; limas will not be done. Drain and set aside.

In a food processor fitted with the metal blade, combine mushrooms and onion. Pulse until finely chopped.

Heat oil and chile in a medium, nonreactive skillet over medium-high heat. Stir in mushroom mixture, cover and cook until juices are released, 3 to 4 minutes. Stir in brown sugar, curry powder, cardamom, coriander, ginger, salt, pepper, turmeric and cayenne. Cook, stirring, over medium-high heat until spices are fragrant, 2 to 3 minutes.

Stir in tomato puree or crushed tomatoes and cook until mixture is bubbling. Remove from heat; blend in sour cream. Add lima beans and mix thoroughly.

Pour mixture into a 2-quart baking dish. Cover with foil and bake until sauce is thick and bubbly and limas are tender, about 45 minutes. Serve hot.

Wine: Bonny Doon Vineyard Clos de Gilroy (California) or a light, fruity California red wine

Mélange of Root Vegetables

Serves 8

WE LIKE THE DELICATE FLAVORS in this simple dish, especially the touch of sweetness from the carrots and parsnips. By the time the vegetables are tender, the braising stock and butter are reduced to a velvety glaze. A sprinkling of herbs and a final splash of lemon juice enliven the vegetables beautifully. They go well with chicken or a simple broiled fish. Or you can even combine them with leftover chicken, some brown rice and more stock for a hearty soup supper. (See photograph, page 93.)

4	tablespoons (½ stick) unsalted butter
4	small parsnips, cut into thirds
4	carrots, cut into thirds
4	medium turnips, trimmed and quartered
1	small celery root, peeled and cut into 8 wedges
1	fennel bulb, trimmed and cut into 8 wedges, plus 1 tablespoon minced fronds
½	cup chicken or vegetable stock, plus more if needed (page 325 or 330)
1	teaspoon fresh thyme or ½ teaspoon dried
2	tablespoons minced fresh flat-leaf parsley
1	teaspoon fresh lemon juice
	Kosher salt and freshly ground white pepper

In a large, heavy skillet with a tight-fitting lid, melt butter over medium heat. Add parsnips, carrots, turnips, celery root, fennel bulb, ½ cup stock and thyme. Cover and cook until stock begins to bubble, 3 to 4 minutes. Reduce heat to low and cook until vegetables are tender, adding more stock if needed, about 25 minutes.

Season with minced fennel fronds, parsley, lemon juice and salt and white pepper. Serve on heated plates.

Wine: Domaine Marcel Deiss Gewürztraminer (France: Alsace) or another Gewürztraminer

Melt-in-Your-Mouth Cabbage, Leeks & Lima Beans

Serves 6

ABBAGE, LEEKS, LIMA BEANS AND SAGE are ever so slowly braised together to make a soft, creamy dish. This is excellent in winter. We love it with crisply roasted chicken. But it is equally delicious tossed with orecchiette or penne pasta, generously sprinkled with grated Parmesan.

6   tablespoons (¾ stick) unsalted butter
1   large yellow onion, thinly sliced
2   plump leeks, well washed, split and thinly sliced
8   cups thinly sliced cabbage (1 large)
2   cups fresh or frozen lima beans
1   tablespoon minced fresh sage or 2 teaspoons dried
½   cup chicken or vegetable stock (page 325 or 330)
2   tablespoons dry white wine
     Kosher salt and freshly ground white pepper

Melt butter in a large, heavy-bottomed, nonreactive skillet or Dutch oven over medium heat. Stir in onion and leeks, cover, reduce heat to low and cook until softened, 4 to 5 minutes. Add cabbage, lima beans and sage; stir well. Tightly cover and reduce heat to low. Cook, stirring several times, for 15 minutes.

Add stock, wine and salt and white pepper; stir and cover. Cook, stirring from time to time, until cabbage is very tender, about 1 hour. Adjust seasonings before serving, adding salt and white pepper if needed.

Wine: Chalk Hill Winery Sauvignon Blanc Chalk Hill (California: Sonoma County), Giuseppe Cortese Dolcetto d'Alba (Italy: Piedmont) or another complex white Sauvignon Blanc or soft and fruity Dolcetto from Piedmont

Scalloped Corn, Lima Beans & Tomatoes

Serves 8-10

WE'VE FOUND *The Buckeye Cookery and Practical Housekeeping* (published in 1877 in Minneapolis, Minnesota) to be a treasure trove of honest American recipes. This mixture of creamy corn, lima beans and tomatoes is inspired by a corn dish called "Bina's Stewed Corn." It's a great choice for late summer, when all the vegetables can be fresh from the garden. Our touch of basil adds another layer of flavor to the finished dish.

1½	cups fresh or frozen lima beans
8	ears fresh sweet corn, shucked
3	tablespoons unsalted butter
3	large tomatoes, peeled, seeded and diced
½	cup heavy cream
¼	cup minced fresh basil
	Kosher salt and freshly ground black pepper
¼	cup sour cream

Combine lima beans with water to cover in a saucepan. Bring to a boil over high heat. Reduce heat and simmer for 5 minutes; limas will not be fully cooked. Drain and set aside.

With a sharp knife, cut corn from cobs, being careful not to cut into cobs. We find that it works best to stand each ear in a shallow baking dish to do this. Be sure to scrape any corn milk from cob as well.

Over low heat, melt butter in a large nonstick skillet. Add lima beans, corn, tomatoes and cream. Cover pan and cook over high heat until liquid begins to bubble. Reduce heat to medium-low. Braise, stirring occasionally, until lima beans and corn are exceptionally tender, 35 to 45 minutes.

Stir in basil, salt and pepper and sour cream. Cook, without boiling, until mixture is piping hot, about 5 minutes. Serve hot.

Wine: Morgadio Albarino Rias Baixas (Spain) or a crisp white wine with concentrated fruit flavors

Curried Vegetables with Ginger & Mint

Serves 4-6

THIS ZIPPY MIXTURE OF VEGETABLES is slowly cooked over low heat while the spices fill your kitchen with warm, appealing aromas. Fresh mint is combined with yogurt to make a luscious finishing sauce.

2-3	tablespoons vegetable oil
1	dried red chile, crumbled
1	teaspoon curry powder
1	teaspoon turmeric
½	teaspoon ground ginger
½	teaspoon freshly ground white pepper
½	teaspoon ground cardamom
6	plump-bulbed green (creaming) onions, bulbs only, or 6 peeled boiling onions, trimmed
3½	cups cauliflower florets
4	medium carrots, cut into thirds
2	medium parsnips, peeled and cut into 1½-inch chunks
	Kosher salt
⅓	cup chicken or vegetable stock (page 325 or 330)
2	teaspoons minced fresh mint or 1 teaspoon dried
½	cup plain yogurt

Combine oil, chile, curry powder, turmeric, ginger, white pepper and cardamom in a large, heavy saucepan. Cook over medium heat, stirring frequently, for 4 minutes to release flavors. Add onions, cauliflower, carrots and parsnips. Sprinkle with salt and add stock. Tightly cover, reduce heat to low and cook, stirring several times, until vegetables are tender, about 20 minutes.

Gently fold in mint and yogurt and serve.

Wine: Handley Cellars Gewürztraminer Anderson Valley (California: Mendocino County) or another California Gewürztraminer

Ragout of Mushrooms, Shallots & Herbs

Serves 4

THIS MUSHROOM STEW can be as simple or as exotic as you wish, depending upon the mushrooms you use. It's a versatile dish that can stand on its own. It is also delicious on toast for lunch, can accompany grilled beef, veal or lamb or is an excellent topping for polenta (page 254). It makes a good base for pasta sauce: Just sauté some escarole in olive oil, add it to the mushrooms (along with some prosciutto, perhaps) and toss it with cooked shells.

1   ounce dried cultivated exotic mushrooms,
       such as cèpes or porcini
3   tablespoons olive oil
1   teaspoon dried thyme
2   plump shallots, minced
1   garlic clove, minced
4-5   ounces fresh cultivated exotic mushrooms,
       such as portobello or shiitake, thinly sliced
1   teaspoon soy sauce
½   cup dry red wine
1   tablespoon unsalted butter
2   tablespoons minced fresh flat-leaf parsley
     Kosher salt and freshly ground black pepper to taste
     Generous pinch of freshly grated nutmeg

Combine dried mushrooms and 1 cup boiling water in a small bowl and set aside for 30 minutes. Remove softened mushrooms and coarsely dice. Strain mushroom soaking liquid through a coffee filter to remove any grit; set aside.

In a medium skillet, heat oil over medium heat. Add thyme, shallots and garlic, tightly cover, reduce heat to low and cook until translucent, about 5 minutes. Stir in fresh mushrooms and soy sauce, cover and cook, stirring from time to time, until mushrooms begin to release their liquid, 10 to 15 minutes.

Add chopped dried mushrooms, cover and cook for 5 minutes. Stir in wine and mushroom soaking liquid; increase heat to high and cook, uncovered, until liquid comes to a vigorous boil. Cook until liquid is reduced by half and mixture thickens somewhat, 3 to 4 minutes.

Remove skillet from heat; stir in butter. Cook vigorously over high heat until sauce thickens, 1 to 2 minutes. Stir in parsley, salt and pepper and nutmeg and serve.

Wine: David Bynum Winery Pinot Noir (California: Sonoma County) or another medium-bodied, fruity Pinot Noir

Eggplant & Garbanzo Stew

(Im-Naz ' Zalee)

Serves 6

THIS LIGHT SYRIAN STEW OF EGGPLANT, garbanzo beans and tomatoes is flavored with mint and allspice. When made a day ahead of serving, the vegetables become permeated with the seasonings. Served hot, the dish can stand on its own or serve as an accompaniment to fluffy rice. It is also wonderfully good cold or at room temperature, especially with the last-minute addition of minced fresh cilantro. The recipe was given to us by Helen and Wedad Shaheen.

1	large eggplant (2½-3 pounds), peeled
½	cup olive oil
1	large Spanish onion, coarsely chopped
1	large carrot, coarsely chopped
1	cup drained canned garbanzo beans (also called chick-peas)
1	plump garlic clove, minced
1	teaspoon kosher salt
½	teaspoon freshly ground black pepper, plus more to taste
¼	teaspoon ground allspice
3	large tomatoes, peeled and coarsely chopped
1	teaspoon dried mint
2	tablespoons minced fresh cilantro

Cut eggplant lengthwise in half; cut lengthwise into 1-inch-wide strips. Cut crosswise into 1½-inch lengths.

In a large nonreactive saucepan, heat oil. Add onion and stir over medium heat until softened, 3 to 4 minutes. Add carrot, garbanzos, garlic, eggplant, salt, ½ teaspoon pepper and allspice. Cover and simmer, stirring occasionally in a folding motion, for 10 minutes.

Add tomatoes and enough water to bring liquid to half the depth of solids. Cover and continue cooking for 20 minutes.

Stir in mint. Cover and cook until eggplant is very tender, about 10 minutes more.

Serve hot, at room temperature or cold. Stir in cilantro just before serving.

Wine: Lamoreaux Landing Wine Cellars Chardonnay Estate Bottled (New York: Finger Lakes) or another medium-bodied crisp and fruity Chardonnay

Summer Eggplant & Tomato Stew

Serves 8-10

To reduce the amount of oil in this dish, we partially cook the eggplants in boiling water. Then we slowly stew the tender flesh with garlic, onions, a touch of zippy pepper, some fresh tomatoes and a splash of lemon juice. When the eggplants have cooled slightly, we add lots of fresh parsley and capers. The dish can be served hot, cold or at room temperature. If you wish, you could toss this with some freshly cooked penne or brown rice for a hearty vegetarian dinner.

3	large eggplants (6-7 pounds total)
3	tablespoons olive oil
1	cup finely chopped sweet onion
2	plump garlic cloves, minced
1	teaspoon fresh thyme leaves or ½ teaspoon dried
1	banana pepper or another medium-hot pepper, seeded and cut into thin rings
4	medium tomatoes, peeled and cut into medium dice
	Kosher salt and freshly ground black pepper
	Juice of ½ lemon
2	tablespoons drained capers
⅓	cup minced fresh flat-leaf parsley

Fill a large pot with generously salted water; bring to a boil over high heat. Add eggplants, cover and reduce heat to low. Simmer eggplants until tender but not mushy, 15 to 20 minutes. Remove from water and cool in cold water. Peel and cut flesh into 1½-inch cubes.

Heat oil in a large nonreactive skillet. Add onion, garlic, thyme and pepper rings. Cover and cook over low heat until onions soften, about 2 minutes. Stir in eggplant, tomatoes, salt and pepper, cover and cook until mixture is very stewy, about 30 minutes.

Stir in lemon juice and adjust seasonings, adding more salt and pepper if desired. Let stew cool slightly. Stir in capers and parsley and serve.

Wine: Havens Wine Cellars Sauvignon Blanc (California: Napa Valley) or another crisp, slightly grassy Sauvignon Blanc

Braised Kale with Caramelized Leeks

Serves 4

THIS RECIPE COMBINES the tang of fresh kale with a touch of browned sweetness from caramelized leeks. It is prepared in a matter of minutes and is a great dish for autumn, when kale is plentiful in the garden. This is a versatile recipe. As one variation, add diced tomatoes during the last 10 minutes of cooking. You could also add pine nuts. Or, if you finish the dish with 2 more tablespoons of olive oil and ⅓ cup cooking water from pasta, you can turn it into a sauce for a shaped pasta like conchiglie (little shells) or orecchiette (little ears).

3	tablespoons olive oil, plus more if needed
1	small dried red chile, crumbled
1	plump garlic clove, minced
2	large leeks, trimmed to include tender greens, split in half, well washed and thinly sliced
8	cups coarsely chopped kale (about ½ pound)
3	tablespoons chicken or vegetable stock (page 325 or 330) or water
	Juice of ½ lemon
	Kosher salt and freshly ground white pepper
	Few grindings of nutmeg

Heat 3 tablespoons oil in a large nonstick skillet over low heat. Add chile and garlic and cook for 2 minutes to release flavors. Increase heat to medium, add leeks and cook, stirring often, for 5 minutes. Add kale, stir to coat with oil; add stock or water and tightly cover. Cook, stirring from time to time, until kale is tender and leeks are caramelized and golden, about 20 minutes.

Sprinkle with lemon juice, season with salt and white pepper and nutmeg and serve.

Wine: Annie and André Brunel Domaine de la Becassonne (France: Rhône) or another medium-bodied white Côtes du Rhône

Braised Snow Pea Pods with Lettuce & Butter

Serves 4-6

Place in the bottom of your sauce-pan, or boiler, several of the outside leaves of lettuce; put your peas in the dish with two ounces of butter in proportion to half a peck of peas; cover the pan or boiler close, and place over the fire; in thirty minutes they are ready for the table. They can either be seasoned in the pan or taken out. Water extracts nearly all the delicious quality of the green pea, and is as fatal to their flavor as it is destructive to a mad dog."

This recipe from Phineas Thornton's *Southern Gardener and Receipt Book*, published in 1845, was the inspiration for our simply delicious dish of sweet and tender pea pods thoroughly braised with a chiffonnade of lettuce in a splash of butter. Should you wish, you can substitute freshly shelled peas (4 cups) for the pods.

3 tablespoons unsalted butter
4 cups very fresh, small snow pea pods, strings removed
1 packed cup shredded leaf lettuce, preferably homegrown
   Kosher salt
1 teaspoon freshly ground white pepper
2 teaspoons fresh minced apple or orange mint (optional)

Melt butter in a heavy, nonstick skillet with a tight-fitting lid. While butter is melting, rinse pea pods and lettuce. Shake off obvious excess moisture, but do not dry. Add lettuce, then peas. Sprinkle with salt and white pepper. Tightly cover and cook over very low heat, without lifting lid, shaking pan occasionally, for 30 minutes.

Stir and check for doneness; pea pods should be completely tender, with no crispness.

Adjust seasonings, adding salt and white pepper if needed; stir in mint if desired. Serve immediately.

Braised Asparagus with Lemon-Egg Butter

Serves 4

WE'LL SHARE A HOUSE SECRET: Fred does wonderful kitchen scullery work. Linda is often too impatient, especially when it comes to asparagus. So when we eat them—and we do so often—Fred peels every stalk. Such careful preparation is appropriate for this springtime dish. We finish the asparagus with a tasty lemon butter thickened by some hard-cooked egg yolk.

1   cup chicken or vegetable stock (page 325 or 330)
1   pound asparagus, trimmed
4   tablespoons (½ stick) butter, melted
    Juice of ½ lemon
1   hard-cooked egg, yolk and white separated;
        yolk mashed, white finely chopped
    Kosher salt and freshly ground white pepper
1   tablespoon minced fresh chives, for garnish

Combine stock and asparagus in a saucepan or skillet just wide enough to hold asparagus. Tightly cover and bring to a boil. Reduce heat to low and simmer until asparagus is just tender, 5 to 7 minutes, depending upon thickness of stalks. About the time asparagus is tender, stock will be nearly reduced to a glaze.

Meanwhile, combine butter and lemon juice in a small bowl. Whisk in mashed egg yolk. If not using immediately, cover and keep warm on stovetop.

Quickly pour off any remaining stock from asparagus. Cover with lemon-egg butter mixture and gently toss to coat well. Season with salt and white pepper.

Divide among serving plates. Sprinkle with chopped egg white and chives.

Buttery Snap Beans with Herbs

Serves 2-4

S
AD TO SAY, WE ARE COOKS, NOT FARMERS. Only tomatoes and herbs grow well every year in our yard, but we keep trying. We always plant a variety of seeds and hold our breath. Happily, our friend Adele Straub, aka The Farmer is Adele, grows gorgeous produce at her organic farm, and she keeps us supplied with splendid products all summer. Her delivery of the season's first yellow and purple beans inspired this recipe for snap beans braised in chicken stock. As with most braised vegetables, the stock reduces into exquisite richness, making a perfect "sauce" for the tender beans. A dab of butter and a generous addition of fresh herbs yields a truly pleasurable dish.

1½	pounds green, yellow and/or purple snap beans
1	cup chicken or vegetable stock (pages 325 or 330)
	Kosher salt and freshly ground white pepper
2	tablespoons unsalted butter
½	cup mixed minced fresh herbs (basil, lemon thyme, tarragon, pineapple sage)

Trim beans and cut into 1-to-2-inch pieces. Heat stock and salt and white pepper in a medium saucepan over high heat. When liquid begins to boil, add beans. Cover, reduce heat to low and simmer until beans are quite tender, 10 to 15 minutes. Stock should be reduced to about 2 tablespoons. Otherwise, increase heat to high and cook, uncovered, for 1 to 2 minutes.

Toss beans with butter and herbs; season with more salt and white pepper and serve.

Gingered Carrots
with Lemon & Thyme

Serves 6-8

THESE TENDER CARROTS are seasoned with touches of lemon and fresh ginger, as well as a hint of white wine. Be sure to buy carrots that still have their tops—you'll know that they are fresh that way. This dish can be prepared a few hours ahead. Just reheat quickly so the carrots don't turn to mush.

2	pounds fresh carrots, cut into 2-inch lengths
3	tablespoons unsalted butter
½	cup finely diced shallots
1	rounded tablespoon grated fresh ginger
	Minced zest and juice of 1 lemon
⅓	cup dry white wine
⅓	cup chicken or vegetable stock (page 325 or 330)
2	teaspoons fresh thyme leaves or 1 teaspoon dried
	Kosher salt and freshly ground white pepper

With a sharp knife, cut each piece of carrot lengthwise into slices about ⅛ inch thick. Set aside.

In a large nonstick skillet fitted with a lid, melt butter over low heat. Add shallots and ginger and cook until shallots are soft, about 4 minutes. Add carrots, lemon zest and juice, wine, stock and thyme. Cover skillet and cook, stirring from time to time, until carrots are tender, about 20 minutes. Season with salt and white pepper and serve.

Braised Yellow Squash with Fresh Herbs

Serves 4

MANY OF THE ORGANIC VEGETABLES we enjoy all summer are grown from heirloom seeds. We are especially partial to yellow squash, harvested young. Because they are so tasty, we treat them simply. What could be better than fresh-from-the-garden, young yellow squash served with splashes of herbs and a dash of shallots?

2 tablespoons olive oil
1 pound mixed small yellow squash,
    cut into ¼-inch-thick slices
1 celery stalk, finely diced
1 plump shallot, minced
2 tablespoons chicken or vegetable stock (page 325 or 330)
¼ cup mixed minced fresh herbs (basil, tarragon,
    thyme and flat-leaf parsley)
Kosher salt and freshly ground black pepper

Heat oil in a large nonstick skillet over medium heat. Add squash, celery and shallot and toss until vegetables are coated with oil. Sprinkle with stock, cover and cook, stirring from time to time, until vegetables are just tender, 5 to 10 minutes.

Stir in herbs and salt and pepper and serve.

Homey Creamed Spinach

Serves 4

SIMPLE AS IT IS, there is something especially satisfying about tender spinach, braised in a creamy sauce with touches of nutmeg and white pepper. We like the tangy taste of evaporated milk, but this dish can also be made with cream.

1½	pounds spinach, well washed, tough stems discarded
3	tablespoons unsalted butter
½	cup minced shallots
1	tablespoon unbleached flour
⅔	cup evaporated milk or heavy cream
⅛	teaspoon freshly grated nutmeg
1	teaspoon kosher salt, plus more to taste
½	teaspoon freshly ground white pepper, plus more to taste

Fill a large pot with 1 to 2 inches of water. Place spinach in a steaming basket or colander. Bring water to a boil; lower steaming basket into pot. Reduce heat to low, cover and cook until spinach is tender, 5 to 10 minutes. Remove spinach from pot and let drain. Coarsely chop and set aside.

Melt butter in a medium, nonreactive skillet over low heat. Add shallots and stir until soft, 3 to 5 minutes. Sprinkle flour over shallots and stir for 1 minute. Increase heat to medium and gradually add evaporated milk or cream, stirring until hot. Add spinach, nutmeg, salt and white pepper. Cover, reduce heat to low and cook until mixture is very creamy, about 10 minutes. Adjust seasonings before serving, adding salt and white pepper if desired.

Fred's Famous Fried Potatoes

Serves 4

FRED HAS BEEN MAKING these tender-on-the-inside but crisp-on-the-outside potatoes for eons—with fish, with steak and especially with breakfast eggs and bacon. To his son Wally, this dish may be the ultimate in comfort foods.

¼ cup vegetable oil, plus more if needed
3-4 very large russet or all-purpose potatoes,
  peeled and thinly sliced
Kosher salt and freshly ground black pepper

Heat ¼ cup oil in a 9- or 10-inch cast-iron skillet. When hot, layer potatoes evenly in skillet. If you cannot see a bit of oil at edges, add a little more. Tightly cover, reduce heat to medium-low and cook until potatoes are crisp on bottom, about 30 minutes.

Turn potatoes with a wide spatula; cover and cook for 5 minutes.

Uncover, increase heat to medium-high and cook until bottom is crisped, about 5 minutes.

Season generously with salt and pepper. Serve on heated plates.

Garlic-Braised New Potatoes with Herbs

Serves 4-6

THESE TENDER HERBED POTATOES are slowly cooked in a heavy saucepan with garlic and butter. Slow heat and a tight-fitting lid are essential to the process. In the summer, when you can buy fresh garlic and new potatoes from a local farm stand, this dish is outstanding. That's when we have a field day combining a wider variety of minced fresh herbs. For example, try adding a little fresh mint and a fistful of basil. And if you have cinnamon basil, all the better. We've been preparing potatoes this way for decades, especially to accompany fish or roasted chicken. The cooking time will vary according to the size of the potatoes. If they are marble-sized, they will cook in about 25 minutes.

16   small yellow, red or purple potatoes
6   tablespoons (¾ stick) unsalted butter
3   plump garlic cloves, sliced into thirds
½   cup minced mixed fresh herbs
        (flat-leaf parsley, basil, thyme, chives)
      Kosher salt and freshly ground black pepper

Thoroughly wash and drain potatoes. In a large, heavy-bottomed saucepan, melt butter over low heat. Add potatoes and garlic. Cover tightly and cook for 25 minutes over very low heat, without lifting lid, tossing potatoes from time to time by holding lid down and shaking pan. Test for tenderness with a skewer. Small potatoes that are about 2 inches in diameter will require about 45 minutes of slow cooking.

When potatoes are done, add herbs and salt and pepper. Stir well to coat potatoes thoroughly with seasonings and serve.

Mashed New Potatoes with Chicken Stock, Herbs & Scallions

Serves 4

THESE MASHED POTATOES are prepared without a speck of butter, but you won't miss it because the fresh herbs and chicken stock give them a rich flavor. A handful of minced fresh scallions adds bright flavor and some crunchy texture.

12   uniform-sized new potatoes, scrubbed
1   cup chicken stock (page 325)
2   teaspoons kosher salt
1   tablespoon olive oil
1   tablespoon minced fresh herbs
        (basil, thyme, rosemary)
    Freshly ground black pepper
2   scallions, trimmed to include 1 inch of green,
        minced

In a medium-sized heavy saucepan, combine potatoes, stock, salt, oil and herbs. Tightly cover and bring to a boil. Reduce heat to low and simmer until potatoes are very tender, about 25 minutes.

Remove from heat and carefully drain liquid into a measuring cup. Using a potato masher, thoroughly mash potatoes. Gradually mash in cooking liquid until potatoes are creamy. Stir in pepper and scallions. Serve.

Lemon-Braised Fennel & Endive

Serves 6-8

THE CRISP ANISE FLAVOR OF FENNEL blends beautifully with the slight bitterness of endive. Braising in a combination of lemon juice and stock adds a delightful freshness to these two very different vegetables.

3 tablespoons olive oil
2 plump shallots, minced
8 small Belgian endives, trimmed
1 large fennel bulb, cut lengthwise into eighths,
      plus 1 tablespoon minced fronds
⅓ cup chicken or vegetable stock (page 325 or 330),
      plus more if needed
1 tablespoon fresh lemon juice
   Minced zest of 1 lemon
1 tablespoon fresh thyme leaves or 2 teaspoons dried
   Kosher salt and freshly ground white pepper
2 tablespoons minced fresh chives, for garnish

Heat oil in a large nonstick skillet with a tight-fitting lid. Add shallots and cook, stirring, over medium heat, until shallots begin to soften, 2 to 3 minutes. Reduce heat to low, add endives and fennel bulb; gently turn to coat lightly with oil.

Add ⅓ cup stock, lemon juice, zest and thyme. Tightly cover and braise over low heat, carefully turning vegetables once and adding more stock if needed, until fork-tender, 20 to 30 minutes. Season with salt and white pepper; sprinkle with chives and minced fennel fronds and serve.

Piquant Rapini

Serves 4

RAPINI, OR BROCCOLI RABE, is one of Linda's favorite vegetables. Although she always enjoys its slight bitterness, Fred prefers it with a little sweetness. We combine it with red wine vinegar and some sweet golden raisins—so we each have our way. The cardamom adds a pleasing note.

2   tablespoons olive oil
2   plump shallots, finely diced
1   bunch (about 1 pound) rapini, tough ends discarded,
        coarsely chopped
3   tablespoons red wine vinegar
¼   cup golden raisins
    Kosher salt and freshly ground black pepper
¼   teaspoon ground cardamom

In a large nonstick skillet, heat oil over medium heat. Add shallots and cook, stirring, until softened, about 1 minute. Stir in rapini.

Add vinegar, raisins, salt and pepper, cardamom and 2 tablespoons water. Cover, reduce heat to low, and cook until rapini is tender, about 15 minutes. Serve immediately.

Red Cabbage with Leeks & Apple Cider

Serves 12

THIS DISH OFTEN APPEARS on our holiday table because its wonderful spices perfume the whole house during its long, slow baking. The buttery-soft cabbage melds beautifully with the leeks. Touches of raspberry vinegar and apple cider add a delicate fruitiness. It goes well with roasted goose or any poultry, and it's also good as part of a buffet table with barbecued brisket or roasted pork.

7	tablespoons unsalted butter
3	plump leeks, split, well washed and thinly sliced crosswise
3-4	pounds red cabbage, cored and thinly sliced (from 1 large)
½	cup raspberry vinegar or another fruit vinegar
⅓	cup packed dark brown sugar
¾	cup apple cider
¾	cup dry red wine
1¼	teaspoons kosher salt
1¼	teaspoons freshly ground white pepper
½	teaspoon ground cinnamon
¼	teaspoon ground cloves

In a large, deep, heavy, nonreactive sauté pan, melt 6 tablespoons butter over low heat. Add leeks, cover, and braise for 5 minutes. Increase heat to medium and braise until leeks are softened, 3 to 4 minutes more. Place cabbage over leeks, tightly cover, and cook over low heat until cabbage begins to soften and leeks just barely begin to brown, about 10 minutes.

Meanwhile, preheat oven to 325 degrees F.

Butter a 3-to-4-quart ovenproof casserole with a lid with remaining 1 tablespoon butter. (You can also use heavy-duty foil to cover dish.)

Stir cabbage and leeks together and spoon into prepared casserole. Set aside.

Combine vinegar and brown sugar in skillet used for cabbage. Place over medium heat and add cider, wine, salt, white pepper, cinnamon and cloves. Increase heat to high and bring liquid to a rolling boil. Continue to boil until sauce just slightly thickens, 2 to 3 minutes. Pour evenly over cabbage mixture.

Tightly cover casserole and place in preheated oven. Braise until cabbage is very soft, about 2 hours. Serve hot.

Simple Spicy Cabbage

Serves 4-6

Slow, moist cooking gives this tender cabbage a buttery texture. There's a hint of smoke from a bit of bacon, while the chile adds a pleasing but subtle heat. But the best is for last—a splash of vinegar for a touch of piquancy.

2	thick slices bacon, finely cut into matchsticks
1	tablespoon olive oil
2	dried red chiles, crumbled
1	large yellow onion, cut in half and thinly sliced
1	small cabbage, preferably savoy, finely shredded
¾	cup chicken or vegetable stock (page 325 or 330)
	Kosher salt and freshly ground white pepper
2	tablespoons red wine vinegar

In large, deep sauté pan or a heavy, nonreactive Dutch oven, cook bacon over medium heat until fat is rendered and pieces are moderately crisp. Drain off all but 1 tablespoon fat; add oil and chiles. Cook, stirring, for 1 minute to release flavors of chiles.

Stir in onion, cabbage, stock and salt and white pepper. Cover and cook until liquid bubbles, 3 to 5 minutes. Reduce heat to low. Cook, stirring occasionally, for 45 minutes.

Stir in vinegar, cover and cook until cabbage is buttery soft, about 15 minutes more.

Adjust seasonings before serving.

Red Onions & Sage

Serves 4-6

A SMALL DRIED CHILE gives a hint of heat to this dish. We cook the onions slowly until they almost fall apart. There's some sage for pleasing pungency and balsamic vinegar for a tangy sweetness. Capers make the dish slightly salty. We serve it at room temperature as a light side dish with roasted poultry or pork or instead of a sauce with grilled chicken, fish or even a burger.

2   tablespoons olive oil
1   small dried red chile, crumbled
2   very large red onions, very thinly sliced
¼   cup dry red wine
1   tablespoon minced fresh sage or 1½ teaspoons dried
1   tablespoon balsamic vinegar
2   tablespoons drained capers
    Kosher salt and freshly ground black pepper

In a large, deep, nonreactive skillet over medium heat, heat oil until hot. Add chile and cook, stirring, for 30 seconds. Reduce heat to low, add onions, wine and sage. Stir gently, cover and cook over low heat, stirring from time to time, until onions are very tender, 20 to 30 minutes.

Remove skillet from heat. Add vinegar, capers and salt and pepper; stir well. Set aside to cool to room temperature. Serve.

Glazed Brussels Sprouts with Black Walnut Butter

Serves 10-12

THE TWO BEST-KNOWN WALNUTS are the English walnut, grown all over the world, and the black walnut, native to America. The English walnut is readily available in bulk year-round. We are, however, partial to its cousin, the black walnut, which is significantly darker and richer in flavor but exceedingly difficult to shell. Happily, because of their popularity in holiday dishes, black walnuts are sold in bulk in metropolitan-area markets from October until January. They are also offered from King Arthur Flour (see Sources, page 336). We always keep several pounds on hand in our freezer.

Chef Richard Perry, who devoted his early culinary life to promoting American food to an enthusiastic St. Louis constituency, introduced us to slowly cooked buttered black walnuts. They've topped a variety of vegetable preparations at our house for years, especially over the holidays. But our favorite is the combination of the gently toasted nuts in butter over tender Brussels sprouts glazed with lemony chicken stock. This is a superb side dish for turkey, goose, duck or pheasant. It's also terrific with fried chicken. You can substitute English walnuts, but they will taste much milder.

8	tablespoons (1 stick) unsalted butter
1	cup broken black walnut meats
2¼	pounds Brussels sprouts, trimmed and quartered
2	tablespoons olive oil
1	cup chicken or vegetable stock (page 325 or 330)
	Juice of ½ lemon
	Kosher salt and freshly ground white pepper

In a heavy, small saucepan, melt butter over very low heat. Add walnuts and cover. Cook, stirring occasionally, until dark, rich brown, 30 to 50 minutes (check after 20 minutes). Nuts should slowly turn dark brown without burning. Set aside.

In a large nonreactive skillet with a tight-fitting lid, combine Brussels sprouts, oil, stock and lemon juice. Tightly cover and bring to a boil. Reduce heat to medium and cook until sprouts are tender, about 10 minutes. Uncover, increase heat and stir until stock has almost evaporated, 3 to 5 minutes.

Warm walnuts and butter and toss with Brussels sprouts. Season with salt and white pepper and serve.

Desserts

Mulled Dried Fruits with Port Wine 302

Minted Basil Peaches Poached in Zinfandel 304

Poached Rosemary Pears with Late-Harvest Riesling & Raisins 305

Spiced Honey-Baked Apples with Black Walnuts & Dried Apricots 306

Maple-Braised Plums, Figs & Blackberries 308

Creamy Almond Rice Pudding 309

Lemony Ginger Dumplings with Blueberry Maple Syrup 310

Apple & Raisin Roly Poly 312

Chocolate Pecan Bread Pudding 314

Lemon Cake with Dried Cherries & Lemon Sauce 316

Christmas Plum Pudding with Hard Sauce 318

Gingered Carrot Cake 320

Mulled Dried Fruits
with Port Wine

Serves 8-12

THIS FRAGRANTLY SPICED DRIED-FRUIT DISH is cooked into moist tenderness in a bath of citrus juices, apple cider and port wine. This recipe is not the Holy Grail; feel free to experiment with other combinations of dried fruits. You might also want to use Cointreau instead of port, or even some applejack or Calvados. The nice thing about this dish is that it will keep very well for several weeks in the refrigerator. Just spoon it into sterilized jars and tightly seal.

	Juice of 2 lemons
	Juice of 2 limes
⅔	cup fresh orange juice
3	cups apple cider
1	cup packed dark brown sugar
1	3-to-4-inch cinnamon stick
4	whole cloves
1	whole allspice
1	tablespoon minced candied ginger
1	teaspoon ground cardamom
½	teaspoon ground coriander
¼	teaspoon freshly grated nutmeg
12	ounces (about 2 cups) dried apricots
8	ounces (about 1½ cups) large dried peaches
8	ounces (about 2 cups) dried cherries
8	ounces (about 2 cups) dried apples
5	ounces (about 1 cup) dried blueberries or cranberries
8	ounces (about 1½ cups) dried figs
1	cup ruby or tawny port wine

In a large, heavy, nonreactive saucepan, combine all citrus juices, cider, brown sugar and all spices. Bring to a boil over high heat. Reduce heat to medium, cover and simmer briskly for 5 minutes.

Add all dried fruits, cover and cook until liquid begins to bubble, about 5 minutes. Reduce heat to low and cook, stirring from time to time, for 15 minutes.

Add port, cover and cook for 15 minutes more.

Remove saucepan from heat and allow fruit to cool for at least 30 minutes. Serve warm or at room temperature.

Minted Basil Peaches Poached in Zinfandel

Serves 6

WHAT COULD BE BETTER than summer peaches gently cooked in red Zinfandel wine, some peppercorns and spices? Fresh basil and mint add a refreshing finish. If you have it, a little lemon verbena is nice too.

6	firm but ripe peaches
1	750-ml bottle red Zinfandel wine
1	cup sugar
1	scant tablespoon white peppercorns
2	teaspoons minced lemongrass or minced zest of 1 lemon
1	teaspoon ground cardamom
½	teaspoon freshly grated nutmeg
2	thin slices fresh ginger
3	whole cloves
⅓	cup mixed minced fresh basil or cinnamon mint and mint (preferably apple or orange mint)
1	tablespoon minced lemon verbena (optional) Edible flowers, for garnish (optional)

Quickly plunge peaches into boiling water. After 5 seconds, transfer to a bowl of chilled water. Peel. Split in half and discard stones.

Combine wine, sugar, peppercorns, lemongrass or zest, cardamom, nutmeg, ginger and cloves in a wide, nonreactive saucepan. Bring liquid to a boil over high heat. Reduce heat to low and gently add peaches. (You may do this in 2 batches.) Tightly cover and simmer, turning after 5 minutes, until peaches are tender, 10 to 12 minutes.

Place a rack over a large platter. Using a slotted spoon, transfer peaches, flat sides down, to rack and let drain.

Return saucepan with liquid to high heat and bring to a boil. Boil until reduced by half and somewhat syrupy, 15 to 25 minutes. Remove from heat; let cool.

Arrange peaches in a shallow dish. Pour sauce through a strainer evenly over peaches. Wrap dish with plastic and store in refrigerator for 2 to 6 hours.

Let come to room temperature for 1 hour before serving.

Divide peaches and sauce among serving dishes. Sprinkle with herbs and flowers, if using.

Poached Rosemary Pears with Late-Harvest Riesling & Raisins

Serves 6

D ESSERT WINE, GINGER AND ORANGE combine to make a poaching liquid for these pears. The liquid is then reduced, and raisins are added for a light sauce. (See photograph, page 96.)

	Juice of 1 lemon
6	ripe but firm pears, preferably Bosc
1	750-ml bottle Late-Harvest Riesling, or another sweet dessert wine
⅔	cup sugar
1	thin slice fresh ginger
	Peel of 1 orange
1	3-inch fresh rosemary branch or 3 branches fresh thyme
1	cup dark raisins
¼	teaspoon freshly grated nutmeg
	Fresh mint leaves, for garnish (optional)

Fill a large, deep bowl with water. Stir in lemon juice and set aside. Peel pears. Carefully core them through bottoms, leaving stems intact. Place in lemon water.

Combine wine, sugar, ginger, orange peel and rosemary or thyme in a deep, nonreactive saucepan. Bring to a boil. Remove pears from lemon water and add to saucepan. Cover and reduce heat to low; simmer until pears are tender, 10 to 14 minutes.

Using a slotted spoon, transfer pears to a serving dish that will hold them in a single layer, stems up.

Add raisins and nutmeg to saucepan. Simmer, uncovered, until liquid reduces by half, 15 to 25 minutes, depending on size of saucepan. Pour mixture over pears. When fruit and sauce are cool, cover with plastic and refrigerate for 2 to 6 hours.

To serve, let fruit come to room temperature. Discard ginger and orange peel. Divide pears among serving bowls. Spoon over raisin sauce and garnish with a mint leaf, if using.

Spiced Honey-Baked Apples with Black Walnuts & Dried Apricots

Serves 6

OST OFTEN, APPLES ARE BAKED uncovered, but we find that baking them under cover creates a modest atmosphere of steam, yielding a more evenly cooked apple with a much more delicate texture. These apples taste as good as they smell. We like to serve them warm, with a dollop of vanilla ice cream, but they are good plain too. To order black walnuts by mail, see King Arthur Flour (Sources, page 336).

2	tablespoons unsalted butter, softened
6	large, beautiful baking apples (Rome, Wolf River)
	Juice of 1 lemon combined with 1½ quarts (6 cups) water
½	cup packed light brown sugar
1	teaspoon ground cinnamon
½	teaspoon ground cardamom
¼	teaspoon ground allspice
⅛	teaspoon freshly grated nutmeg
½	cup apple cider
⅓	cup honey
½	cup chopped black walnuts or English walnuts
½	cup finely diced dried apricots
1	tablespoon finely chopped candied ginger
3	tablespoons unsalted butter, melted
	Vanilla ice cream and sprigs of fresh mint, for serving

Use butter to thoroughly cover bottom and sides of a baking dish that is just large enough to hold apples.

Carefully core apples without cutting all the way through bottoms. Pare away a ¾-inch band of skin around each apple about ⅓ down from tops. Place apples in lemon water and set aside.

Preheat oven to 425 degrees F.

In a small saucepan, combine brown sugar and spices and blend thoroughly. Stir in cider and honey and cook over high heat, stirring constantly, until mixture comes to a boil. Reduce heat to medium and simmer briskly for 2 minutes. Set syrup aside.

In a small mixing bowl, blend together walnuts, apricots, ginger and butter.

Remove apples from water, drain thoroughly and pat dry. Quickly distribute filling among hollowed cores, pressing lightly with your finger to pack. Place stuffed apples in baking dish and spoon 1 tablespoon of syrup over each apple. Pour remaining syrup into bottom of pan. Cover baking dish with heavy-duty foil. Bake for 30 minutes.

Uncover and baste with syrup. Bake, uncovered, until apples are tender when pierced with a thin skewer, about 15 minutes.

Remove pan to a rack to cool. Serve apples in shallow bowls generously topped with syrup, ice cream and a sprig of fresh mint.

Maple-Braised Plums, Figs & Blackberries

Serves 6

THESE FRUITS are braised in a bay-scented, maple-sweetened bath of apple juice and crème de cassis. A light sprinkling of ground pepper brings contrast to the sweet sauce. Served warm, the fruits are especially pleasing when topped with a small scoop of ice cream and a sprinkling of tasty pistachio nuts.

2	tablespoons unsalted butter, softened
1	pint blackberries, cleaned and sorted
2	tablespoons packed dark brown sugar
6	ripe plums, split and pitted
12	small or 6 large figs
⅔	cup apple juice
⅓	cup maple syrup
⅓	cup crème de cassis
1	tablespoon freshly ground black pepper
2	bay leaves
	Vanilla ice cream and chopped pistachio nuts, for serving

Use butter to lavishly coat a 10-inch round pie pan or 9-inch-square baking dish. Preheat oven to 350 degrees F.

Toss together berries and brown sugar in a small bowl; set aside.

With a sharp knife or skewer, score each plum half and fig in several places. Place plums, cut side down, in dish. Scatter figs over plums. Sprinkle evenly with berries.

Combine apple juice, maple syrup, cassis, pepper and bay leaves in a saucepan; bring to a boil over high heat. Reduce heat to medium and simmer briskly until sauce thickens slightly, 3 to 5 minutes. Evenly pour sauce over fruit. Securely cover pie pan or baking dish with foil. Bake until plums are tender, 45 to 60 minutes.

Let cool, uncovered, for 15 to 20 minutes. Remove bay leaves. Divide among individual serving bowls. Serve with a small scoop of ice cream; sprinkle with pistachios.

Creamy Almond Rice Pudding

Serves 4-6

T HIS RICE PUDDING tastes just the way Linda remembers it from when she was a child. The covered double-boiler cooking method results in an exceptionally flavorful, creamy pudding. The recipe is adapted from one in Linda and Lowell Raun's book, *Lowell Farm's Pure Rice Cookbook*. The Rauns, who live in El Campo, Texas, are organic rice farmers who grow superb jasmine rice (see Sources, page 335). According to Linda Raun, rice pudding is a traditional Christmas dessert in Denmark. One almond is added to the whole pot; the person who finds it is said to have a year of good luck.

1	cup jasmine rice
½	cup sugar
½	teaspoon salt
5	cups milk
1	teaspoon almond extract
1	almond
⅔	cup golden raisins (optional)
1-2	tablespoons cinnamon sugar

Combine rice, sugar, salt, milk and almond extract in the top of a double boiler set over simmering water. Cover and cook, stirring every 15 minutes, until rice is soft, mixture is thick and liquid is absorbed, about 2 hours.

Remove double boiler from heat. Stir in almond and raisins, if using. Cover rice and let stand, over the water, for 20 minutes.

Pour pudding into a 1½-quart serving dish. Sprinkle with cinnamon sugar, chill until cold and serve.

Lemony Ginger Dumplings with Blueberry Maple Syrup

Makes 12 dumplings; serves 8-10

BASED ON OUR FAMILY BISCUIT DOUGH, these unusual dessert dumplings are flavored with lemon and ginger and then steamed in a lightly sweetened cooking liquid. They are topped with a sauce of blueberries and maple syrup. The inspiration comes from a recipe in one of Elsie Masterton's charming books, *Blueberry Hill Menu Cookbook* (Thomas Y. Crowell, 1963).

Blueberry Maple Syrup

1	cup maple syrup
1	pint blueberries, cleaned and sorted
1	tablespoon unsalted butter

Dumpling Cooking Liquid

½	cup sugar
	Juice and grated zest of 2 lemons
	or 1 lemongrass stalk, split
1	3-inch cinnamon stick

Dumplings

1½	cups unbleached flour
4	teaspoons baking powder
1	tablespoon sugar
1	teaspoon ground ginger
½	teaspoon baking soda
½	teaspoon kosher salt
1½	tablespoons solid shortening
	Minced zest of 1 lemon
¾	cup buttermilk

To make syrup: Combine maple syrup, blueberries and butter in a small, nonreactive saucepan; bring to a boil. Cover and remove from heat.

To make dumpling cooking liquid: Fill a wok that has a cover or a large pot two-thirds full of water. Add sugar, lemon juice and zest or lemongrass and cinnamon stick; bring to a boil over high heat.

Meanwhile, make dumplings: In a food processor fitted with the metal blade or a mixing bowl, combine flour, baking powder, sugar, ginger, baking soda and salt. Pulsing quickly or using 2 knives or a pastry blender, cut shortening into flour mixture until flour is texture of cornmeal. Lightly toss with lemon zest. Add buttermilk and lightly blend together, pulsing or with a fork, until it forms a soft ball.

Lightly sprinkle work surface with flour. Pat pastry into a 9-x-6-x-½-inch-thick rectangle. Cut into 12 pieces that are 3 x 1½ inches.

Drop dumplings into boiling liquid. Cover, reduce heat to medium and cook for 40 minutes. (Dumplings will become firm inside in 15 minutes, but they will become lighter with further cooking.)

Using a slotted spoon, transfer dumplings to serving bowls. Top generously with blueberry-maple syrup. Serve hot or warm.

Apple & Raisin Roly Poly

Serves 8-10

ROLY POLYS, steamed rolled pastries usually filled with fruit, were common in the last century when most American housewives had a pudding cloth—a piece of heavy muslin often actually stitched into a tube. Inspired by a recipe in the 1877 *Buckeye Cookery and Practical Housekeeping*, this one is filled with apples and raisins. When steamed, the biscuit pastry dough expands and becomes airy and light. Be sure to serve the dessert warm, timing it to be finished about 30 minutes before you need it.

Rosewater is available in specialty or Middle Eastern markets or by mail order from King Arthur Flour (see Sources, page 336).

¾	cup unbleached flour, plus more if needed
1	teaspoon rosewater or lemon oil (optional)
1	fresh rosemary branch or slice of fresh ginger (optional)

Dough

1	large egg
½	cup buttermilk
1½	cups unbleached flour, plus more if needed
3	tablespoons sugar
2	teaspoons baking powder
½	teaspoon baking soda
½	teaspoon salt
1	teaspoon minced lemon zest
3	tablespoons solid shortening or lard

Filling

2½	cups diced peeled apples
½	cup dark or golden raisins
1	tablespoon minced crystallized ginger
2	teaspoons minced fresh lemon verbena or lemon zest
3	tablespoons sugar
½	teaspoon ground cinnamon
¼	teaspoon freshly grated nutmeg
2	tablespoons unsalted butter, cut into small bits

Vanilla ice cream or applesauce, for serving

Cut a triple layer of cheesecloth or muslin into a 14-inch square. Dip into boiling water, wring dry and open up on a work surface. Sprinkle evenly, but lightly, with flour. Rub flour in with your fingertips. Repeat several times.

Set a steaming rack or basket in a wide pot or wok 12 inches in diameter or larger. Fill with water to reach 1 inch below rack. Add rosewater or lemon oil and rosemary or ginger if desired.

To prepare dough: Combine egg with buttermilk in a small bowl and set aside.

In a food processor fitted with the metal blade, combine 1½ cups flour, sugar, baking powder, baking soda, salt and lemon zest; blend. Add shortening or lard and pulse 5 times. With motor running, add buttermilk mixture, blending just until evenly mixed. If mixing by hand, cut shortening into flour mixture using a pastry blender or 2 knives until mixture resembles cornmeal. Add buttermilk, and using a fork, quickly mix just until evenly blended. With your fingers, gently gather dough together into a ball.

Flour a work surface. Scrape dough onto it and gently knead, adding flour as needed to make a dough that is only slightly tacky but still very soft. Form into a ball, wrap in wax paper and chill until needed.

To prepare filling: Combine all ingredients in a large mixing bowl and blend thoroughly. Set aside.

To assemble roly poly: Evenly sprinkle flour over cheesecloth or muslin once again and rub it in gently with your fingertips.

Pat dough into a square; place in center of cloth. Roll pastry into a 12-inch square. Distribute filling evenly, leaving a 1-inch margin all around. Using cheesecloth to help you, tightly roll up pastry. Fold under ends; pinch to seal. Gently ease roll down to lower edge of cloth and loosely roll up in cheesecloth, taking care to leave enough slack for expansion of dough. Tie ends with kitchen twine.

Bring water to a rolling boil over high heat. Place roly poly on rack, cover and reduce heat to low so water steadily simmers.

Steam for at least 1½ hours, adding more water as needed. Roly poly is done when it feels firm to touch and a toothpick inserted into it slides in without resistance and comes out clean.

Remove from steamer and let rest on a rack for 15 to 30 minutes. Unwrap. Slice and serve warm with ice cream or applesauce.

Chocolate Pecan Bread Pudding

Serves 10-12

THIS DESSERT IS FOR SERIOUS CHOCOLATE LOVERS. A cross between a pudding and a soufflé, it almost floats from the dish into your mouth. With some good vanilla ice cream, it's fit for royalty.

To make fresh bread crumbs, we take large chunks of the challah (Jewish egg bread, available in most bakeries) and rub them against a large-holed grater. While we like the flavor of challah, if it's not available, you can use another seedless white bread. The bread pudding can be prepared in advance and re-steamed for 30 to 40 minutes to heat it through.

¼	cup coarsely chopped pecans, toasted
1	tablespoon packed dark brown sugar
6	cups fresh challah crumbs
6	tablespoons (¾ stick) unsalted butter, melted
3	cups half-and-half
5	large eggs, separated
1¼	cups sugar
¼	cup rum
2	teaspoons vanilla extract
8	ounces bittersweet or semisweet chocolate, chopped, melted and cooled
½	cup heavy cream
	Vanilla ice cream, for serving

Set a steaming rack or basket in a wide pot. Fill pot with water to reach just to bottom of rack. Bring water to a boil before cooking.

Thoroughly butter a 10-to-12-cup pudding mold or a deep heatproof bowl. In a small bowl, blend together pecans and brown sugar. Sprinkle evenly over bottom of mold. Set aside.

In a large mixing bowl, toss challah crumbs with melted butter. Add half-and-half and mix. Set aside.

In another large bowl, combine egg yolks, 1 cup sugar, rum and vanilla; whip well. Add melted chocolate and heavy cream; blend well. Pour over challah mixture and mix thoroughly.

With an electric mixer, whip egg whites until foamy. Gradually add remaining ¼ cup sugar and beat until stiff but not dry. Fold beaten egg whites into challah mixture.

Pour pudding into prepared mold. Place a sheet of wax paper over top and tightly cover with lid. Place on rack in steamer. Cover and steam for 1¼ hours, or until a knife inserted into center comes out clean. Transfer to a rack and let rest for 30 minutes.

Invert pudding onto a warm platter and remove mold. Cut into wedges and serve warm, topped with ice cream.

Lemon Cake with Dried Cherries & Lemon Sauce

Serves 12-14

THE LEMON FLAVOR OF THIS WARM STEAMED CAKE is nicely complemented by the dried cherries and subtle spices. Popular in the early eighteenth century, steamed cakes were often made with large amounts of cornmeal and dried bread crumbs. Inspired by a recipe in the late Richard Sax's *Classic Home Desserts*, we also incorporate fresh whole wheat crumbs, instead of plain dry ones. Not only do they add more flavor, they contribute to the cake's lightness. While Linda thinks this cake is fine on its own, Fred prefers it with some vanilla ice cream or the sauce suggested here.

1	cup unbleached flour
½	cup unbleached pastry flour
1	cup sugar
2½	teaspoons baking powder
1	teaspoon ground cardamom
¼	teaspoon freshly grated nutmeg
¼	teaspoon ground mace
¼	teaspoon kosher salt
1	cup coarse fresh whole wheat bread crumbs
½	cup stone-ground yellow cornmeal
¾	cup dried cherries
3	large eggs
	Minced zest of 3 lemons
6	tablespoons (¾ stick) unsalted butter, melted
½	cup fresh lemon juice, plus more if needed
1	cup milk

Sauce

½	cup sugar
3	tablespoons cornstarch
½	cup fresh lemon juice, plus more if needed
½	cup kirsch liqueur or brandy

Set a steaming rack or basket in a wide pot. Fill pot with water to reach just to bottom of rack. Thoroughly butter a 10-to-12-cup pudding mold or a deep heatproof bowl.

Sift together flours, sugar, baking powder, cardamom, nutmeg, mace and salt into a large mixing bowl. Add bread crumbs, cornmeal and cherries; lightly mix with a whisk.

With an electric mixer, beat together eggs and lemon zest until fluffy. Beat in melted butter; beat in lemon juice. Add one-fourth of flour mixture to egg mixture and blend. Add ⅓ cup milk, then another one-fourth of flour. Blend. Repeat twice more, alternating milk and flour and ending with flour.

Pour mixture into mold, smoothing top. Leave at least 1½ inches head room for cake to expand. Tightly cover. Place mold on rack in pot. Cover pot and bring water to a boil over high heat. Reduce heat to low so water simmers, just enough to maintain constant steam. Steam, adding hot water as needed, until a toothpick inserted into center of cake comes out clean, 2 to 2¼ hours.

Remove cake from pot and set on a wire rack. Uncover and let stand for 10 to 15 minutes.

To make sauce: Combine sugar and cornstarch in a heavy, nonreactive saucepan. Gradually whisk in lemon juice, ½ cup cold water and kirsch or brandy. Cook, whisking, over medium heat until thickened, 5 to 10 minutes. If sauce is too thick, thin with equal amounts of juice and water. Keep warm.

Invert cake onto a heated serving platter and remove mold. Slice and serve with warm sauce.

Christmas Plum Pudding with Hard Sauce

Serves 12-18

SIMILAR IN TEXTURE AND FLAVOR TO A FRUITCAKE, this dense dessert is filled with dried fruits, redolent with a host of exotic spices. It has been our Christmas dessert since our first holiday together. We make it right after Thanksgiving, splashing it with rum every week until Christmas. Its last splash is warmed and ignited, and Fred marches into the darkened dining room with the flaming pudding in all its glory. We follow this with a glass of vintage port.

1	cup golden raisins
1	cup finely chopped dried apricots
1	cup sliced glacéed cherries
½	cup chopped candied fruits
¾	cup chopped dates
½	cup chopped figs
¾	cup Myers's dark rum, plus up to 1½ cups, for aging
2	tablespoons unsalted butter, softened, for buttering mold
½	cup chopped black walnuts or English walnuts
¼	cup chopped candied orange peel
¼	cup chopped crystallized ginger
½	pound beef suet, finely grated
5	large egg yolks, beaten
¼	cup packed dark brown sugar
1	cup stale ladyfinger crumbs
½	cup unbleached pastry flour, sifted
1	teaspoon freshly grated nutmeg
1	teaspoon ground cinnamon
½	teaspoon ground cloves
½	teaspoon ground mace
⅓	cup heavy cream
6	large egg whites, beaten until stiff but not dry

Hard Sauce

1   pound (4 sticks) unsalted butter, softened

3-4   cups confectioners' sugar

3   tablespoons Myers's dark rum, plus ¼ cup for flaming

Sprig of holly, for garnish (optional)

In a large mixing bowl, combine raisins, apricots, cherries, candied fruits, dates and figs. Toss with ¾ cup rum. Cover bowl with plastic and macerate overnight at room temperature.

Set a steaming rack or basket in a deep pot. Fill pot with water to reach just to bottom of rack. Thoroughly butter a 10-to-12-cup pudding mold or a deep heatproof bowl using 2 tablespoons butter.

Stir walnuts, orange peel, ginger and suet into bowl with macerated fruit; blend thoroughly. Stir in egg yolks, brown sugar, ladyfinger crumbs, flour, nutmeg, cinnamon, cloves, mace and cream. Blend again. Fold in beaten egg whites.

Spoon mixture into mold. Cover with wax paper; top with a tight-fitting lid or heavy-duty foil. Place on rack in pot. Bring water to a boil. Tightly cover, reduce heat to low and steam pudding for 3½ hours, adding more water as needed. Remove mold from pot and cool. Pour ¼ cup rum over top.

Cover and store in refrigerator for 3 to 5 weeks. Moisten each week with another ¼ cup rum.

To serve, bring pudding to room temperature. Prepare pot for steaming. Steam pudding for 1 hour before serving to heat through.

Meanwhile, make hard sauce: Cream butter with an electric mixer. Gradually beat in confectioners' sugar until sauce is thick and creamy. Beat in 3 tablespoons rum. Spoon into an attractive serving bowl.

Unmold plum pudding on a heatproof serving platter. Place holly sprig in center if desired. Carefully warm remaining ¼ cup rum in a small saucepan. Pour over the pudding, and averting your face, ignite. Make your grand entrance into a darkened room.

Serve with hard sauce on the side.

Gingered Carrot Cake

Serves 10-12

THIS STEAMED CARROT CAKE is inspired by Mabel Vernon's carrot pudding recipe in Billie Burn's *Stirrin' the Pots on Daufuskie*. It is light in texture, studded with raisins and delightfully seasoned. (See photograph, page 92.)

2	cups finely grated carrots
¾	cup drained grated white potatoes
1	cup dark raisins or dried currants
1	large egg
7	tablespoons unsalted butter, melted
1	cup unbleached flour
1	cup sugar
1	teaspoon freshly grated nutmeg
1	teaspoon ground cloves
1	teaspoon ground cinnamon
1	teaspoon ground ginger
1	teaspoon baking soda
¾	teaspoon kosher salt
	Applesauce or cinnamon ice cream, for serving

Set a steaming rack in a deep pot. Fill pot with water to reach just to bottom of rack. Thoroughly butter a 10-to-12-cup pudding mold or a deep heatproof bowl.

In a large bowl, combine carrots, potatoes, raisins or currants, egg and melted butter. Place remaining ingredients in a sifter, sift in and stir until combined.

Spoon mixture into mold. Cover with wax paper and a lid. Place on rack. Bring water to a boil over high heat. Reduce heat to low and steam over simmering water, replenishing water as needed, for 3 hours; a toothpick inserted in middle will come out clean.

Transfer mold to a rack and let cool, covered, for 30 minutes.

Remove lid and paper. Invert onto a warm serving platter. Cut into wedges and top with applesauce or ice cream.

Appendix

Basics

Fresh Tomato Puree 324

Rich Chicken Stock 325

Dark Brown Duck Stock 326

Rich Fish Stock 327

Dark Brown Beef or Veal Stock 328

Rich Vegetable Stock 330

Bouquet Garni 331

Confit Seasonings 332

Fresh Tomato Puree

Makes about 4 cups

LINDA ALWAYS PLANTS TOO MANY TOMATOES. Besides the San Marzano (red) pear, we have several bushes of yellow pear tomato varieties. Our garden contains red, yellow and orange heirlooms with names like Big Rainbow, Mortgage Lifter, Yellow Marglobe and Oxheart. In the end, we always have more luscious tomatoes than two people and their friends can consume. This simple recipe allows us to capture the wonderful freshness of our right-from-the-vine tomatoes. We freeze the puree in 1-, 2- and 4-cup containers so that throughout the winter, we have it on hand for pasta sauce and soups and meats. To make the puree, we usually use a mix of tomatoes, including a generous portion of the paste-producing pear-shaped types, in order to get a more flavorful sauce. We do not season the puree; we think it tastes fresher this way.

1 tablespoon olive oil
3 quarts mixed fresh vine-ripened tomatoes,
   cut in half

Coat a heavy, nonreactive 3-quart saucepan with oil; add tomatoes. Cover with a tight-fitting lid and cook over very low heat, stirring occasionally, until tomatoes fall apart, about 45 minutes. Let cool.

Puree through a food mill to separate skins and seeds from pulp. (Alternatively, puree in a food processor fitted with the metal blade and strain.)

If using only paste tomatoes, pour puree into freezer containers, cover and freeze. If using a mixture of tomatoes, return puree to saucepan and simmer, uncovered, until reduced and thickened, 20 to 30 minutes. Cool.

Cool to room temperature. Ladle into freezer containers, cover and freeze for up to 1 year.

Rich Chicken Stock

Makes 2 quarts

W E PREPARE LARGE AMOUNTS OF STOCK AT A TIME, freezing it in containers ranging in size from 1 cup to 1 quart. We do not add salt, preferring the lighter, fresher taste of unsalted stock.

6	pounds chicken bones
2	large yellow onions, unpeeled
2	whole cloves
8	whole carrots
2	whole celery stalks
1	leek, trimmed, split and well washed
1	whole parsnip
1	whole turnip
1	bunch fresh flat-leaf parsley
10	black peppercorns, bruised
5	white peppercorns, bruised
2	fresh thyme sprigs
1	bay leaf

Place chicken bones and 5 quarts water in a large stockpot; bring to a boil over high heat. Reduce heat to medium-low and skim froth as it forms on top of pot. Replenish any liquid you discard by adding warm water to pot.

Stud each onion with 1 clove and add to pot along with all remaining ingredients. Reduce heat, cover and simmer for 8 hours.

Line a colander with a double layer of dampened cheesecloth; strain stock into a large saucepan. Discard solids. Bring stock to a boil; reduce heat to a brisk simmer. Continue to simmer, uncovered, until reduced to 2 quarts, about 1 hour. (If you wish, you can reduce stock to 1 quart for an even richer result.)

Cool to room temperature. Ladle into freezer containers, cover and freeze for up to 1 year.

Dark Brown Duck Stock

Makes 1½-2 quarts

BESIDES BEING PERFECT FOR Casserole of Ducks with Carrots, Onions & Turnips (page 142) and Duck Legs Braised with Baby Lettuces (page 146), this dark brown stock is a good base for any sauce for roasted duck. Ask your butcher for carcasses when he or she bones the breasts.

Grill the legs and thighs and store the remaining bones in the freezer until you are ready to make stock.

4	duck carcasses, broken into pieces
	Giblets, if available
6	carrots, cut into chunks
3	celery stalks
2	large onions, quartered
2	parsnips, cut into chunks
2	turnips, cut into chunks
1	tablespoon duck fat or olive oil
1	bunch fresh flat-leaf parsley
10	black peppercorns, bruised with bottom of a heavy pot
1	bay leaf
1	whole clove

Preheat oven to 450 degrees F.

In a large roasting pan, roast duck carcasses and giblets, uncovered, turning frequently, until lightly browned, about 30 minutes.

Meanwhile, toss carrots, celery, onions, parsnips and turnips with fat or oil.

After carcasses have roasted for 30 minutes, add vegetables. Continue roasting until vegetables are dark brown, about 1 hour.

Transfer browned duck, giblets and vegetables to a large stockpot. Add cold water to cover; bring to a boil over high heat. Remove froth as it forms, replenishing any liquid you discard with an equal amount of warm water. When froth no longer forms, add remaining ingredients, partially cover and simmer for 3 hours.

Strain liquid through a double layer of dampened cheesecloth into a large saucepan. Discard solids. Briskly simmer stock until reduced to 1½ to 2 quarts, about 1 hour.

Cool to room temperature. Skim off surface fat. Ladle into freezer containers, cover and freeze for up to 1 year.

Rich Fish Stock

Makes 3 quarts

L ET YOUR FISH MERCHANT KNOW A FEW DAYS AHEAD OF TIME that you want to make fish stock so that he or she has time to gather some good fish heads and carcasses for you. Do not use strong, oily fish like tuna or mackerel.

4	cups finely chopped onions
2	cups coarsely chopped carrots
2	cups coarsely chopped celery
6	pounds fresh fish heads, bones and trimmings
8	celery stalks
14	white peppercorns, bruised with bottom of a heavy pot
4	fresh thyme sprigs
2	bay leaves
2	teaspoons fennel seeds
2	3-inch strips orange peel
3	cups Sauvignon Blanc

Place onions, carrots, celery and 1 quart water in a large nonreactive stockpot. Tightly cover and bring to a boil. Immediately reduce heat to low and simmer for 15 minutes.

Add 4 quarts water and all remaining ingredients; bring to a boil. Reduce heat to a brisk simmer, and skim froth as it forms. When froth no longer forms, place cover slightly ajar, and cook for 1 hour.

Remove pot from heat. Use a slotted spoon or skimmer to remove as many solids as possible. Line a colander with a double layer of dampened cheesecloth; strain stock into a clean pan; discard solids.

Simmer stock briskly, uncovered, until reduced to 3 quarts, about 1 hour.

Cool to room temperature. Ladle into freezer containers, cover and freeze for up to 1 year.

Dark Brown Beef or Veal Stock

Makes 2 quarts

WE FIND IT USEFUL to have many containers of this rich beef stock in the freezer. The veal stock is the base for Veal Roast with Leek & Caramelized Onion Gravy (page 186). As with all our stocks, we do not add salt, preferring to leave the seasoning for the final dish.

6	pounds beef or veal marrowbones
2	pounds beef knuckle
1	pound beef or veal soup meat
1	bunch (1-1½ pounds) carrots
3	large yellow onions, unpeeled, quartered
3	large whole tomatoes
3	whole parsnips
3	whole celery stalks
3	plump garlic cloves, unpeeled
1	bunch fresh flat-leaf parsley
10	black peppercorns, bruised with bottom of heavy pot
2	fresh thyme sprigs or ½ teaspoon dried
1	whole clove
1	bay leaf

Preheat oven to 425 degrees F.

Combine bones and meat in a large, shallow roasting pan and roast, turning often, until very lightly browned, about 45 minutes.

Add carrots, onions, tomatoes, parsnips, celery and garlic to pan. Continue to roast, turning frequently, until bones and vegetables are a dark, rich brown, about 2 hours.

With a slotted spoon or skimmer, transfer solids to a large stockpot. Pour off fat from roasting pan, add 1 cup water and deglaze by stirring over high heat, scraping any loose browned bits that adhere to bottom.

Pour mixture into stockpot and add 6 quarts water. Bring to a boil. Reduce heat to medium and simmer briskly, skimming any froth that forms on surface, until froth no longer forms. Reduce heat to low, add parsley, peppercorns, thyme, clove and bay leaf. Place cover ajar and simmer over low heat for 8 to 10 hours.

Line a colander with a double layer of dampened cheesecloth; strain stock and discard solids. If stock measures more than 2 quarts, return it to a large saucepan, bring to a boil, reduce heat to medium and simmer briskly until reduced to 2 quarts.

Chill for at least 6 hours or overnight to congeal fat. Remove any fat from surface.

Ladle into freezer containers, cover tightly and freeze for up to 1 year.

Rich Vegetable Stock

Makes about 2 quarts

SAVE YOUR VEGETABLE TRIMMINGS for a few days so you can enrich the stockpot.

10	large whole carrots, coarsely chopped
3	large whole yellow onions
2	large whole turnips, cut into chunks
2	large whole zucchini
2	large leeks, split, well washed and trimmed to include tender green
2	cups vegetable trimmings, such as pea pods, asparagus bottoms, scallions
1	celery bunch, cut into chunks
1	large parsnip, cut into chunks
1	bunch fresh flat-leaf parsley
1	bouquet garni (opposite page)
1	tablespoon mixed black and white peppercorns

Combine all ingredients and 3½ quarts water in a large stockpot. Cover and bring to a boil over high heat. Reduce heat to low and simmer for 2½ hours.

Line a colander with a double layer of dampened cheesecloth; strain stock into clean pan. Discard solids.

Simmer stock, uncovered, until reduced to 2 quarts, about 1 hour.

Cool to room temperature. Ladle into freezer containers, cover and freeze for up to 1 year.

Bouquet Garni

WHILE THE HERBS IN THIS CLASSIC SEASONING MIXTURE of French cuisine may vary slightly, they generally include a sprig or two of parsley and thyme and a bay leaf. The herbs are either tied together with a string or wrapped and secured in a piece of cheesecloth. Sometimes, we throw the loose herbs into the pot and fish them out later.

If we don't have fresh thyme and must use dried, we make a cheesecloth pouch: Cut a 4-inch square of cheesecloth. In the center, place 1 bay leaf, 2 sprigs of fresh flat-leaf parsley and ½ teaspoon dried thyme. Gather the corners and tie them together to form a pouch.

You can also purchase prepared, dried bouquet garnis from specialty markets and Williams-Sonoma (see Sources, page 336).

Confit Seasonings

IN THE SOUTHWEST OF FRANCE, farmers still prepare a variety of *confits*—duck, goose, pork—all cured with spices and herbs and slowly cooked in their own rendered fat. The preserved meat is then stored in crocks. Over the years, we've developed our own blend of confit seasonings that we often use to flavor meats cooked under cover.

8	whole juniper berries
4	whole cloves
2	teaspoons fennel seeds
1	12-inch cinnamon stick, broken in half
2	whole allspice
1	teaspoon finely ground fresh black pepper
½	teaspoon freshly grated nutmeg
½	teaspoon ground ginger
½	teaspoon ground cardamom
½	teaspoon ground coriander

Combine seasonings in a spice grinder or use a mortar and pestle; finely grind. Place in a clean jar, tightly cover and store for up to 3 months.

Sources

Sweet Onions, Shallots, Garlic & Leeks

The Allium Connection
1339 Swainwood Drive
Glenview, Illinois 60025
(708) 729-4823
John F. Swenson
  A variety of French shallots.

Kingsfield Gardens
Blue Mounds, Wisconsin 53517
(608) 924-9341
Richard Abernethy and Erika Koenigsaecker
  Organically grown shallots, both the hard-to-find French gray shallot and large red shallots, and a variety of exceptionally clean and flavorful leeks (late summer through late autumn).

Robison Ranch
P.O. Box 1018
Walla Walla, Washington 99362
(509) 525-8807
Jim Robison
  An excellent source for plump shallots (all year) and garlic (August through early fall) as well as Walla Walla sweet onions (July, early August).

Specialty Food Products

Dean & DeLuca
560 Broadway
New York, New York 10012
(212) 431-1691
  With various locations outside of New York, this company is still among the finest sources in the country for all specialty products, including cheeses, vinegars, imported olive oils, exotic grains, dried mushrooms, mushrooms, fruits, chiles, chile powder, specialty Mediterranean olives, anchovies, polenta and Arborio rice.

The West Point Market
1711 West Market Street
Akron, Ohio 44313
(800) 838-2156
  Well known in the specialty-food industry, this market is a fine source for hard-to-find products, such as fruit vinegars, high-quality olive oils, exotic grains, dried beans and flours, chile powder and specialty Mediterranean olives. The market also sells a wide variety of imported cheese and chocolate.

Meats, Poultry & Shellfish

Mr. Brisket
2156 South Taylor Road
Cleveland Heights, Ohio 44118
(216) 932-8620

High-quality beef, veal, lamb, pork, chicken, ducks, geese and turkeys delivered overnight to homes around the country. Owner Sanford Herskovitz is also an enthusiastic source for information about meat.

S. Wallace Edwards & Sons Inc.
P.O. Box 25
Surry, Virginia 23883
(800) 222-4267

Founded in the 1920s, this family-owned Virginia ham company prides itself on its hands-on production of cured and smoked hams, sausages and bacon. Edwards' hams are cured with as little nitrate and salt as possible and are hickory-smoked. Wigwam ham has the longest aging process—one year. Edwards' especially meaty bacon is dry-cured, not injected with water and chemicals, and is hickory-smoked.

Taylor United
SE 130 Lynch Road
Shelton, Washington 98584
(360) 426-6178

A popular source for shellfish, including farmed oysters and "Mediterranean" mussels, which are especially meaty and tender.

Grains, Beans & Flours

Arrowhead Mills
Box 2059
Hereford, Texas 79045
(806) 364-0730

One of the best producers of certified organic flours, grains and beans. They can advise you about purchasing their products from retailers in your region or can ship directly to your home.

The Fowler's Milling Company
12500 Fowler's Mill Road
Chardon, Ohio 44024
(216) 286-2024
Rick Erickson

An excellent source for stone-ground flours, medium-grind yellow cornmeal and grits.

Lowell Farms
311 Avenue A
El Campo, Texas 77437
(800) 484-9213, ID# 7423
Lowell and Linda Raun

These rice farmers grow and sell certified organic white jasmine and brown jasmine rice.

Manitok Wild Rice
Box 97, Highway 59
Callaway, Minnesota 56521
(800) 726-1863

Authentic, certified organic lake-grown wild rice, harvested and packaged by hand. The Manitok cooperative was formed by the White Earth Band of the Ojibway tribe, and the income from the sales of the rice goes to the tribe.

Books & Utensils

Kitchen Arts & Letters

1435 Lexington Avenue

New York, New York 10128

(212) 876-5550

Fax (212) 876-3584

Nahum Waxman

If a book about food and wine is in print, Waxman will probably have it. The store also searches for out-of-print books without charge.

Wine and Food Library

1207 West Madison

Ann Arbor, Michigan 48103

(313) 663-4894

Jan and Dan Longone

Rare and out-of-print cookery and wine books searched without charge.

King Arthur Flour Baker's Catalogue

P.O. Box 876

Norwich, Vermont 05055

(800) 827-6836

An excellent source for the Pullman bread pan (a covered pan for baking sandwich bread), baking utensils, flours, syrups, yeasts, herbs, black walnuts and rosewater.

The Oriental Pantry

423 Great Road

Acton, Massachusetts 01720

(800) 828-0368

Joyce Chen's Good Earth (Yunnan) Pot as well as many other Chinese cooking utensils and ingredients.

Sur la Table

84 Pine Street

Seattle, Washington 98101

(206) 448-2244

Fax (206) 448-2245

This Seattle store is a cook's dream, an outstanding mail-order source for cooking and baking utensils. It carries an excellent selection of Le Creuset Dutch ovens and plain cast-iron Dutch ovens.

Williams-Sonoma

P.O. Box 7044

San Francisco, California 94120-7044

(800) 541-2233

Cookware and baking utensils as well as specialty oils, grains and flours.

Don Drumm Studio and Gallery

437 Crouse Street

Akron, Ohio 44311

(216) 253-6268

Don Drumm's cast-aluminum casseroles and cooking utensils are available in galleries around the country or can be ordered by mail.

Bill Sax

The Knolls

South Hadley, Massachusetts 01075

(413) 532-4236

Bill Sax's flameware casseroles and cooking utensils are available in fine craft galleries around the country. His Massachusetts studio is open to the public, and he often appears at large regional craft fairs. Call for more information; some of his work can be ordered by phone.

Bibliography

Anderson, Jean. *The Food of Portugal.* New York: William Morrow, 1986.

Bean, Barbara. *The Electric Slow Cooker Cookbook.* Chicago: Henry Regnery, 1975.

Bianchini, Francesco, and Corbetta, Francesco. *The Fruits of the Earth.* London: Bloomsbury Books, 1973.

Bitting, Katherine Golden. *Gastronomic Bibliography.* San Francisco: 1939. (Limited edition facsimile. Mansfield, Connecticut: Maurizio Martino Publisher.)

Blake, Anthony. "The Cooking Chemist; The Chemistry of Good Taste." *The Chemical Intelligencer.* New York: Springer-Verlag, 1995.

Bridge, Fred, and Tibbetts, Jean F. *The Well-Tooled Kitchen.* New York: William Morrow, 1991.

Brothwell, Don and Patricia. *Food in Antiquity: A Survey of the Diet of Early Peoples.* New York: Frederick A. Praeger, 1969.

Brown, Theresa C. *Modern Domestic Cookery: A Collection of Receipts Suitable for All Classes of Housewives.* Charleston, South Carolina: Edward Perry, 1871. (Facsimile. Williamston, South Carolina: The Journal, 1985.)

Bryan, Lettice. *The Kentucky Housewife.* Cincinnati, Ohio: Shepard & Stearns, 1839. (Facsimile. Introduction by Bill Neal. Columbia, South Carolina: University of South Carolina Press, 1991.)

The Buckeye Cookery and Practical Housekeeping. Minneapolis, Minnesota: Buckeye Publishing, 1877. (Facsimile. Austin, Texas: Steck-Warlick, 1970.)

Burn, Billie. *Stirrin' the Pots on Daufuskie.* Daufuskie Island, South Carolina: Billie Burn, 1985.

Chen, Helen. *Chinese Home Cooking.* New York: Hearst Books, 1993.

Claiborne, Craig. *The New York Times Food Encyclopedia.* New York: Times Books, 1985.

Collquitt, Harriet Ross. *The Savannah Cook.* New York: Farrar & Rinehart, 1933.

David, Elizabeth. *Elizabeth David Classics.* New York: Alfred A. Knopf, 1980.

Davidson, Alan, general editor. *The Cook's Room.* New York: HarperCollins, 1991.

De Voe, Thomas F. *The Market Book.* New York: Burt Franklin, 1862. Reprint, 1969.

Digby, John and Joan, editors. *Food for Thought: An Anthology of Writings Inspired by Food.* New York: William Morrow, 1987.

Drummond, J.C. *The Englishman's Food: A History of Five Centuries of English Diet.* London: Readers Union, 1959.

Durrell, Alexis. *Crockery Cooking.* New York: Weathervane Books, 1975.

Edgerton, John. *Southern Food.* New York: Alfred A. Knopf, 1987.

Elkort, Martin. *The Secret Life of Food: A Feast of Food and Drink History, Folklore and Fact.* Los Angeles: Jeremy P. Tarcher, 1991.

Farb, Peter, and Armelagos, George. *Consuming Passions: The Anthropology of Eating.* Boston: Houghton Mifflin, 1980.

Farley, John. *The Art of Cookery.* London: Scatcherd and Letterman, 1807. (Facsimile. Edited by Ann Haly. East Sussex, England: Southover Press, 1988.)

The First Texas Cook Book. Houston, Texas: The First Presbyterian Church of Houston, 1883. (Facsimile. Austin, Texas: Eakin Press, 1986.)

Fisher, Abby. *What Mrs. Fisher Knows about Old Southern Cooking*. San Francisco: Women's Co-Operative Printing Office, 1881. (Facsimile. Edited by Karen Hess. Bedford, Massachusetts: Applewood Press, 1995.)

Flexner, Marion. *Out of Kentucky Kitchens*. New York: Franklin Watts, 1949.

Flexner, Marion. *Dixie Dishes*. Boston: Hale, Cushman & Flint, 1941.

Gay, Lettie, editor; Rett, Blanche S., recipe collector. *200 Years of Charleston Cooking*. New York: Random House, 1934.

Harris, Marvin. *Good to Eat: Riddles of Food and Culture*. New York: Simon & Schuster, 1985.

Harvey, Adell, and Gonzalez, Mari. *Sacred Chow*. Nashville: Abingdon Press, 1987.

Hazan, Marcella. *Essentials of Classic Italian Cooking*. New York: Alfred A. Knopf, 1992.

Heath, Henry B., and Reineccius, Gary. *Flavor, Chemistry and Technology*. Westport, Connecticut: AVI Publishing, 1986.

Hess, Karen. *The Carolina Rice Kitchen: The African Connection*. (Featuring in facsimile the *Carolina Rice Cookbook*.) Columbia, South Carolina: University of South Carolina Press, 1992.

Hirsch, Alan R. "Scents of Childhood." *Chicago Medicine*, May 21, 1995.

Hirsch, Alan R. "Nostalgia, the Odors of Childhood and Society." *Psychiatric Times*, August 1992.

Hirsch, Alan R. "The Good Old Smells." *The International Journal of Aromatherapy*, Autumn 1992.

Hirsch, Alan R. "Nostalgia: A Neuropsychiatric Understanding." *Advances in Consumer Research*, Volume 19, 1992.

Hyman, Mavis. *Indian-Jewish Cooking*. London: Hyman Publishers, n.d.

Jones, Evan. *American Food: The Gastronomic Story*. New York: Vintage Books, 1981.

Junior League of Nashville. *Nashville Seasons Cook Book*. Nashville, Tennessee: The Junior League of Nashville, 1964.

Lang, Jenifer Harvey, editor. *Larousse Gastronomique*. New York: Crown, 1988.

Leslie, Eliza (A Lady of Philadelphia). *Seventy-Five Receipts, for Pastry, Cakes, and Sweetmeats*. Boston: Munroe and Francis, 1828. (Facsimile: Bedford, Massachusetts: Applewood Books.)

Lifshey, Earl. *The Housewares Story*. Chicago: National Housewares Manufacturers Association, 1973.

Longone, Janice Bluestein and Daniel T. *American Cookbooks and Wine Books, 1797–1950*. Ann Arbor, Michigan: The Clements Library & The Wine and Food Library, 1984.

Luard, Elisabeth. *The Old World Kitchen*. New York: Bantam, 1987.

Luchetti, Cathy. *Home on the Range: A Culinary History of the American West*. New York: Villard Books, 1993.

McGee, Harold. *On Food and Cooking: The Science and Lore of the Kitchen*. New York: Scribner's, 1984.

Manière, Jacques; Lyness, Stephanie, translator. *The Art of Cooking with Steam*. New York: William Morrow, 1995.

Marks, Copeland. *Sephardic Cooking*. New York: Donald I. Fine, 1992.

Marshall, Lillian. *The Courier-Journal & Times Cookbook*. Louisville, Kentucky: The Courier-Journal and Louisville Times Company, 1971.

Marshall, Lydie Pinoy. *Cooking with Lydie Marshall*. New York: Alfred A. Knopf, 1982.

Maryland's Way. Annapolis, Maryland: The Hammond-Harwood House Association, 1963.

Masterton, Elsie. *Blueberry Hill Menu Cookbook*. New York: Thomas Y. Crowell, 1963.

Nathan, Joan. *An American Folklife Cookbook*. New York: Schocken Books, 1984.

Neal, Bill. *Biscuits, Spoonbread, and Sweet Potato Pie*. New York: Alfred A. Knopf, 1990.

Neal, Bill. *Southern Cooking*. Chapel Hill, North Carolina: The University of North Carolina Press, 1985.

Parliment, Thomas H., editor. *Thermally Generated Flavors*. American Chemical Society, Symposium Series 543. Washington, D.C., 1994.

Porter, Mrs. M.E. *Mrs. Porter's New Southern Cookery Book*. Philadelphia: John E. Potter, 1871. (Facsimile. Edited by Louis Szathmáry. New York: Promontory Press, 1974.)

Pullar, Philippa. *Consuming Passions: Being an Historic Inquiry into Certain English Appetites*. Boston: Little Brown, 1970.

Randolph, Mary. *The Virginia Housewife*. Baltimore: Plaskitt & Cugle, 1828. (Facsimile. Birmingham, Alabama: Oxmoor House, 1984.)

Reed, Ethel. *Pioneer Kitchen, A Frontier Cookbook*. Frontier Heritage Press, 1971.

Robotti, Frances D., and Peter J. *French Cooking in the New World*. Garden City, New York: Doubleday, 1967.

Root, Waverley. *Food*. New York: Simon & Schuster, 1980.

Rutledge, Sarah. *The Carolina Housewife*. Charleston, South Carolina: W.R. Babcock, 1847. (Facsimile. Edited by Anna Wells Rutledge. Columbia, South Carolina: University of South Carolina Press, 1979.)

Sax, Richard. *Classic Home Desserts*. Shelburne, Vermont: Chapters, 1994.

Schumacher, John. *John Schumacher's New Prague Hotel Cookbook*. New Prague, Minnesota: International Cuisine Publishers, 1991.

Scott, Natalie V. *200 Years of New Orleans Cooking*. New York: Jonathan Cape & Harrison Smith, 1931.

Simmons, Amelia. *American Cookery*. Hartford, Connecticut: Hudson & Goodwin, 1796. (Facsimile. Mineola, New York: Dover Publications, 1984.)

Simonds, Nina. *Classic Chinese Cuisine*. Rev. ed. Shelburne, Vermont: Chapters, 1994.

Sokolov, Raymond. Recipes by Susan R. Friedland. *The Jewish-American Kitchen*. New York: Stewart, Tabori & Chang, 1989.

Soyer, Alexis. *Soyer's Cookery Book*. London: George Routledge, 1854. (Facsimile. Forward by James Beard. New York: David McKay, 1959.)

Stern, Jane and Michael. *Goodfood*. New York: Alfred A. Knopf, 1983.

Tannahill, Reay. *Food in History*. New York: Stein & Day, 1973.

Thorne, John. *Outlaw Cook*. New York: Farrar Straus Giroux, 1992.

Thornton, Phineas. *The Southern Gardener and Receipt Book*. Newark, New Jersey: A.L. Dennis, 1845. (Facsimile. Birmingham, Alabama: Oxmoor House, 1984.)

Ude, Louis Eustache. *The French Cook*. Philadelphia: Carey, Lea and Carey, 1828. (Facsimile. New York: Arco Publishing, 1978.)

Waller, George R., and others, ed. *The Maillard Reaction in Foods and Nutrition*. American Chemical Society, Symposium Series 215. Washington, D.C., 1983.

Weaver, William Woys. *Pennsylvania Dutch Country Cooking*. New York: Abbeville Press, 1993.

Weaver, William Woys. *America Eats: Forms of Edible Folk Art*. New York: Harper & Row, 1989.

Weaver, William Woys. *Sauerkraut Yankees*. Philadelphia: University of Pennsylvania Press, 1983.

Wells, Patricia. *Trattoria*. New York: William Morrow, 1993.

Wolf, Burton, and others. *The Cooks' Catalogue*. New York: Harper & Row, 1975.

Index

Alsatian Sauerkraut & Pork, Braised
  (*Choucroute Garni*), 240; *photo*, 90

Appetizers. *See* Starters

Apple & Raisin Roly Poly, 312

Apples with Black Walnuts & Dried Apricots,
  Spiced Honey-Baked, 306

Arroz con Pollo (Casserole of Spanish-Style
  Chicken & Brown Rice), 130

Artichokes
  Barigoule, 34; *photo*, 95
  Provençal, Casserole of, 36

Asian-Style Stuffed Flounder, Steamed, 80

Asparagus
  with Lemon-Egg Butter, Braised, 286
  Soup, Summer, with Tarragon, 40

Autumn Vegetable Stew, 272

Baked
  Foil-, Sweet Onions with Mushrooms,
    Shallots & Herbs, 28
  Slow-, Barbecued Beans, 260
  Steak, 152
  Veal Chops with Mushrooms, 192

Barbecued Beans, Slow-Baked, 260

Basic Recipes, 324-32
  Beef or Veal Stock, Dark Brown, 328
  Bouquet Garni, 331
  Chicken Stock, Rich, 325
  Confit Seasonings, 332
  Duck Stock, Dark Brown, 326
  Fish Stock, Rich, 327
  Tomato Puree, Fresh, 324
  Vegetable Stock, Rich, 330

Bean(s), 255-64
  Barbecued, Slow-Baked, 260
  Black, Soup with Sherry, Kentucky, 54

Chicken, Garlic & Herbs, Silky Slow-
  Cooked Stew, 136

Five-Bean Chili, 258

Green, Lamb with, 218

Lima
  Cabbage & Leeks, Braised, Melt-in-
    Your-Mouth, 277
  Dried, & Tomatoes with Sage, Basil &
    Garlic, Stew of, 262
  & Mushrooms, Curried, Ragout of, 274
  Scalloped Corn & Tomatoes, 278

Red, with Spicy Sausage, 256

Snap, with Herbs, Buttery, 287

White, Pureed, 264

Beef, 152-78
  Brisket, Garlic-Studded, with Tomatoes,
    Red Wine & Onions, 160
  Cabbage Rolls, Mom's, 176
  Corned, & Cabbage, 162; *photo*, 89
  Daube, Gascon, with Onions, Prunes &
    Carrots, 168
  Flank Steak Deluxe, 153
  Flank Steak Stuffed with Corn & Herbs,
    154
  Goulash, Simple (*Gulyás*), 166
  Italian Potted, with Basil & Garlic, 156
  Meat Loaf, Dutch-Oven, 163
  Meatball Curry, Fragrant Calcutta (*Kofta*),
    178
  Meatballs, Grandma Bess's, 26
  Oven-Braised Chili (brisket), 164
  Sauerbraten, 158
  Short Ribs
    Beer-Braised, with Onions & Shallots,
      174
    Oklahoma-Style Breaded, 172

Stew with Caramelized RoLot
    Vegetable Sauce, 170
  Steak, Baked, 152
  or Veal Stock, Dark Brown, 328
Beer-Braised
  Short Ribs with Onions & Shallots, 174
  Veal Brisket with Onions & Parsnips, 184
Bisque. *See* Soup
Black Bean Soup with Sherry, Kentucky, 54
Blanquette of Veal, 188
Bluefish, Ginger-Steamed, with Pepper &
  Cilantro, 78
Bouquet Garni, 331
Braised
  Alsatian Sauerkraut & Pork (*Choucroute
    Garni*), 240; *photo*, 90
  Asparagus with Lemon-Egg Butter, 286
  Beer-, Short Ribs with Onions & Shallots,
    174
  Beer-, Veal Brisket with Onions &
    Parsnips, 184
  Cabbage, Leeks & Lima Beans, Melt-in-
    Your-Mouth, 27
  Chianti-, Pork Chops Stuffed with Sun-
    Dried Tomatoes & Ham, 238
  Duck Legs with Baby Lettuces, 146
  Eggplant Stuffed with Lamb, Pine Nuts &
    Mint, 220
  Fennel-, Pork Roast with Apples, Endive &
    Herbs, 226
  Flageolets with Herbs, Shallots & Lemon,
    263
  Garlic-, New Potatoes with Herbs, 292
  Halibut with Sake, 106
  Kale with Caramelized Leeks, 284
  Lamb with Okra, Indian-Style Spicy, 212
  Lemon-, Fennel & Endive, 294
  Lentils & Caramelized Onions, Veal
    Shanks with, 198

Maple-, Plums, Figs & Blackberries, 308
Mélange of Root Vegetables, 276; *photo*, 93
Oven-, Chili, 164
Oven-, Salmon, with *Labnee* & Herb-
  Cucumber Sauce, 102
Parchment-, Snapper with Fennel, 98
Pork Chops with Apples & Cabbage, 232;
  photo, 94
Pork Chops & Mushrooms in Mustard
  Cream Sauce, 230
Snow Pea Pods with Lettuce & Butter, 285
Tomato-, Swordfish, with Onions &
  Anchovies, 107
Trout with Onions & Peppers, 76
Yellow Squash with Fresh Herbs, 289
braising (technique), 10
Bread 266-68
  Brown, Daufuskie Island, 266
  Corn, Under-Cover, 267
  Pullman (Lydie's *Pain de Mie*), 268
Bread Pudding, Chocolate Pecan, 314
Brisket
  Garlic-Studded, with Tomatoes, Red Wine
    & Onions, 160
  Veal, Beer-Braised, with Onions &
    Parsnips, 184
  Veal, Spice-Rubbed, with Red Wine Sauce,
    182
Brown Rice in a Spanish Sauce, Casserole of,
  251
browning main ingredients, 12
Brussels Sprouts, Glazed, with Black Walnut
  Butter, 299

Cabbage
  Corned Beef &, 162; *photo*, 89
  Leeks & Lima Beans, Braised, Melt-in-
    Your-Mouth, 277
  Red, with Leeks & Apple Cider, 296

Rolls, Mom's, 176

Scallions & Carrots, Pot Stickers with, 32;
   photo, 82

Simple Spicy, 297

Cake

   Carrot, Gingered, 320; *photo*, 92

   Lemon, with Dried Cherries & Lemon
      Sauce, 316

Carrot(s)

   Cake, Gingered, 320; *photo*, 92

   Gingered, with Lemon & Thyme, 288

   Soup, Puree of (*Potage Crécy*), 42

casserole (dish), 13

Cauliflower Bisque, 58

Chianti-Braised Pork Chops Stuffed with
   Sun-Dried Tomatoes & Ham, 238

Chicken(s), 112-36

   Baby, Pot-Roasted, with Garlic, Root
      Vegetables & Herbs, 114

   Beans, Garlic & Herbs, Silky Slow-Cooked
      Stew, 136

   Curried, Old Kentucky, 132

   Fricassee, Nana's, 126

   Hunter's Style (*Pollo alla Cacciatora*), 123

   Oven-Barbecued, 122

   Peppered, with Curried Onion & Mustard
      Sauce, 128

   Potted Stuffed, & Vegetables, 118; *photo*,
      front cover

   & Shrimp Gumbo, 124

   Skillet-Fried, with Creamy Cracklin' Gravy,
      112

   Smothered, with Andouille Sausage,
      Onions & Peppers, 120

   Spanish-Style, & Brown Rice, Casserole of
      (*Arroz con Pollo*), 130

   Stew with Virginia Ham, Mushrooms, Peas
      & Cornmeal Dumplings, 134

   Stock, Rich, 325

Yunnan Pot, with Bok Choy & Snow Peas,
   116; *photo*, 87

Chili

   Five-Bean, 258

   Oven-Braised, 164

   of Smoked Turkey & Peppers, 140

Chocolate Pecan Bread Pudding, 314

Choucroute Garni (Braised Alsatian Sauerkraut
   & Pork), 240; *photo*, 90

Chowder. *See* Soup

Christmas Plum Pudding with Hard Sauce,
   318

Clam Chowder, New England, 44

Clams, & Lobster, Spicy Steamed, with Corn,
   70

Confit Seasonings, 332

cooking techniques, slow moist, 9-11

cookware for slow cooking, 13-15

Corn

   Bread, Under-Cover, 267

   Scalloped, Lima Beans & Tomatoes, 278

Corned Beef & Cabbage, 162; *photo*, 89

Cornmeal. *See* Polenta

covered dishes, short history of, 11-12

Curry(ied)

   Chicken, Old Kentucky, 132

   Lima Beans & Mushrooms, Ragout of, 274

   Meatball, Fragrant Calcutta (*Kofta*), 178

   Vegetables with Ginger & Mint, 279

Daufuskie Island Brown Bread, 266

Dessert, 302-20

   Apple & Raisin Roly Poly, 312

   Apples with Black Walnuts & Dried
      Apricots, Spiced Honey-Baked, 306

   Carrot Cake, Gingered, 320; *photo*, 92

   Chocolate Pecan Bread Pudding, 314

   Fruits, Mulled Dried, with Port Wine, 302

Lemon Cake with Dried Cherries & Lemon Sauce, 316

Lemony Ginger Dumplings with Blueberry Maple Syrup, 310

Maple-Braised Plums, Figs & Blackberries, 308

Peaches Poached in Zinfandel, Minted Basil, 304

Pears, Poached Rosemary, with Late-Harvest Riesling & Raisins, 305; *photo*, 96

Plum Pudding, Christmas, with Hard Sauce, 318

Rice Pudding, Creamy Almond, 309

Deviled Turkey Legs with Olive Pan Sauce, 138

Duck(s)

with Carrots, Onions & Turnips, Casserole of, 142

Legs Braised with Baby Lettuces, 146

Stock, Dark Brown, 326

& Wild Rice Casserole, 144

Dumplings, Lemony Ginger, with Blueberry Maple Syrup, 310

Dutch oven, cooking in, 11, 13

Dutch-Oven Meat Loaf, 163

Egg Noodles, Silky Farfel with Peas & Carrots, 265

Eggplant

Braised, Stuffed with Lamb, Pine Nuts & Mint, 220

& Garbanzo Stew (*Im-Naz' Zalee*), 282

& Tomato Stew, Summer, 283

electric slow cooker, 13

Endive & Fennel, Lemon-Braised, 294

Escarole & Squash, Spicy Pork Stew with, 242

Farfel, Silky, with Peas & Carrots, 265

Fennel

-Braised Pork Roast with Apples, Endive & Herbs, 226

& Endive, Lemon-Braised, 294

Fish. *See also* Shellfish

Bluefish, Ginger-Steamed, with Pepper & Cilantro, 78

Chowder with Chard & Corn, Creamy, 46; *photo*, 91

Flounder, Steamed Asian-Style Stuffed, 80

Halibut with Sake, Braised, 106

Lemon Sole *en Papillote*, Fragrant, 79

Salmon

Herbed, Poached in Red Wine, 77

Orange & Ginger Steamed, 100; *photo*, 83

Oven-Braised, with *Labnee* (Yogurt Cheese) & Herb-Cucumber Sauce, 102

& Spinach Chowder with Yellow Potatoes & Scallions, 43

Teriyaki with Spinach & Scallions, 97

Salt Cod in Garlic Sauce with Potatoes & Raisins, 30

Shad Roe with Crispy Bacon & Lemon Sauce, 108

Snapper, Parchment-Braised, with Fennel, 98

Stew, Mediterranean, 72

Stew, Portuguese (*Caldeirada*), 74

Stock, Rich, 327

Swordfish, Tomato-Braised, with Onions & Anchovies, 107

Trout, Braised, with Onions & Peppers, 76

Tuna Provençal, 104

Five-Bean Chili, 258

Flageolets, Braised, with Herbs, Shallots & Lemon, 263

Flank Steak

Deluxe, 153

Stuffed with Corn & Herbs, 154
Flounder, Stuffed, Steamed Asian-Style, 80
foil-or-parchment baking (technique), 11
Fried Potatoes, Fred's Famous, 291
Fruits, Mulled Dried, with Port Wine, 302

Garbanzo & Eggplant Stew (*Im-Naz' Zalee*), 282
Garlic
   -Braised New Potatoes with Herbs, 292
   -Studded Brisket with Tomatoes, Red Wine & Onions, 160
Gascon Beef Daube with Onions, Prunes & Carrots, 168
Ginger-Steamed Bluefish with Pepper & Cilantro, 78
Gingered
   Carrot Cake, 320; *photo*, 92
   Carrots with Lemon & Thyme, 288
   Pork Loin with Sweet Potatoes & Prunes, 228
Glazed Brussels Sprouts with Black Walnut Butter, 299
Goulash, Simple (*Gulyás*), 166
Grains. *See* Grits; Polenta; Rice
Grape Leaves Shaheen, Stuffed (*Yub' Ruck*), 24
Green Beans, Lamb with, 218
Grits Pudding, Steamed Spicy, 252
Gulyás (Simple Goulash), 166
Gumbo
   Chicken & Shrimp, 124
   Oyster & Sausage, with Okra & Corn, 62

Halibut with Sake, Braised, 106
Ham, Smoked, & Shrimp Jambalaya, 64
Herbed Salmon Poached in Red Wine, 77
Hungarian Sauerkraut Soup, Spicy, 56

Indian-Style Spicy Braised Lamb with Okra, 212
Italian
   Osso Bucco Milanese, Joey's, 194; *photo*, 86
   Potted Beef with Basil & Garlic, 156
   Venetian-Style Shrimp with Olive Paste Croutons, 20

Jambalaya, Shrimp & Smoked Ham, 64

Kale with Caramelized Leeks, Braised, 284
Kentucky
   Black Bean Soup with Sherry, 54
   Old, Curried Chicken, 132
Kofta (Fragrant Calcutta Meatball Curry), 178

Lamb, 202-20
   with Green Beans, 218
   Indian-Style Spicy Braised, with Okra, 212
   Leg of
      with Potatoes & Onions, 202
      Savory, with Shallots, Turnips & Carrots, 203
      Stuffed Boneless, with Sweet Potatoes, 206
      with White Wine, Prosciutto, Coriander & Rosemary, 204
   Pine Nuts & Mint, Braised Eggplant Stuffed with, 220
   Ragout of, with Mushrooms, Onions & Red Wine, 210
   Shanks, Rosemary, with White Wine, Leeks & Shallots, 214
   Shanks, Spiced, in Red Wine, 216
   Springtime Stew of (*Printanier Navarin*), 208; *photo*, 85
Leek(s)
   and Caramelized Onion Gravy, Veal Roast with, 186

& Potato Soup with Sage, 47

Red Cabbage with, and Apple Cider, 296

Lemon

-Braised Fennel & Endive, 294

Cake with Dried Cherries & Lemon Sauce, 316

Sole *en Papillote*, Fragrant, 79

Veal Shanks with White Wine, 196

Lemony Ginger Dumplings with Blueberry Maple Syrup, 310

Lentils on Rice (*Im-Jud' Dara*), 255

Lima Beans

Cabbage & Leeks, Braised, Melt-in-Your-Mouth, 277

Dried, & Tomatoes with Sage, Basil & Garlic, Stew of, 262

& Mushrooms, Curried, & Mushrooms, Ragout of, 274

Scalloped Corn & Tomatoes, 278

Lobsters & Clams, Spicy Steamed, with Corn, 70

Maillard, Louis-Camille, 12

Maple-Braised Plums, Figs & Blackberries, 308

McGee, Harold, 12

Meat Loaf, Dutch-Oven, 163

Meatball Curry, Fragrant Calcutta (*Kofta*), 178

Meatballs, Grandma Bess's, 26

Mediterranean

Fish Stew, 72

Veal Stew with Black Olives, 190

"middle meat," 12

Minted Basil Peaches Poached in Zinfandel, 304

moist cooking techniques, slow, 9–11

Mulled Dried Fruits with Port Wine, 302

Mushroom-Stuffed Pork Chops with Escarole & Onion Sauce, 236

Mushrooms, Shallots & Herbs, Ragout of, 280

Mussel Stew with Tomatoes & Tarragon, 68

New England Clam Chowder, 44

Oklahoma-Style Breaded Short Ribs, 172

On Food and Cooking, 12

Onions

Red, & Sage, 298

Sweet, Foil-Baked, with Mushrooms, Shallots & Herbs, 28

Orange & Ginger Steamed Salmon, 100; *photo*, 83

Osso Bucco Milanese, Joey's, 194; *photo*, 86

Oven

-Barbecued Chicken, 122

-Braised Chili, 164

-Braised Salmon, with *Labnee* & Herb-Cucumber Sauce, 102

Oyster & Sausage Gumbo with Okra & Corn, 62

Pain de Mie, Lydie's (Pullman Bread), 268

en Papillote, Lemon Sole, Fragrant, 79

Parchment-Braised Snapper with Fennel, 98

parchment-or-foil-baking (technique), 11

Peaches Poached in Zinfandel, Minted Basil, 304

Pears, Poached Rosemary, with Late-Harvest Riesling & Raisins, 305; *photo*, 96

Pea Soup, Fresh, with Mint, 41

Peppered Chicken with Curried Onion & Mustard Sauce, 128

Pheasant Stuffed with Wild Rice, Leeks & Cabbage, 148

Plum Pudding, Christmas, with Hard Sauce, 318

Plums, Figs & Blackberries, Maple Braised, 308

Poached
   Herbed Salmon in Red Wine, 77
   Peaches in Zinfandel, Minted Basil, 304
   Rosemary Pears with Late-Harvest Riesling
      & Raisins, 305; *photo*, 96
poaching (technique), 11
Pokagama Soup (tomato, beef and barley), 50
Polenta with Mascarpone, Creamy, 254
Pollo alla Cacciatora (Chicken Hunter's Style),
   123
Pork, 224-42
   Chops
      Braised, with Apples & Cabbage, 232;
         photo, 94
      Braised, & Mushrooms in Mustard
         Cream Sauce, 230
      Chianti-Braised, Stuffed with Sun-
         Dried Tomatoes & Ham, 238
      Mushroom-Stuffed, with Escarole &
         Onion Sauce, 236
      in Savory Plum Sauce, 234
   Loaf, Country (Rustic Terrine), 22
   Loin, Gingered, with Sweet Potatoes &
      Prunes, 228
   Roast, Fennel-Braised, with Apples, Endive
      & Herbs, 226
   Roast Loin of, with Black-Eyed Peas, Plum
      Tomatoes & Rosemary, 224
   & Sauerkraut, Braised Alsatian (*Choucroute
      Garni*), 240; *photo*, 90
   Stew, Spicy, with Hubbard Squash &
      Escarole, 242
Portuguese Fish Stew (*Caldeirada*), 74
Pot-Roasted Baby Chickens with Garlic, Root
   Vegetables & Herbs, 114
Pot Stickers with Cabbage, Scallions &
   Carrots, 32; *photo*, 82
Potage Crécy (Puree of Carrot Soup), 42
Potato(es)

Fried, Fred's Famous, 291
& Leek Soup with Sage, 47
New, Garlic-Braised, with Herbs, 292
New, Mashed, with Chicken Stock, Herbs
   & Scallions, 293
Potted Stuffed Chicken & Vegetables, 118;
   photo, cover
pottery cookware, 13
Poultry. *See* Chicken; Duck; Pheasant; Turkey
Printanier Navarin (Springtime Stew of
   Lamb), 208; *photo*, 85
Pullman Bread (Lydie's *Pain de Mie*), 268
Pumpkin & Apple Bisque with Crispy Leeks,
   Fresh, 48; *photo*, 84
Pureed White Beans, 264

Ragout
   of Curried Lima Beans & Mushrooms, 274
   of Lamb with Mushrooms, Onions & Red
      Wine, 210
   of Mushrooms, Shallots & Herbs, 280
Red
   Beans with Spicy Sausage, 256
   Cabbage with Leeks & Apple Cider, 296
   Onions & Sage, 298
Rice. *See also* Risotto
   Lentils on, (*Im-Jud' Dara*), 255
   Pudding, Creamy Almond, 309
Risotto, Covered
   Green, 250
   with Spicy Sausage, Sun-Dried Tomatoes
      & Escarole, 248
   with Wild Mushrooms & Radicchio, 246;
      photo, 88
Roast
   Leg of Lamb with White Wine, Prosciutto,
      Coriander & Rosemary, 204
   Loin of Pork with Black-Eyed Peas, Plum
      Tomatoes & Rosemary, 224

Pork, Fennel-Braised, with Apples, Endive
& Herbs, 226
Veal with Leek & Caramelized Onion
Gravy, 186
Root Vegetables, Mélange of, 276; *photo*, 93
Rosemary
Lamb Shanks with White Wine, Leeks &
Shallots, 214
Leg of Lamb with White Wine, Prosciutto,
Coriander &, 204
Loin of Pork with Black-Eyed Peas, Plum
Tomatoes &, 224
Pears, Poached, with Late-Harvest Riesling
& Raisins, 305; *photo*, 96
Rutabaga Soup with Caramelized Shallots,
Creamy, 57

Salmon
Herbed, Poached in Red Wine, 77
Orange & Ginger Steamed, 100; *photo*, 83
Oven-Braised, with *Labnee* (Yogurt
Cheese) & Herb-Cucumber Sauce, 102
& Spinach Chowder with Yellow Potatoes
& Scallions, 43
Teriyaki with Spinach & Scallions, 97
Salt Cod in Garlic Sauce with Potatoes &
Raisins, 30
Sauerbraten, 158
Sauerkraut
Alsatian, & Pork, Braised (*Choucroute
Garni*), 240; *photo*, 90
Soup, Spicy Hungarian, 56
Sausage
Andouille, Onions & Peppers, Smothered
Chicken with, 120
& Oyster Gumbo with Okra & Corn, 62
Spicy, Red Beans with, 256
Spicy, Sun-Dried Tomatoes & Escarole,
Covered Risotto with, 248

Scalloped Corn, Lima Beans & Tomatoes, 278
Scallops, Tea-Smoked, 18
Seafood. *See* Shellfish
Shad Roe with Crispy Bacon & Lemon Sauce,
108
Shellfish, 62-79. *See also* Fish
Clam Chowder, New England, 44
Lobsters, Spicy Steamed, & Clams with
Corn, 70
Mussel Stew with Tomatoes & Tarragon,
68
Oyster & Sausage Gumbo with Okra &
Corn, 62
Shrimp
& Chicken Gumbo, 124
& Smoked Ham Jambalaya, 64
with Snow Peas & Corn, 66
Venetian-Style, with Olive Paste
Croutons, 20
Squid Marinara, 69
Short Ribs
Beer-Braised, with Onions & Shallots, 174
Oklahoma-Style Breaded, 172
Stew with Caramelized Root Vegetable
Sauce, 170
Shrimp
& Chicken Gumbo, 124
& Smoked Ham Jambalaya, 64
with Snow Peas & Corn, 66
Venetian-Style, with Olive Paste Croutons,
20
Skillet-Fried Chicken with Creamy Cracklin'
Gravy, 112
slow cooker, electric, 13
slow moist cooking techniques, 9-11
Smoked
Ham & Shrimp Jambalaya, 64
Scallops, Tea-, 18
Turkey & Peppers, Chili of, 140

smoking (technique), 11

Smothered Chicken with Andouille Sausage, Onions & Peppers, 120

Snap Beans with Herbs, Buttery, 287

Snapper, Parchment-Braised, with Fennel, 98

Snow Pea Pods with Lettuce & Butter, Braised, 285

Soup, 40-59. *See also* Stew

    Asparagus, Summer, with Tarragon, 40

    Black Bean, with Sherry, Kentucky, 54

    Cauliflower Bisque, 58

    Fish Chowder with Chard & Corn, Creamy, 46; *photo*, 91

    Hungarian Sauerkraut, Spicy, 56

    New England Clam Chowder, 44

    Pea, Fresh, with Mint, 41

    Pokagama (tomato, beef and barley), 50

    Potage Crécy (Puree of Carrot), 42

    Potato & Leek, with Sage, 47

    Pumpkin & Apple Bisque with Crispy Leeks, Fresh, 48; *photo*, 84

    Rutabaga with Caramelized Shallots, Creamy, 57

    Salmon & Spinach Chowder with Yellow Potatoes & Scallions, 43

    of Split Peas, Big, 52

    Vegetable Stew, Winter, 59

sources (books, food supplies, utensils), 334-36

Spanish-Style Chicken & Brown Rice, Casserole of (*Arroz con Pollo*), 130

Spice-Rubbed Veal Brisket with Red Wine Sauce, 182

Spiced

    Honey-Baked Apples with Black Walnuts & Dried Apricots, 306

    Lamb Shanks in Red Wine, 216

Spinach

    Homey Creamed, 290

& Salmon Chowder with Yellow Potatoes & Scallions, 43

Split Peas, Big Soup of, 52

Springtime Stew of Lamb (*Printanier Navarin*), 208; *photo*, 85

Squash

    Braised Yellow, with Fresh Herbs, 289

    Hubbard, & Escarole, Spicy Pork Stew with, 242

Squid Marinara, 69

Starters, 18-36

    Artichokes Barigoule, 34; *photo*, 95

    Artichokes Provençal, Casserole of, 36

    Grape Leaves Shaheen, Stuffed (*Yub ' Ruck*), 24

    Meatballs, Grandma Bess's, 26

    Onions, Sweet, Foil-Baked, with Mushrooms, Shallots & Herbs, 28

    Pot Stickers with Cabbage, Scallions & Carrots, 32; *photo*, 82

    Rustic Terrine (Country Pork Loaf), 22

    Salt Cod in Garlic Sauce with Potatoes & Raisins, 30

    Shrimp, Venetian-Style, with Olive Paste Croutons, 20

    Tea-Smoked Scallops, 18

Steak. *See also* Beef; Flank Steak

    Baked, 152

Steamed

    Bluefish with Pepper & Cilantro, Ginger-, 78

    Flounder, Stuffed, Asian-Style, 80

    Grits Pudding, Steamed, 252

    Lemon Sole, Fragrant, *en Papillote*, 79

    Lobsters & Clams with Corn, Spicy, 70

    Salmon, Orange & Ginger, 100; *photo*, 83

steaming (technique), 11

Stew. *See also* Soup

Beef Daube, Gascon, with Onions, Prunes & Carrots, 168

of Chicken, Beans, Garlic & Herbs, Silky Slow-Cooked, 136, 136

Chicken, with Virginia Ham, Mushrooms, Peas & Cornmeal Dumplings, 134

of Dried Lima Beans & Tomatoes with Sage, Basil & Garlic, 262

Eggplant & Garbanzo (*Im-Naz' Zalee*), 282

Eggplant & Tomato, Summer, 283

Fish, Mediterranean, 72

Fish, Portuguese (*Caldeirada*), 74

Gumbo, Chicken & Shrimp, 124

Lamb, Ragout of, with Mushrooms, Onions & Red Wine, 210

of Lamb, Springtime (*Printanier Navarin*), 208; *photo*, 85

Mussel, with Tomatoes & Tarragon, 68

Pork, Spicy, with Hubbard Squash & Escarole, 242

Ragout of Mushrooms, Shallots & Herbs, 280

Short Ribs, with Caramelized Root Vegetable Sauce, 170

Vegetable, Autumn, 272

Winter Vegetable, 59

stewing (technique), 10

Stock

Beef or Veal, Dark Brown, 328

Chicken, Rich, 325

Duck, Dark Brown, 326

Fish, Rich, 327

Vegetable, Rich, 330

Summer

Asparagus Soup with Tarragon, 40

Eggplant & Tomato Stew, 283

Swordfish, Tomato-Braised, with Onions & Anchovies, 107

Tea-Smoked Scallops, 18

Terrine, Rustic (Country Pork Loaf), 22

Tomato

& Eggplant Stew, Summer, 283

Puree, Fresh, 324

Trout, Braised, with Onions & Peppers, 76

Tuna Provençal, 104

Turkey

Legs, Deviled with Olive Pan Sauce, 138

Smoked, & Peppers, Chili of, 140

Veal, 182-98

or Beef Stock, Dark Brown, 328

Blanquette of, 188

Brisket, Beer-Braised, with Onions & Parsnips, 184

Brisket, Spice-Rubbed, with Red Wine Sauce, 182

Chops with Mushrooms, Baked, 192

Meat Loaf, Dutch-Oven, 163

Meatball(s)

Chicken Fricassee, Nana's, 126

Curry, Fragrant Calcutta (*Kofta*), 178

Grandma Bess's, 26

Osso Bucco Milanese, Joey's, 194; *photo*, 86

Roast with Leek & Caramelized Onion Gravy, 186

Shanks with Braised Lentils & Caramelized Onions, 198

Shanks, Lemon, with White Wine, 196

Stew with Black Olives, Mediterranean, 190

Vegetable(s)

Curried, with Ginger & Mint, 279

Entrees, 272-84

Root, Mélange of, 276; *photo*, 93

Side Dishes, 285-99

Stew, Autumn, 272

Stew, Winter, 59

Stock, Rich, 330
Venetian-Style Shrimp with Olive Paste
    Croutons, 20

White Beans, Pureed, 264
Wild Mushrooms & Radicchio, Covered
    Risotto with, 246; *photo*, 88
Wild Rice
    & Duck Casserole, 144
    Leeks & Cabbage, Pheasant Stuffed with,
    148

Winter Vegetable Stew, 59
wok, cooking in, 13-14

Yellow Squash, Braised, with Fresh Herbs, 289
Yogurt Cheese (*Labnee*), Oven-Braised
    Salmon with, & Herb-Cucumber Sauce, 102
Yunnan Pot Chicken with Bok Choy & Snow
    Peas, 116; *photo*, 87